American Literary Environmentalism

American Literary Environmentalism

BY DAVID MAZEL

The University of Georgia Press
Athens and London

© 2000 by the University of Georgia Press
Athens, Georgia 30602
All rights reserved
Designed by Sandra Strother Hudson
Set in Scala and Scala Sans by G&S Typesetters
Printed and bound by Maple-Vail
The paper in this book meets the guidelines for
permanence and durability of the Committee on
Production Guidelines for Book Longevity of the
Council on Library Resources.

Printed in the United States of America
04 03 02 01 00 C 5 4 3 2 1

Library of Congress Cataloging-in-Publication Data

Mazel, David.
American literary environmentalism / by David Mazel.
     p.   cm.
Based on the author's thesis (Louisiana State University).
Includes bibliographical references and index.
ISBN 0-8203-2180-x (alk. paper)
1. American literature—History and criticism.   2. Environmental
literature—United States—History and criticism.   3. Environmental
protection in literature.   4. Environmental policy in literature.
5. Wilderness areas in literature.   6. Landscape in literature.
7. Ecology in literature.   8. Nature in literature.   I. Title.
PS169.E25 M39   2000
810.9′36 21—dc21   99-043730

British Library Cataloging-in-Publication Data available

For

Sanford Mazel

. . . the poem makes meanings of the rock,
Of such mixed motion and such imagery
That its barrenness becomes a thousand things . . .
—Wallace Stevens, "The Rock"

Contents

Acknowledgments

Many people helped to shape this book. For their patience and expert editorial feedback, I must thank first of all Dana Nelson and the other faculty members who served on my dissertation committee at Louisiana State University: Daniel Fogel, Carl Freedman, Kent Mathewson, Elsie Michie, and Paul Paskoff. My work has benefited from the suggestions of several other insightful readers as well, among them Cheryll Glotfelty, SueEllen Campbell, and Ann Ronald. Tom Lyon, Scott Slovic, John Tallmadge, Michael Branch, and David Robertson have helped in ways they may not be aware of, but for which I thank them nonetheless. The American Studies Association and Western Literature Association assisted me financially in presenting portions of my initial draft of this book at their respective national conferences. I owe special thanks to the members of my Baton Rouge writing group—Catherine Williamson, Janet Wondra, Joanna Barszewska Marshall, and Leonard Vraniak—as well as to my American literature students, who so perceptively challenged my thinking about the texts we studied together. I must acknowledge finally the support and encouragement of my friends Phyllis Ann Thompson, Chris Healy, Drayton Vincent, Ximena Gallardo, RickBob Stahl, SueBob Peterson, and most of all my father, Sanford Mazel.

Early versions of some of the material in this book first appeared in *Reading the Earth: New Directions in the Study of Literature and Environment*, edited by Michael Branch, Rochelle Johnson, Daniel Patterson, and Scott Slovic (University of Idaho Press, 1998); *Reading Under the Sign of Nature*, edited by Hank Harrington and John Tallmadge (University of Utah Press, 1999); and *James Fenimore Cooper Society Miscellaneous Papers* 7 (August 1996).

Introduction

> This myth of the human "condition" rests on a very old mystifi-
> cation, which always consists in placing Nature at the bottom of
> History. Any classic humanism postulates that in scratching the
> history of men a little, the relativity of their institutions or the
> superficial diversity of their skins . . . one very quickly reaches the
> solid rock of a universal human nature. Progressive humanism,
> on the contrary, must always remember to reverse the terms of
> this very old imposture, constantly to scour Nature, its "laws" and
> its "limits" in order to discover History there, and at last to estab-
> lish Nature itself as historical.
> —Roland Barthes, *Mythologies*

Shortly after Independence Day in 1876, as news of the an-
nihilation of the Seventh Cavalry at the Little Bighorn intruded upon the nation's centennial celebration, a New York newspaper published Walt Whitman's
"Death-Sonnet for Custer." The poem addressed its eastern readers from a distant and embattled West,

> *From far Dakota's canyons,*
> *Lands of the wild ravine, the dusky Sioux, the lonesome stretch, the silence . . .*
> *The battle-bulletin,*
> *The Indian ambuscade, the craft, the fatal environment.*[1]

In glorifying Custer's death and putting a patriotic spin on his "fatal environment," Whitman conflates an act of resistance to United States imperialism
with what has since become a *canonical* landscape. His poem speaks of "far"
lands, of what is not present at the scene of reading and can therefore only be
represented, and its representation utilizes a language at once romantic and
racist, a language scarcely able to distinguish people from place: the ravine is

"wild" and the Sioux are "dusky," and both seem equally insignificant within the vastness of the landscape itself. The wildness and the duskiness seem to function in concert, as parallel markers of what is really important: the very otherness of a grand western environment in which the canyons, the Sioux, and the Sioux's resistance are all of a piece.

Whitman uses the term *environment* in the sonnet with a precision fundamental to this study. While the term "literally refers," as Richard Slotkin argues in his incisive reading of the poem, to Custer's "being surrounded and killed by Indians," Whitman intends it also to convey "the idea that Custer's death completes a meaningful myth-historical design, a grand fable of national redemption and Christian self-sacrifice, acted out in the most traditional of American settings. And it is essential to the illusion of this myth that Custer's fate seem somehow implicit in the environment, a moral and ideological lesson which seems to emerge from the very nature of things—as if Nature or God composed the story and assigned its meanings, rather than men." Environment blends with history as together they are "infused with meaning in the form of a story" (11). Like that other durable myth, "the frontier," this storied American "environment" can be made the subject of a sort of literary history or genealogy, and one aim of this book is to take some initial steps toward such a history. This book is not, however, about some myth *of* the environment, as if the environment were an ontologically stable, foundational entity we have a myth *about*. Rather, the environment is *itself* a myth, a "grand fable," a complex fiction, a widely shared, occasionally contested, and literally ubiquitous narrative. More precisely, this study treats the environment as a discursive construction, something whose "reality" derives from the ways we write, speak, and think about it.

It will not do, however, to say that the environment is *merely* a discursive construction, for that would be to discount the tremendous power of discourse to shape the world and the people who inhabit it. On the one hand, the constructive power of environmental discourse is something for which we might be thankful; the "environment," after all, is more or less coextensive with the environmental movement, and thus with an entire constellation of genuinely admirable political reforms. On the other hand, as critics ranging from Andrew Ross to Joni Seager have shown, that movement has had its regressive aspects as well, and this book will supplement their critiques by exploring how the fundamental ideological underpinnings of the environment *itself* work to undermine environmentalism's most potentially progressive ideals.[2] I will not treat the environment as a separate and passive "nature" that is acted upon by free-willed human agents. Instead, proceeding in the spirit of Michel Foucault, I will examine the role of environmental discourse in constituting human subjects simultaneously with producing "the environment" as an object of environmental discourse. I will view the environment as part of an "environing" cultural complex within which and by means of which particular, historically contingent forms of agency and subjectivity are constituted in the first place. All too often, this process of "subjectification" functions normatively by keeping us from imagining better alternatives to the world in which we live.

The environment's durability as a discursive construct has presumably rested on just this sort of conservative ideological efficacy, and nowhere is this more evident than in traditional environmentalism's focus on "nature," particularly that supposedly "pure" form of nature known as "wilderness." This emphasis has often led environmentalism to undermine its most progressive aims by obscuring and enabling the economic, political, and historical relationships at the root of both environmental destruction and human oppression. Nature, as Roland Barthes noted so long ago, is forever blinding us to History. This study more particularly concerns itself with the way the environment has helped to mask "the subordination of society to the imperatives of capitalist development," as Slotkin puts it, and thereby helped convince us to accept the inevitability of natural processes as a substitute for "the complexities of capital formation" and "class and interest-group competition" (47). In the early national period that is this work's primary focus, the idea of the natural environment provided Euro-American men with a new and ideologically advantageous understanding of their activities in the New World. Perhaps more accurately, that idea provided those early nation builders a useful stance from which to *mis*understand their activities. It mystified rather than clarified their relationships to both the land and the people they worked to subordinate upon the land.

Critiquing "Nature"

As the quotation marks around the term *nature* suggest, this study can be seen as an intervention in the debate that has recently raged over the problematics of nature and the cultural politics of environmentalism. The postmodernist position in this controversy is perhaps most clearly staked out by William Cronon's 1995 collection, *Uncommon Ground,* whose contributors argue in various ways that nature is both a "self-conscious cultural construction" (39) and thoroughly contested terrain (51). Their fear is that environmentalism's refusal to problematize its fundamental concepts has led to an *ideological* abuse of nature that is ultimately just as objectionable as nature's *physical* destruction. To the extent that nature is treated by traditional environmentalism as a self-evident "moral imperative," argues Cronon, it is liable to be valued for "its capacity to take disputed values and make them seem innate, essential, eternal, nonnegotiable" (36)—and, therefore, all too frequently invoked to close off legitimate debates such as those concerning environmental sexism and racism. By legitimizing and foregrounding such debate, however, the critique of "nature" and "the environment" might produce a reinvigorated environmentalism "more aware of its own history and cultural assumptions" (26), an environmentalism less eager to mistake the desires of specifically positioned social subjects for "human" or "natural" universals. The result of such a critique would be an environmentalism both more democratic and more politically effective. "At a time when threats to the environment have never been greater, it may be tempting to believe that people need to be mounting the barricades rather than asking abstract questions," Cronon admits. He adds, however, that "without asking such questions, it will be hard to know which barricades to mount, and harder still to persuade large numbers of people to mount them with us" (22).

In response to such sentiments, Gary Lease and Michael E. Soulé edited a collection of their own, *Reinventing Nature? Responses to Postmodern Deconstruction* (1995). Lease and Soulé argue that without a "real" environment there can be no real environmentalism. The poststructuralist critique of nature plays into the hands of the "capitalist right," they add, and might prove to be "just as destructive to nature as bulldozers and chain saws" (xv–xvi). Contributors to the volume insist on the autonomy and prediscursive "reality" of a universal nature and inveigh against the "sophomoric" "nihilism and relativism" of deconstruction (154). Many appear to harbor the hope that implacable ecological "realities" might somehow provide an antidote to what they deem a postmodern pathology infecting the academy.[3]

This ecocritical dispute echoes the earlier feminist debate over the constructedness of ideas such as "woman" and "female"—a debate in which "sex" was invoked as both the originary "nature" of gender and the politically indispensable ground of feminism. In *Bodies that Matter,* Judith Butler summarizes the essentialist objections to her own deconstruction of the biological category of "sex," objections that neatly prefigure the questions that would be raised by Lease and Soulé concerning the ontological status of "nature." "One hears warnings like the following," Butler notes. "If everything is discourse, what happens to the body? If everything is a text, what about violence and bodily injury?" Such questions are crucial because so many believe "that in order for feminism to proceed as a critical practice, it must ground itself in the sexed specificity of the female body. Even as the category of sex is always reinscribed as gender, that sex must still be presumed as the irreducible point of departure for the various cultural constructions it has come to bear. And this presumption of the material irreducibility of sex has seemed to ground and to authorize feminist epistemologies and ethics" (28). The arguments made in *Reinventing Nature?* seem to run along a parallel track.[4] If nature is a text, what about plainly evident environmental destruction? If environmentalism has been grounded in the "irreducible materiality" of the natural environment—above all, in what is thought of as nature's culturally unmarked "body," the wilderness— what could possibly ground environmentalist praxis in the aftermath of that body's deconstruction? Like Cronon, I suggest that problematizing "wilderness" need no more endanger environmentalism than Butler's critique of "sex" need endanger feminism. Environmentalism will instead be democratized and enriched by such critique.

Butler concedes that the term *woman* as grounded in "sex" has proved politically useful. She believes, however, that the term does not become useless in the wake of its deconstruction. Instead it becomes a term "whose uses are no longer reified as 'referents,' and which stand a chance of being opened up," of signifying in new and unpredictable ways. Feminist activists and theorists alike will continue to use the concept "tactically." But knowing that one is inevitably "used and positioned" by that term, one will also subject it "to a critique which interrogates the exclusionary operations"—the thoughtless assumptions about whiteness, heterosexuality, and so on—through which it is constructed. This is a necessary critique, for without it feminism vitiates its progressive aims, blinding itself to the exclusionary processes that "put it in play" (29). I would make the same argument concerning the environment: that it will serve in a postmodern environmentalism as a sort of useful fiction, necessary but necessarily *revisable* as we come to better understand the conservative and often exclusionary assumptions that have infiltrated its basic conceptual vocabulary. Only through a better understanding of these processes can environmentalism amount to a fully progressive and truly broad-based politics.

In both feminism and environmentalism, the constructionism debate has not focused solely on theorizing the movements' respective objects, "woman" and "nature." It has also centered on new theories of materiality itself, and on closely related issues concerning postmodern approaches to agency and political resistance. Essentialist critics have demanded answers to such questions as: "If gender is constructed, then who is doing the constructing?" and "If the subject is constructed, then who is constructing the subject?" (*Bodies* 7). Who, in other words, can be a politically effective *agent* in these new formulations? Because similar suspicions are sure to haunt the kind of poststructuralist eco-criticism performed in this book, I will examine Butler's response at some length here. She notes, first, that such questions misunderstand agency. They mistakenly suppose that there must preexist an "I" or "we" who constructs the gendered body, whereas in fact there cannot be a subject at all who has not *already* undergone the social processes that construct gender. Thus, "[s]ubjected to gender," but also "subjectivated by gender, the 'I' neither precedes nor follows the process of this gendering, but emerges only within and as the matrix of gender relations themselves" (*Bodies* 7). My own ecocriticism approaches environmental discourse as an analogous matrix, a set of performed relations between "nature" and "culture" (or "civilization") within which is constituted the "we" of an "environmentalized" subjectivity.

Butler insists that the essentialism/constructivism debate is really beside the point. The key is not in arguing over whether everything is a construct, but rather in understanding more clearly "the constitutive force of exclusion, erasure, violent foreclosure, abjection and its disruptive return." Within the discourses of sex, these processes of exclusion, erasure, foreclosure, and abjection work to naturalize a discursive object—"sex"—and particular, gendered subjects—"men" and "women" (8). In environmentalism, similar processes have worked to constitute a seemingly real object, "the environment," along with an "environmentalized" or "ecologized" subject, by which I mean an "I" or a "we" who has been "subjectivated" within environmentalist discourse.

This book examines (although not systematically) the operation of each of the specific processes in Butler's list of "constitutive forces." The very idea of environment, as we shall see, depends upon an *exclusion* that separates the environment from the speaker who is environed. The American environment in particular, at the beginning of its history, is constituted through the *abjection* of specific classes of human beings and through the violence of concomitant *foreclosures*—as when, for example, people's lands are usurped in order to create first a *nation* and later a set of *national* parks.[5] Environmentalism has typically *erased* such abjection from its own history, but as we also shall see, the voices thereby silenced have a habit of *returning* to *disrupt* the naturalized, apparently stable boundaries of the environment.

What finally are we to make of the "body" of nature, of the seemingly indisputable materiality of wilderness country which by its very definition is said to be unencumbered by any "merely cultural" inflection or overlay? I will treat the wilderness landscape the way Butler treats the "naturally" sexed human body, "not as a site or surface, but as *a process of materialization that stabilizes over time to produce the effect of boundary, fixity, and surface we call matter.*" Materiality in this formulation is an *effect* produced through "the repeated and violent inscription of cultural intelligibility," by means of "certain highly regulated practices" (2). In the case of the natural environment, these reiterative and "highly regulated" practices are epitomized by National Park Service "interpretation," which I examine in chapter 1. But where the "regulatory norms of 'sex' work in a performative fashion to constitute the materiality of bodies" as part of "the consolidation of the heterosexual imperative" (2), I suggest that the materiality of the environment has hitherto been constituted in the interest of a white capitalist patriarchy. Not unproblematically so, however; as Butler emphasizes, the very reiteration needed to maintain the illusion of the material body inevitably opens potentially destabilizing "gaps and fissures," which always threaten to put the effects of materiality "into a potentially productive crisis" (10) that can be exploited by radical politics. This may seem a rarefied opportunity for political action, wholly peculiar to postmodern thought and utterly foreign to early environmentalism, yet something very much like it is thematized in some of the early literary works analyzed here, most notably in James Fenimore Cooper's *The Last of the Mohicans* and Theresa Yelverton's *Zanita*. The curious episodes of nature-culture cross-dressing in these novels are most readily explained as attempts by marginalized voices to parody the iterative materialization of the "nature" used to justify a political order. Nature, much like sex, is not real at all but *performative,* and hence as malleable as any other constructed category.

What does all this have to do with the debate between environmental essentialists and constructionists? The point is simply that the constructivist approach need not impede environmental politics; it does not wipe out the possibility of effective political agency, but rather reconfigures such agency "as a reiterative or rearticulatory practice" like that we shall see depicted in several early environmental texts. Agency and resistance in this formulation reside most fundamentally in the way people revise and retell the nation's environmental narratives. Such revisions can leave intact a "nature" worth protecting, while also working "to expose the self-grounding presumptions" of the subject—so that we may preserve nature without simultaneously preserving objectionable elements of the social order.

Critiquing "Nation"

Environmental discourse constitutes not only a specifically American *nature* but also a particular conception of an American *nation*, and ecocriticism can thus be aligned with the contemporary critique of the "national narrative." The latter term, as Donald Pease has explained it, refers broadly to a textual process constructing "imaginary relations to actual sociopolitical conditions to effect imagined communities called national peoples." In the particular case of the early United States, this ideological work entailed the deployment of an "image repertoire" that could "interconnect an exceptional national subject (American Adam) with a representative national scene (Virgin Land) and an exemplary national motive (errand into the wilderness). The composite result of the interaction of these images was the mythological entity—Nature's Nation—whose citizens believed, by way of the supreme fiction called natural law, that the ruling assumptions of their national compact (Liberty, Equality, Social Justice) could be understood as indistinguishable from the sovereign creative power of nature" (3–4). I will examine the relation between this "exceptional national subject" and a specific portion of the national narrative, the portion that has construed most literally the idea of "nature." I suggest that this extremely durable conceit—the United States as Nature's Nation, forged in a Virgin Wilderness—both gave a peculiar force to and derived a particular legitimacy from the early environmental narratives that claimed to engage American "nature" most concretely and directly. What we recognize today as the precursors of American nature writing in turn played a crucial and still largely unexamined role in constructing and revising a national subjectivity. It did so not by faithfully representing the environment "itself," however, but by discursively constituting that environment within, as Pease puts it, "a social symbolic order that systematically separated an abstract, disembodied subject from resistant materialities, such as race, class, and gender" (3).

There was a particularly urgent need for such a new, "American" subjectivity during the early national period, when it was widely felt that the discovery of a "natural" or "latent" American identity might justify the rebellion against

Britain and legitimate the nation created afterward. (Because the revolution was conceived in part as a rebellion against the Crown's patriarchal authority—a patriarchal authority the new nation's early leaders wished to reestablish now that they were the patriarchs—there was also a need to formulate a distinctly American ideal of masculinity.) The early nation builders hoped that the nascent American literature would function as a "national narrative," one that would help to "make the concept of a 'home' for 'a people' appear intrinsic and natural rather than contingent and, ultimately, fictive."[6]

It was not only the new nation's literature, however, that was pressed into the service of the national narrative; its very *environment* was called on as well. In the chapters that follow I examine an ambitious (albeit diffuse) cultural project that was at once environmentalist, nationalist, and narratorial. This project was rooted in the colonial "errand into the wilderness" and reached a culmination of sorts with the creation in 1864 of the world's first national park at Yosemite.[7] Environmentalists traditionally mark the latter event as a milestone of the political history of the environment's *preservation;* I set it down also as a key moment in the environment's *discursive construction* and *political function.* As we shall see in chapter 5, the park's founding was motivated in part by an explicit recognition of the efficacy of the wilderness landscape in constructing a desired national subject.

Yosemite's early history provides a clear example—though certainly not the only example—of how the American wilderness was enlisted as an official component of what Lauren Berlant has termed the National Symbolic. As part of "the fantasy-work of national identity," Berlant explains, the National Symbolic functions to create a "heritage" that, however fictional, is at once believable and emotionally compelling (2–3). It permits otherwise divided peoples to "share not just a history, or a political allegiance, but a set of forms and the affect that makes these forms meaningful." The scope and importance of the National Symbolic justify quoting Berlant's definition at some length, if only to indicate the range of closely related issues necessarily touched on by the sort of ecocriticism I will perform in the pages that follow. The National Symbolic refers to "the order of discursive practices whose reign within a national space produces, and also refers to, the 'law' in which the accident of birth within a geographic/ political boundary transforms individuals into subjects of a collectively-held history. Its traditional icons, its metaphors, its heroes, its rituals, and its narratives provide an alphabet for a collective consciousness or national subjectivity; through the National Symbolic the historical nation aspires to achieve the inevitability of the status of natural law, a birthright. This pseudo-genetic condition not only affects profoundly the citizen's subjective experience of her/his political rights, but also of civil life, private life, the life of the body itself" (20). The National Symbolic in general and the "environment" in particular serve to intertwine history, iconography, narrative, subjectivity, landscape, and the body—producing a ubiquitous, environing array of disciplinary mechanisms that subtly enmesh politics with nature and public policy with seemingly private personal experience.

By the mid-1800s, Berlant argues, this diverse "order of discursive practices" had come to operate more or less as it does today, as a "technology of collective identity" (8), most notably, for my purposes, "through the double articulation of subjectivity and landscape" (35). The "double articulation of subjectivity and landscape" is a key concept in this study, and analyzing it will entail understanding "the crucial interface between the state and the person as affectively invested and experienced" (13). What I term "literary environmentalism" produces just such an affective "investment"—among other ways, via a popularized aesthetics of landscape appreciation. It does so in particular through the articulation, dissemination, and selective interpretation of an environmental "canon" whose core, not surprisingly, is the national parks—for what more natural interface could there be between the state and the affectively invested citizen than an awe-inspiring *national* park? Chapter 1 explores how environmental interpretation evolved as a nationalistic landscape politics carried on, consciously and systematically, by a burgeoning National Park Service bureaucracy. This deployment of the parks has been so successful that, as Ansel Adams once remarked with unintended ambiguity, "it is *difficult to conceive of America without them*" (15, my emphasis). At the same time, whatever is constructed can also be deconstructed, and the environmental narrative is as liable as any other text to the destabilizing effects of textuality. Wilderness environments and the subjectivities they ground always-already bear the seeds of their own subversion; it is always possible to *re*imagine America through the environment. The environment is always potentially contested terrain.

An Environmental Prehistory

By circling around Berlant's notion of the "double articulation of subjectivity and landscape," approaching it from a variety of angles, I aim to practice a poststructuralist ecocriticism—a way of reading environmental literature *and* canonical landscapes—that attends concurrently to the discursive construction of both an American environment and an American subjectivity. Such a project involves an analysis of what might be called the prehistory of the environmental movement, an examination of the shifting constructions of that movement's object, the environment "itself," from the early colonial period to the creation of the first national park. It also entails an analysis of that environment as a powerful site for naturalizing constructs of race, class, nationality, and gender. I will be arguing in general that efforts to write the environment in these terms—efforts to deploy and control the land's meanings—are often indistinguishable from efforts to appropriate the land itself. To that end I will return repeatedly to the key figure of the environmental interpreter, who might be a real figure such as a park ranger, or a literary figure such as James Fenimore Cooper's Natty Bumppo or Theresa Yelverton's Oswald Naunton. In either case, the interpreter enunciates and authorizes an interpretive stance loosely summarized by the equation *interpretation = whiteness + masculinity = ownership*.

This study is a highly selective examination, confined more or less to the American colonial period and the nineteenth century, of various aspects of the "double articulation of subjectivity and landscape." Though the material is largely arranged in chronological order, I do not mean to give the impression that this study traces a linear history. Rather than exhaustively delineating the creation of the environmental component of the National Symbolic—a tall order—I wish merely to explore a few of the ways early environmental discourse participated in its creation, and to touch upon some of the many ancillary issues raised by that participation. There is, for example, the question of just how the American wilderness—once thought of as utterly opaque, a region by definition devoid of reliable signification—came to be thought of first as transparently readable text and then as something very much like a set of Great Books. This question, as we shall see, is closely related to questions not only of race, class, and gender, but also of the body and of the performativity and commodification of nature, all in a tightly interwoven complex of issues that call for a variety of reading strategies and defy a strictly linear analysis. Part of my project is simply to suggest by example the sheer variety of work that might be done by a poststructuralist ecocriticism.

My aim is not to be exhaustive, then, but merely suggestive. Certainly I do not pretend that the texts I have chosen are representative; genuine representativeness of such a broad phenomenon as literary environmentalism, in fact, seems neither possible nor particularly desirable. In choosing texts to analyze, I focused not on dense, highly individualistic, and traditionally literary works of "genius," but rather on popular works widely read and readily accepted in their own day. Here I have followed Philip Fisher, whose *Hard Facts* theorizes the sort of cultural work I am interested in as a "transforming power" emanating from a kind of literary "ordinariness" (8). Typically standing apart from the main currents of popular sentiment, the literary genius is "unable to bring about the work of the cultural present" because such work is at root "the process by which the unimaginable becomes, finally, the obvious." This is the opposite of what one would look for in a radical biocentrist such as John Muir or an individualist social critic like Henry David Thoreau—much of whose power lay in rendering the obvious into the extraordinary.[8]

As a discursive vehicle for social discipline, literary environmentalism is a form of cultural work most readily traceable in the popular rather than the high-literary text, in the words of the socially integrated rather than the alienated or critical. About Thoreau and Muir, then, this book has comparatively little to say, notwithstanding the power of their writings and the degree to which they have dominated previous discussions of American environmentalism. Writers more amenable to my purpose range instead from soldier-explorers like John Underhill and Lafayette Bunnell, who lacked literary greatness but quite revealingly chronicled crucial events in the discursive construction of the American environment; to breezy popular novelists such as Theresa Yelverton, who wrote engagingly enough but was forgotten after her own time and remains largely unread today; to authors who were best-sellers in their own day and have remained, if not fully canonical, at least on the radar of American literary history: Mary White Rowlandson, James Fenimore Cooper, and Clarence King. Yelverton and King have the advantage that the Yosemite landscape they helped write remains a tremendously popular text in its own right. Unlike much of the landscape of, say, Cooper's New York, Yosemite is still "in print" and still widely "read" in what is passed off as the "original edition." Of course, I realize the danger in generalizing on the basis of any such limited sample, however judiciously chosen. Stephen Greenblatt once noted that "we seize upon a handful of arresting figures" because they seem "to promise access to larger cultural patterns"; we begin with grand designs, but wind up hoping simply that the story we tell is not "entirely of our own critical invention" (6). Ultimately, of course, this book *is* my own story, but I hope it is at least an interesting and suggestive one.

I do not pretend to have written a full-fledged genealogy of the environment; my goals have been more modest. I hope first of all simply to demonstrate that the environment *has* a history, that it is not simply "out there" waiting to be either destroyed or preserved but rather that it brings considerable historical and ideological baggage to any discussion about it. I hope more particularly to suggest how the environment came to be so fully and efficaciously *interpretable*—that is, how it came to be first *readable by* and then *disciplinary of* a modern "American" subject—and how it might be reinterpreted in the future.

Chapter 1 gives a brief genealogy of the environment constructed by the National Park Service, characterizing Park Service "interpretation," as it is called, as the explication of a canon of Great Landscape Texts.

Chapter 2 theorizes "literary environmentalism"—the discursive processes that produce the environment as a disciplinary object while simultaneously constructing an "ecologized" or "environmentalized" subjectivity. This chapter examines the links between ecological literacy, ideology, and subjectivity before analyzing the literary environmentalism of a putatively "postnatural" text, Bill McKibben's *The End of Nature*.

Chapter 3 delineates some of literary environmentalism's specific narratological and psychosociological bases; it concludes with readings of two colonial texts whose literary environmentalism strikes me as paradigmatic. The first of these, John Underhill's *Newes from America* (1638), is a combined promotional pamphlet and account of the Pequot War that writes the New England wilderness via tropes of gender and race that explicitly link the environment's *description* to its *possession*. The second, Mary Rowlandson's *Narrative of the Captivity* (1682), recapitulates these figures but also considerably complicates them. Lacking the blustering self-assurance of Underhill's account, Rowlandson's writing is tentative and nuanced, marked by hesitations and resistances that suggest the ongoing possibility of rewriting the American environment and radically reconceiving the subjectivity it would ground.

Chapter 4 is an extended reading of an influential text that brilliantly and self-reflexively thematizes its own writing of the American environment of the early national period: James Fenimore Cooper's *The Last of the Mohicans*. Building on earlier treatments of Cooper by such critics as Leslie Fiedler, John F. Lynen,

Philip Fisher, and Shirley Samuels, I pay particular attention to the novel's construction of a gendered and racialized wilderness that, in its "virgin" purity, could serve as the ground of a perpetual regeneration of a "pure" white American citizenry and civilization. But however much *Mohicans* tries to naturalize its visions of racial and natural purity—and however much it tries to make its wilderness landscape self-originating—the abjected, elusive, and profoundly troublesome figure of Magua always manages to frustrate such aims. Magua's reappearances and disruptions steadily erode the novel's confidence in the "reality" of the wilderness it writes, reducing the story toward the end to a series of skits and masquerades that destabilize its underlying categorizations of "nature" and "culture." The novel suggests thereby that wild nature (and not just the identities formulated in opposition to it) is fully *performative* in the sense developed by Judith Butler. In addition, while Fisher argues that the cultural work of the Leatherstocking novels effected "moral and perceptual change" in readers "by means of moral and perceptual practice, which includes repetition" (4), I argue that *Mohicans* makes this performative "rehearsal" one of its themes.

Chapter 5 examines four noncanonical texts related by their contributions to the canonicity of a fifth: Yosemite Valley, the world's first national park. Considered together, these four individual excursions add up to a more comprehensive reading of the Yosemite landscape "itself"—that is, Yosemite as it had already been constructed *before* John Muir encountered it and made it the heart of his wilderness-centered environmentalism. Lafayette Bunnell's account of the Mariposa War (1851–1852), *Discovery of the Yosemite and the Indian War of 1851 Which Led to that Event,* demonstrates the role of aesthetic landscape discourse in neutralizing the genocidal horrors of a paradigmatically violent "environment," the Euro-American invasion and conquest of Yosemite. The new park's first management report, Frederick Law Olmsted's "The Yosemite Valley and the Mariposa Big Tree Grove" (1865), implicates the very idea of the national park in a disciplinary process that might be called "social sanitation through outdoor recreation"—an environmentally progressive but socially conservative form of class politics that had already proved effective in the urban East by the time Olmsted adapted it to the wilderness of the West.

Continuing this theme of the East writing the West, I turn to Clarence King's *Mountaineering in the Sierra Nevada* (1872) to explore the links between early environmentalism, the new literary realism, and the exigencies of a fast-maturing corporate capitalism. Using his surveying and mountaineering activities as figures for reading and writing as well as for struggle, competition, progress, and domination, King brilliantly constructs the California landscapes now canonized as national parks. Simultaneously, however, he mystifies the social and economic developments that were to so completely transform the remainder of the state, and uses the landscape to naturalize a particular vision of masculinity. The chapter concludes with a discussion of Theresa Yelverton's *Zanita: A Tale of the Yo-Semite* (1872), a sentimental novel based loosely on the life of Florence Hutchings, the first "white" child born in Yosemite Valley. Anticipating some of the insights of today's ecofeminism, *Zanita* interrogates the constitutive boundary between the wild and the civilized and challenges the traditional association of women and nature. I argue in Butlerian terms that Yelverton's "wild" child, Zanita, signifies the abjection necessary for the materialization of gender and nature. (The novel's foregrounding of abjection contrasts sharply with John Muir's more problematic treatment of the abjected figures in his own Yosemite classic, *My First Summer in the Sierra;* while Muir accords those characters scarcely any voice at all, Yelverton places them on center stage.) The hyperbolic performances of Zanita serve in particular to disrupt her father's prototypical environmental interpretations, thereby destabilizing the interpretive equation that links whiteness, masculinity, and ownership.

The Conclusion takes up the question of the "postnatural" again as it has been developed in Rebecca Solnit's postmodern environmentalist memoir, *Savage Dreams.* In contrast to Bill McKibben, Solnit rejects the concept of an originary nature and adopts a much more promising mode for a genuinely postnatural environmental writing. *Savage Dreams* refuses to seek in nature the sorts of lessons and remedies that are in fact available only through a conscious engagement with one's own culture. Removing contemporary readers of the Yosemite environment from the timeless realm of the sublime and radically resituating them in history—in what she terms the "hidden wars of the American West"—Solnit makes a point of recovering the voices that have been silenced by more traditional forms of environmental literature.

Chapter One

Canonizing Landscape

> Whoever expounds a text . . . is an interpreter. And no such person
> can go about the work of interpretation without some awareness
> of forces which limit, or try to limit, what he may say. . . . I am
> describing the world as it is or as we all know it, and am doing so
> only because its familiarity may have come to conceal from us its
> mode of operation.
> —Frank Kermode, "Institutional Control of Interpretation"

In the Introduction I suggested that "the environment" and "wilderness" are effects of environmental discourse, and that such things become "natural" to us only through the reiterative work of the discourses that deal with or speak for them. The natural environment seems natural only because it is continually reconstituted as such, on a daily basis and at seemingly benign levels of perception, within interlocking systems of signs generated and perpetuated by living institutions. In the case of the environment, such systems and institutions include nature writers and publishers, environmental organizations, and the National Park Service. The professed aims of these institutions are typically the celebration and preservation of nature; they do not consciously concern themselves with the discursive construction of subjectivity—much less with documenting that literary-environmental concern. But the National Park Service is different. As a taxpayer-supported government bureaucracy that is required to record its activities and justify its expenditures to the public, it has left a paper trail documenting both its methods and its aims, leaving a memory trace of literary environmentalism that is elsewhere more deeply effaced.

Canonizing Landscape

The American environment has been fundamentally gendered and racialized by largely unconscious narrative and psycho-sociological processes (see chapter 2). It possesses certain political valences by the mere virtue of having been brought into discourse by concretely situated human beings. Underpinning this basic level of environmental politics is another, implied by the notion of the environment's *totality*, of its supposedly consisting of *everything* that surrounds one. But this totality cannot in practice refer exhaustively to the infinity that still remains after a finite and central subset—some "I" or "we"—is abstracted from everything else; as the object of the study and concern and political action of environmentalism, the environment must be finite and particularized. Any politically actionable environment, that is, rests upon two creations of difference: an initial discrimination of an outside from an inside, and a secondary marking off and foregrounding of some targeted portion of the remaining totality. But what part shall we thus privilege with our attention? Out of an infinitude of "environing" material, what is to *count* as environment? Surely not everyone will agree on what counts; if there appears to be agreement, one may reasonably suspect that not everyone has been in on the choosing. In engaging this level of environmental politics, the critic is free to challenge claims of universality and objectivity, to ask not just, What has come to *matter*? but also, What has come to matter to *whom*? The critic is also free to ask whether what comes to count as the environment is that which matters to the culturally dominant, and finally to explore the ways in which the construction of the environment is itself an exercise of cultural power.

All this speaks to the insinuation of politics not merely into explicit environmentalist practice—where we are used to seeing and analyzing it—but into the *environment itself*, where it remains inaccessible to any universalizing ecocriticism. Underlying my own approach is the conviction that the critic should highlight this more elusive politics. Ecocriticism should help us realize that our environmental concerns are not exclusively of the order of, Shall this forest be preserved? or, Shall this river be dammed?—important as such questions are—but also of the order of, What has counted as the environment, and what *may* count? Who marks off its conceptual boundaries, and under what authority, and for what reasons? Have those boundaries and that authority been contested, and if so, by whom? With what success, and by virtue of what strategies of resistance?

These questions of boundary and authority will sound familiar to anyone who has followed the recent controversies concerning the literary canon and notions of "cultural literacy." Part of what is at stake in this book is the realization that the national parks constitute an environmental *canon*—a collection of

Great Landscape Texts whose meanings and importance have long been considered transparent and unchallengeable, and whose political utility has been to embody a particular vision of the nation that has so reverently preserved them. Until quite recently, these canonical environments have been read and taught almost exclusively in ways that today's cultural conservatives would approve—as if they "transcend[ed] accidents of class, race, and gender," in the words of Lynne Cheney, the Reagan-era director of the National Endowment for the Humanities, and as if they embodied "truths" that could "speak to us all" (14).

Conservatives value the idea of such truths precisely for their stabilizing political utility, because they appear to unify an otherwise fractured and stratified society. As Cheney's successor William Bennett put it (with doubtless unintentional irony), studying the Great Books makes us all "shareholders in our civilization" (4). More than a century ago, Frederick Law Olmsted said much the same thing—about beautiful natural scenery. Himself a wealthy member of the New York elite, Olmsted was quite literally a *shareholder* in his civilization; he was also the first superintendent of the new Yosemite Park, and he felt that landscapes like Yosemite's should be made available to as many people as possible—should be widely read and widely taught—precisely because they exemplified great truths that could help unify a badly divided nation. (He outlined these views during the Civil War.) They could also be the means to an aesthetic and moral education that would help reduce crime, elevate the public taste, and iron out class distinctions.[1]

In thus arguing for the edifying powers of canonical scenery, Olmsted did not see himself as conservative, however. He felt that he was arguing against a certain type of reactionary park opponent, "the ignorant exclusive" who, in the words of Olmsted's mentor, the landscape architect Andrew Jackson Downing, had "no faith in the refinement of a republic" and would prefer to see marvelous landscapes pass into private ownership. Downing had earlier argued in favor of preserving New York's Central Park as a public space; Olmsted, extending a developing ideology of public outdoor recreation from the urban to the wilderness setting, quotes Downing at length in his pioneering 1865 report on the management of the Yosemite Park. Downing had predicted that antipark elitists would eventually be proved wrong and would "stand abashed . . . before a whole people whose system of voluntary education embraces (combined with perfect individual freedom) not only schools of rudimentary knowledge, but common enjoyments for all classes in the higher realms of art, letters, science, social recreations and enjoyments. Were our legislators but wise enough to understand, today, the destinies of the New World, the gentility of Sir Philip Sidney, made universal, would be not half so much a miracle fifty years hence in America, as the idea of a whole nation of laboring men reading and writing was, in his day, in England" (qtd. in Olmsted 21). Downing and Olmsted saw the early park movements as part of a larger array of liberal-democratic reforms. Downing's words raise several interesting points. His invocation of a universal literacy (and Olmsted's foregrounding of that invocation in his own report) is just one more turn on the trope of the Book of Nature; the two men's managerial vision rests upon a suspect teleology of "progress"; and the insistence on the "voluntary" nature of a literacy compatible with "perfect individual freedom" might be seen as actually betraying a certain anxiety about literacy and freedom. Certainly park creation forecloses on privatization, which Olmsted's class would otherwise consider the preferred disposition of attractive real estate; Olmsted correctly divined, however, that the immediate loss was more than compensated for by the projected edification of "all classes." He argued in essence that the disciplining of the rabble, refining itself during its own scant leisure time by unwittingly subjecting itself to the benign influence of the landscape, would produce far more surplus value than would be lost through preservation.

Olmsted's comparison of the *parks* movement in the United States to England's early *literacy* movement points up the way that the most spectacular New World landscapes were to be transformed into a canon of Great Texts that could discipline an entire society. This transformation has been so successful, and its conservative roots so completely effaced, that today seemingly progressive environmental educators are heard to argue that "ecological literacy" must be "made universal." Without it, they insist, there can be neither a genuine "ecological identity" nor the genuinely effective environmentalism such an identity makes possible. "The idea of ecological identity," as Mitchell Thomashow puts it in discussing what I term "ecologicality," "is complementary and parallel to ecological literacy" (176), and such literacy ensures a widely shared "'knowledge base' of environmental studies" (172) as the common ground for political action (xiii). In their ecological identity work, therefore, Thomashow and his students use "personal experiences and [their] interpretations of the great texts of environmentalism as a means for common reflection" (xi).

Such work links landscape to reading and aligns both with the work of E. D. Hirsch's "cultural literacy," which Hirsch too simplistically theorizes as "information that our culture has found useful, and therefore worth preserving," as facts which can quite objectively "be identified and defined" (ix). This information "is not a mystery" and "can be taught to all" (xiv). As with the landscapes that become national parks, Hirsch calls for considerable selectivity in deciding what is to be preserved and what may go by the wayside, so that "[o]nly a small fraction" of a culture's "information" "gains a secure place on the memory shelves of the culturally literate." The importance of that select fraction, however, "is beyond question," precisely because it serves as a "collective memory [that] allows people to communicate, to work together, and to live together" in "shared communities." Cultural literacy is in this sense "a distinguishing characteristic of a national culture" (ix); indeed, it "helped create the nation-state" and "can perpetuate it and make it thrive."[2]

Neither the concept of literacy nor its consequences, however, are as straightforward as Hirsch and theorists like him seem to believe. Literacy can no longer be viewed as simply a disinterested provision of skills giving access to information; it must be seen instead as a complex and highly interested organization of reading and writing activities in the interests of the state.[3] The same is true of the closely associated idea of canonicity. The creation of literary canons can no longer be conceived as the straightforward preservation and celebration of a culture's "best" works, because canons are not formed solely, or even primarily, through the exercise of evaluative judgment. John Guillory, in fact, has shown that "the question of judgment" is precisely the *wrong* question to ask in analyzing the formation of a canon. While canonization "does presuppose acts of judgment," such "acts are necessary rather than sufficient to constitute a process of canon-formation": "An individual's judgment that a work is great does nothing in itself to preserve that work, unless that judgment is made in a certain institutional context, a setting in which it is possible to insure the *reproduction* of that work, its continual reintroduction to generations of readers. The work of preservation has other more complex social contexts than the immediate responses of readers to texts. The question to ask is then: 'In what social context or institution . . . does the process of canon-formation occur?'" (237). Part of the critic's job, as Guillory and many others have suggested, is "to understand the historical circumstances determining the constitution of the literary canon." The critic must bear in mind that "the social practices of reading and writing," in addition to being highly iterative, "are systematically regulated"—not by "acts of individual judgment" but by "the concerted operations of social institutions" (239). National Park Service interpretation can be analyzed as just such an institution, responsible for regulating the reading of the environment and endlessly reconstructing and reiterating its meanings. In the larger context of literacy as a contingent, thoroughly political, and contested sphere, we can examine the specifically *environmental* canonicity produced by the National Park Service.

Reading and Writing Nature in the National Park Service

Environmental interpretation has roots in the late nineteenth-century nature study movement championed by such educators as Liberty Hyde Bailey and Anna Botsford Comstock. (As we shall see in chapter 5, the nature interpreter was a familiar enough figure to be satirized in popular fiction at least as early as 1872.) The institutionalizing of interpretation, however, begins more properly with Enos Mills, "the father of nature guiding," who as early as 1889 was conducting educational field trips in what would later become Rocky Mountain National Park. Mills worked in an unofficial capacity, but following the creation of the Park Service in 1916 he argued publicly that guides such as himself should be taken on as regular employees (H. Weaver 29). Park Service director Stephen Mather was cool to the idea at first, only gradually coming to see in interpretation a way to build appreciation for the parks among a public whose commitment to wilderness preservation was still shaky. Mather seems to have first realized the full potential of interpretation during a 1919 lecture by the ornithologist Loye Holmes Miller, whose superb presentation had attracted an audience both large and enthusiastic—a combination that was "exactly what Mather was seeking" to counter the influence of "those persons who would selfishly destroy park values." (One notices even this early the subtle shift from preserving the "environment itself" to preserving its "values.") Mather asked Miller to bring his show to Yosemite, where he would be designated a "special ranger" and paid a salary. Miller agreed and worked in the summer of 1920 as the first officially sponsored national park interpreter (Weaver 29–32; Mackintosh 7).

Miller's employment marked the beginning of the "carefully directed and planned public contact work" that would quickly spread from Yosemite to Yellowstone and then the other parks to become "the most direct and most important function of the service." Over the following decades, with the help of sizable private grants and donations, interpretation was integrated into the park system as a whole.[4] To coordinate interpretive activities, Mather in 1921 appointed Ansel Hall to serve as chief of the service's Education Division. Two years later, Mather upgraded this division and placed it on an equal footing with the Park Service's two other major administrative units, the Division of Engineering and the Division of Landscape Architecture. Almost from the beginning, that is, the Park Service treated the discursive construction of the park environment just as seriously as the material construction of any other park facility (Weaver 32; Mackintosh 13).

Hall began at once to systematize interpretation. He set up a training program, the Yosemite School of Natural History, and formulated criteria for applicants for the new position of Ranger Naturalist. (Prerequisite to the Yosemite program, for example, were at least two years of college.) Hall also organized the Yosemite Museum Association, which was later replaced by the Yosemite Natural History Association, whose many tasks included gathering and disseminating information on the park's natural and human history, contributing to the educational activities of the Yosemite Nature Guide Service, promoting scientific investigation, maintaining a library, studying and preserving the customs and legends of the Native Americans of the region, and publishing *Yosemite Nature Notes* in cooperation with the Park Service (Mackintosh 10, 13–14). The association functioned as a sort of clearinghouse, assembling and relating the work of a heterogeneous group of academic specialists—biologists, historians, educators, anthropologists, and sociologists—in ways that were invaluable to the more modestly educated rank-and-file of park interpreters.[5] Similar associations sprang up at other parks, forming a broad, interdiscursive institutional base for more refined and authoritative constructions of the various park environments.

From the beginning, interpretation was driven not so much by the park visitor's desire to learn as by the Park Service's desire to educate and persuade, to use the public's interest in spectacular scenery to build support for preservation.[6] By the 1950s, interpretation had become an overt environmental politics, ostensibly grounded in the 1916 legislation establishing the Park Service, whose two major objectives were "to provide for the enjoyment" of and "to use and conserve" the parks. In fulfillment of the first aim, as then-director Conrad Wirth wrote in 1953 (in presciently Hirschean language), interpretation gave the visitor the "background of information necessary for his fullest understanding, enjoyment, and appreciation of these areas." In fulfillment of the second, as Wirth adds in an equally telling phrase, interpretation served as an "offensive weapon in preventing intrusion and adverse use" of parklands. For interpretation "to contribute to preservation" in this way was seen as both "obligation and opportunity" (Mackintosh 105).

This sense of interpretation as an *opportunity* had grown apace with the steady increase of tourism in the parks, particularly following World War II. By 1957 the historian Christopher Crittenden—noting that annual park visitation had surpassed 250 million—could welcome interpretation as a "new means of reaching our people," a "new channel of mass communication." To this "great and wonderful opportunity," Crittenden adds approvingly, interpretive professionals had responded with a flurry of activity, developing "new and very effective techniques and methods of telling their story," experimenting "with many things: with different methods of restoring or reconstructing historic buildings, with ingenious maps and dioramas. . . . They have introduced special lighting and sound effects. In toto they have tried out scores and hundreds of devices in order that objects might become to the visitor seeable and hearable. Did all these things just happen . . . without rhyme or reason? Obviously they did not. They are merely evidence of a new approach, a new philosophy. This latter is interpretation, the effort to make real and vivid to our people our common heritage" (qtd. in Tilden xii). The service's interpretive intent remained the same: not merely to reify a baldly constructed nature but, as Frank Kermode says of literary interpreters, "to establish harmony between canonized texts" (78)—to enlist each park landscape in a totalizing framework, to inscribe it within a particular metanarrative and thereby naturalize a particular liberal-humanist notion of "our common heritage."

The Park Service's new narrative technology, that is, held great promise for "the double articulation of subjectivity and landscape." While welcome and useful, however, all this activity posed special problems—as, for example, when the new techniques proved just as exciting as the natural objects being interpreted, overwhelming the message with the medium. And in a rapidly expanding interpretive bureaucracy rife with experimentation, fragmentation seemed inevitable. How was the service to monitor and unify the content of its message? Interpretation could not be allowed to "just happen"; it would henceforth have to be more carefully systematized and more closely managed. That in turn would require "a new philosophy," a unifying theory that would be provided largely by Freeman Tilden's *Interpreting Our Heritage* (1956)—a book still highly regarded by park interpreters and widely used in their training.[7]

Tilden thought of interpretation as multimedia narrative, an active, innovative, and responsive storytelling practice in which the interpreter must become adept at "making a few words tell a full and moving story" (57). The "lifeblood of satisfying interpretation," he insisted, "flows from the proper and ingenious use" of "devices of language" such as metaphor, simile, and analogy (30). The process is thus more literary than scientific, but science nonetheless remains useful as an authorizing device, inasmuch as it fosters "a vision of the continuity of law which looks like a purpose in nature" (28). What *sort* of purpose are we supposed to envision in nature? Tilden approvingly cites an interpretive ranger who, ostensibly speaking of processes of erosion and plant succession, "told a thrilling story of the way the rock under our feet was attacked by the physical and organic forces; how vegetation begins; the creation of little harboring places in the rocks; the coming of grasses, of shrubs, finally of trees. Our grasses, our forests" (39). Without too much effort, nudged by the images of the "rock" and the "little harboring places," we can detect here an allegorical retelling of the familiar story of the arrival of the persecuted Pilgrims at Plymouth Bay, and the subsequent raising of villages, towns, and cities—a providential metanarrative of conquest, progress, and civilization mapped first onto the historical field of the appropriation and development of *our* nation, and then onto the naturalizing field of the park environment in a way that constitutes a communal "we" while linking the interpretation of the land to its ownership. This, writes Tilden, was stellar interpretation, capable of holding its audience of travel-weary sightseers in "rapt attention" (39).

Textualizing Landscape

As head of the Reagan-era National Endowment for the Humanities, William Bennett argued strenuously for a conservative approach to the literary canon. In doing so he used a revealing landscape metaphor: "If the teacher is the guide," he insisted, "the curriculum is the path. A good curriculum marks the point of significance so that the student does not wander aimlessly over the terrain" (6). In the field of environmental interpretation, Bennett's metaphor is literally instantiated (and his conservative pedagogy neatly realized) in the interpretive genre known as the self-guided trail, or SGT. The SGT, which came into its own "as a major component of the overall interpretive program" because of "budget problems [and] lack of personnel," is an integration of "natural" and written signs into a single linear narrative, "a meandering footpath along which the visitor's attention is drawn to interesting or unusual features which might otherwise be overlooked or not fully appreciated." Though designed to place visitors "in direct contact with the park or forest resource" (Sharpe 247), such trails obviously afford a highly mediated contact, with their natural elements carefully preselected and then foregrounded and glossed by the written sign. Out of a multidimensional and anarchic web is thus distilled a linear sequence of signifiers, ordered into an apparently coherent and monologic text that "will develop an awareness of what makes up that environment" (250).

In designing an SGT, interpretive personnel are encouraged to "put a story together" that "will unfold logically as the visitor moves from station to station" (Sharpe 254). To tell such a story well—to maintain reader interest and achieve narrative closure—the interpreter must pay attention to the written trail markers' location as well as their content. This is a matter of syntax: the markers must be "oriented perfectly so there is no misunderstanding about what is being interpreted" (266); and of suspense: the interpreter should "[w]ind the trail around rock outcrops, trees, or other features," since the story is "more exciting if you can only see short segments at any one time" (254). In addition to such formal considerations, the interpreter must take care in general not to undermine the Park Service's designs upon the reader. One training text, for example, warns against laying out an SGT by "mark[ing] the trees along the route with paint or axe blazes," because doing so "*disfigures* the trees" (254)—damaging the trees themselves, to be sure, but also, as my added italics are meant to suggest, disrupting their efficacy as figures, as signifiers of a pristine environment.

The putative strength of interpretive devices like the SGT is that they bring visitors into unmediated contact with the park environment. In the words of Hermon Carey Bumpus, one of the nation's pioneering interpretive professionals, "The controlling fact governing the development of educational work in the National Parks is that within these reservations multitudes are brought directly in contact with striking examples of Nature's handicraft. To lead people away from direct contact with nature, to beguile them into a building where they are surrounded by artifacts . . . is contrary to the spirit of this enterprise. The real museum is outside the walls of the building and the purpose of museum work is to render the out-of-doors intelligible" (104). However, as such oxymorons as *Nature's handicraft* and *make real* suggest, this theory of interpretation is deeply conflicted. On the one hand, Tilden insists that interpretation in the field is superior to education in the classroom precisely because it is only in the field that the student "meets the Thing itself" (3). This is the popular notion of the natural environment as a site of complete, unmediated, fully materialized presence.

On the other hand, even though interpreters "work closely with the [natural] feature itself" and are "in direct contact with" the park visitor, they nonetheless "have a lot of media to rely on" (Sharpe 6)—and of what use are media but to *mediate* between viewer and scene? Despite the putative reality and presence of the park environment, visitors "depend on park interpreters to tell them what it's all about" (United States, *Personal* 4). To "stand at the rim of the Grand Canyon of the Colorado is to experience a spiritual elevation that could come from no human description of the colossal chasm," but it nonetheless requires the work of a vast institution, of "[t]housands of naturalists," to reveal "something of the beauty and wonder, the inspiration and spiritual meaning that lie behind what the visitor can with his senses perceive" (Tilden 3–4). With what, then, is the visitor in *direct* contact? Not the real after all, it seems, but only some inconsequential surface, for the "true interpreter" must lead the visitor "beyond the apparent to the real" (8). The visitor depends upon the interpreter's presumed ability, as Frank Kermode puts it in the case of the literary text, "to elicit senses not available to persons of ordinary perceptions" (78). Interpreters are "in the business of conducting readers out of the sphere of the manifest" (85)—and, in the case of the nature interpreter, into the highly mediated sphere of environmental discourse. In doing so, writes Tilden, the effective interpreter "pares away all the obfuscating minor detail and drives straight toward the perfection" of the story (31). Interpretation is thus a highly selective process of foregrounding and suppression. This fact suggests a strategy for a poststructuralist ecocriticism or green cultural studies: to inquire into what has been deemed "minor" or "irrelevant" to the "perfection" of interpretive stories, and to ask by whom and for what reasons such decisions have been made. Such a criticism would attempt to bare the more subtly concealed devices of literary environmentalism, to recover enough of its "obfuscating" details to breach the closure of its texts and keep the environment openly problematic.

Tilden quotes the following motto from a Park Service administrative manual: "Through interpretation, understanding; through understanding, appreciation; through appreciation, protection" (38). Omitted here is the implied step that brings the interpretive process full circle: "through protection, interpretation." With the circle closed in this way, interpretation is no longer a mere intermediate step toward the goal of protection, for in preserving landscapes we also preserve the "grounds" of the stories we tell about them. We must now consider the possibility that we value the stories at least as much as we do the environment "itself," that while literary environmentalism clearly tells stories in order to protect the landscape, it also preserves the landscape in order to tell (and endlessly retell) the stories. In this formulation—to simplify—the task of the environmental historian is to ask what happens when someone alters the environment, while the task of the ecocritic is to explore what happens when someone tries to alter the stories, and to give those stories a critical history by recovering their contexts.

One could also outline the ecocritic's task in terms of literary canonicity. To conservatives such as William Bennett and Lynne Cheney, canonical works quite pointedly do *not* speak of the specifics of existence in racialized, gendered, and class-stratified societies. Rather they "tell us how men and women . . . have grappled with life's enduring, fundamental questions," by which typically is meant the usual boilerplate: "What is justice? . . . What is courage? What is noble?" (Bennett 3). Great Books are not to be taught in an "ideological manner," "as if they were . . . subordinated to particular prejudices" (16), but rather in ways that allow us to "protect and transmit a legacy" thought to be damaged by genuinely critical readings (17). According to Cheney, criticism that aims "to expose and refute . . . biases" is not legitimate intellectual activity at all but rather an unacceptable "form of political activism" (12). But what is unacceptable to Cheney seems to be precisely what is necessary, and the questions I wish to ask of our Great Landscape Texts are very like the questions she explicitly proscribes: "What groups did the authors of these works represent? How did their works enhance the social power of those groups over others?" (12).

For a contemporary example of how such biases are encoded in the environment, consider a Woolrich clothing advertisement that appeared in a number of outdoor recreation magazines in 1991. The advertisement depicts a rugged-looking male model shouldering a mountain bike as he splashes across a wilderness stream. Above him are the words, "Out here there are no perceptions. Only reality." Below him we read, "There's no pretending. You either have what it takes to make it in the out-of-doors, or you don't. It's called authenticity. Given that people have been wearing our outdoor wear since 1830, it seems fair to say we've earned that distinction." The model is muscular and energetic; he appears to be impervious to the elements and intimately familiar with the machine he carries over his shoulder. What this advertisement posits as authenticity, that is, seems more accurately to be a perfectly familiar form of masculinity. And despite the ad's thoroughly disingenuous claim that in the outdoors "[t]here's no pretending," this faux authenticity is fully *performative*. Not only is the photo clearly staged, but just as clearly we are supposed to divine that "what it takes to make it in the out-of-doors" is more than just masculine hardihood—it is also a matter of donning the right *clothes*. Nor is it hard to see that this performativity works, ultimately, in the interest of capitalism, for the ad's "authenticity" appears in that particular form of masculinity known as *rugged individualism*. The outdoorsman's fate in the perilous world of nature, like that of the worker in a "free market," is putatively *in his own hands;* survival is seen not as a matter of social determination but as a result of individual virtue and prowess. The natural environment functions here as a stage for rehearsing the myth of American meritocracy: you either have what it takes to make it or you don't. The ad's most immediate aim, of course, is to bolster the fortunes of Woolrich and its investors; what has "earned the distinction" of authenticity is neither the environment nor the outdoorsman nor even the outdoorsman's clothing, but the *company*. More generally this deployment of the environment, this simultaneous materialization of nature and masculinity, works to preserve the ideological underpinnings of corporate capitalism itself.

A Heritage Preserved for *Him*

The rugged model in the Woolrich advertisement is a good example of what Andrew Ross has termed "the Great White Dude." Stressing the way environmentalism has functioned generally as a masculine preserve, Ross identifies it as "the only one of the new social movements where straight white males, even self-identified rednecks, have felt at home in their voice or their bodies. . . . Angry white men have found an accommodating haven under the big tent of environmentalist science, where they are not automatically required to address questions about race, class, gender, and sexuality." The ecology movement is thus the "one place on the map of progressive politics where the Great White Dude can hang his hat, while indulging in varying degrees in the wilderness cults traditionally associated with the making of heroic, white, male identities" (Ross, "Great" 174).

Environmental interpretation's job, as National Park Service director Conrad Wirth wrote in 1957, is "presenting, for the benefit of every American, an interpretation of the unique heritage preserved for him in the National Park System" (qtd. in Tilden vii). Given environmentalism's masculine bias, we should hardly be surprised to find Wirth promising that interpretation will benefit *every* American by illuminating a heritage preserved for *him*. It is true that a considerable number of women have worked in interpretation—since at least 1917, when the federal government licensed Esther Burnell as a nature guide in what today is Rocky Mountain National Park. By the 1980s, in fact, the number of women in the profession equaled or exceeded the number of men (Sharpe 10; Mackintosh 74). But this apparent gender equality owed less to an enlightened Park Service mentality than to the development of an interpretive ghetto created as male rangers who associated natural history work "with qualities lacking in 'he-men'" gravitated toward other positions. (In addition, interpretive positions were not on the fast track for career advancement.) Women, on the other hand, were considered in all the usual ways to be especially suited to the work. Where men were considered "too independent and hard to control," for example, women were thought to be "natural hostesses, more outgoing." One supervisor, citing "studies in industry," claimed that women were better able "to perform duties of a repetitive and routine nature," and another found them "more susceptible to instruction, more obedient, and . . . less of a management problem" (Mackintosh 16, 73–74).

With their presence in interpretation an expression less of equality than of stereotyping, it is not surprising that feminist rangers only comparatively recently began to contest interpretive constructions of gender. It was not until the 1970s that interpreters at Morristown National Historical Park in New Jersey appropriated that park's rural landscape to ground a chapter of herstory, pointedly casting women as active and capable agents by stressing their role in the American Revolution as "both camp followers and those left to manage daily farms while the men were fighting." Such innovations were received cautiously within the profession, which displayed a sense of reaction and containment even where it was apparently sympathetic. While admitting that "the presence of women has desirably expanded and enriched interpretive content," administrators stressed that care must "be taken that *undue* emphasis is not given *tangential* female roles at the expense of *primary* park themes" (emphases mine). This comment presaged a more general retrenchment that would occur when James Watt ran the Department of the Interior. "As late as 1979," says one observer, "environmental education [had been] an essential management function for every park." But during the Reagan years, "a back-to-basics movement" squeezed out all but the most traditional forms of interpretation, "frown[ing] on programs not directly based on park resources or extending too far beyond them." The interpreter's job once again became only "to interpret the resources and themes of our parks, not to function as . . . spokespeople for special causes" (Mackintosh 71–75). Morristown's modestly feminist interpretation was eclipsed as "female roles" in the nation's history were deemed merely "tangential" concerns of a "special cause."

Environmental constructions have been contested along lines of race as well as gender, as is clearly evident in events at Little Bighorn National Monument, a park whose very name was until quite recently a matter of bitter dispute. Little Bighorn, of course, is the location of George Armstrong Custer's "fatal environment," the 1876 battle in which Sioux and Cheyenne warriors defeated the troops of the United States Cavalry. In 1879 the War Department declared the site a national cemetery and erected a memorial to the dead cavalrymen, but no memorial was set up to honor the Indian dead, and the monument itself, in a deviation from the usual custom, was named not after the location (as at Gettysburg, Antietam, Pearl Harbor, and so on) but after the losing commander, Custer.

In 1925, a Northern Cheyenne woman petitioned the secretary of war to allow the placement of a memorial to her father, who had died in the 1876 battle. The War Department did not answer, and the issue apparently lay dormant until the American Indian Movement renewed the woman's request in 1976. By this time the site had come under the management of the National Park Service. Like the War Department, the Park Service ignored the petition; in response, AIM first placed an unauthorized plaque of its own at the perimeter of the site and later, in 1991, conducted a protest march at the monument. By this time Ben Nighthorse Campbell had been elected as the nation's first Native American senator, and Barbara Booher had been appointed monument superintendent (only the second Native American to attain such a rank within the National Park Service). That same year, six decades after the original request and only after a rancorous debate, Campbell sponsored and Congress approved legislation authorizing the construction of an Indian memorial and renaming the site Little Bighorn Battlefield National Monument.[8]

Even after the name change, interpretation at the site continued to operate within racist institutional constraints. In 1989, one of the monument's rangers, Randy Parker, reported that he had been instructed to stop recommending Dee Brown's *Bury My Heart at Wounded Knee* to visitors as background reading. What Parker thought would help visitors to a more balanced understanding of Indian-white relations had been deemed "too biased" by the monument's park historian; furthermore, the book was not for sale at the visitor center's bookstore. Superintendent Booher supported Parker but had limited authority over the bookstore, which—in an arrangement typical of the national park system—was operated by an independent nonprofit group, in this case the Custer Battlefield Historical and Museum Association. In response to a letter-writing campaign begun by Parker, the association's book-review committee finally took up the matter, and voted 4–3 not to carry the book. (None of the committee members was a Native American.) Booher then asked the association's board of directors to override the review committee; they too voted against the book, by the even greater margin of 5–1 (Lockhart 11A).

Interpretation at the monument has changed markedly, however, since 1994, when the existing contract for commercial monument tours expired and Little Bighorn College submitted the winning bid. This tribal community college, working in conjunction with the Crow Agency and the Park Service, hired a number of local residents and trained them to work as interpreters. According to manager Mardell Plainfeather, the revamped monument tours now provide "a whole new perspective" for the thousands of tourists who take them. In addition to highlighting the heroism and sacrifice of Sioux warriors and United States soldiers alike, the guides recommend a variety of books and "often talk about what it's like for the modern Indian on the reservation." The guides adroitly historicize the battle itself, noting that it took place at a time of economic depression and widespread charges of corruption in the Grant administration. Guide Elias Goes Ahead tells visitors that the national mood, coupled with "Custer's prominence and popularity," prompted officials to seek a scapegoat for the Little Bighorn debacle. Thus one of the general's subordinates, Marcus Reno, was court-martialed and dishonorably discharged after the battle, "although even the warriors said he did the right thing" in pulling back from the lopsided engagement. Goes Ahead also credits Custer's troops with making a "formidable line" on Greasy Grass Ridge, while also pointing out matter-of-factly that Companies F and E deliberately attacked a group of women and children—adding in an equally measured tone that "the boys and women drove them back." The story is vividly and convincingly told (Struckman 24A).

The environmental narrative at Little Bighorn has clearly been contested and revised along politically progressive lines. Such narratives can also, however, be revised in accordance with much more conservative beliefs. A case in point is Grand Canyon Creationary Catastrophe Interpretive Tours, conducted by Cecil Allen Roy of Ash Fork, Arizona.[9] Roy was educated at the Hawaiian Mission Academy in Honolulu and at Walla Walla Community College, where he received an associate of arts degree in civil engineering technology. He is also, as he puts it, "a rock hound and amateur geologist." His commitment to the belief that the Book of Genesis provides a scientifically accurate account of the earth's creation led him to object to the way National Park Service interpreters align the spectacular Grand Canyon landscape with "the evolutionary propaganda that pervades the country." His own tours, by contrast, interpret the canyon "within the Biblical Paradigm" ("Grand Canyon" 26). (The tours, ranging up to three days in length, are tailored to families, groups, and schools; with tour rates ranging from thirty to fifty dollars per group, Roy is clearly not in it just for the money.)

Effective interpretation, as Freeman Tilden made clear, rests upon a broad, interdiscursive institutional base capable of educating interpreters and legitimizing their pronouncements. Where the Park Service relies on mainstream geology, Roy relies on creation science, whose adherents have for decades been busily constructing just such an institutional base of their own—a still-expanding network of conservative Christian colleges and private foundations—such as the Creation Research Society, whose Van Andel Creation Research Center is a featured stop on many of his tours.

Roy's creation science assumes as a matter of faith "that sometime within the last 7000 years, God created life on this planet in 6 days and that a global catastrophe killed the birds and land-based animals during the year long Flood catastrophe." Roy claims that "the windows of heaven opened" and "a long string of very large asteroid and comet fragments began striking the Earth at an estimated 4 per day for 150 days. Those exploding in air burned and flattened everything below. Those striking the land sent rock and debris into outer space and leveled everything around for hundreds of miles. Giant mega-tsunami swept ashore from those smashing into the seas. Fountains of water exploded into space and then rained down in torrents, causing global flooding. The many explosions broke apart the earth's crust and created outlets such as the Grand Canyon for "waters driven high ashore" that would otherwise be unable "to drain back to the seas." It's a wonderful story, as carefully crafted and vividly told as Elias Goes Ahead's thrilling account of Custer's demise on Last Stand Hill. That the vast majority of professional scientists find scant evidence for it is beside the point. Mainstream geology and creation science are distinct discourses, each with its own enabling assumptions, its own criteria for evaluating evidence, and its own uses. One Grand Canyon narrative is currently hegemonic, the other marginalized; the outcome of the contest between them will hinge less on the landscape of the canyon "itself" than on the still-evolving structure of the social landscape.

This brief look at National Park Service interpretation has, I hope, begun to show how literary environmentalism participates in the constitution of national subjects even as it "materializes" the environment itself. Its motives are at once narrowly environmentalist and more broadly political— and not always progressive. In fact, to borrow Judith Butler's terminology, it most commonly and repeatedly reveals itself as an "exclusionary matrix" producing the (implicitly white and male) national subject and the "natural" body of the environment. Its modus operandi is both narrative and iterative: it tells officially sanctioned, institutionally generated stories, and—faced always with the disruptive return of the presences it has excluded—it necessarily tells them over and over again.

Chapter Two

Ecocritical Theory

It made the slovenly wilderness
Surround that hill
—Wallace Stevens, "Anecdote of the Jar"

Until recently, no critic of environmental literature would have
questioned the ontological priority of the environment (or of nature, the wilderness, or "the ecology") as the object of and the motivation for the environmental movement. As should by now be clear, however, this study approaches the
environment not as the prediscursive origin and cause of environmental discourse but as an effect of that discourse. The environment is not a simple reflection or projection of human desires and interests, but neither does it transcend
those desires and interests. As a set of represented relations, an idea rather than
a presence, it becomes manifest as what Michel Foucault calls a *dispositif,* a category that organizes around itself the heterogeneous disciplines that claim (in
this case) the environment as their common object of study and concern. The
environment is that particular abstraction that can be studied not only by those
we think of as environmentalists per se—not, that is, just by those who work to
protect it—but by all those whose pronouncements have described it and elaborated on it and validated it as worthy of attention in the first place: the artists
who find it beautiful; the scientists who find it complex, interconnected, and
fragile; the theologians who find it spiritually regenerating (however much they
may once have found it, as uncontrolled nature, vile and dangerous); the sociologists who find it an anodyne for urban anxiety; and so on.

Traditional readings of Wallace Stevens's "Anecdote," quoted in the epigraph, link the environment's *representation* to its *possession* in instructive
ways. The famous jar retrieves its wilderness surroundings from "perceptual
chaos," thereby rendering those surroundings visible to the observer even as
it achieves dominion over them.[1] In much the same sense, the environment

makes objects, processes, disciplines, and languages sprawl intelligibly around it, creating a sense of order, relation, and ownership out of an otherwise slovenly complex of words and things. It functions as one of the "privileged settings" described by Philip Fisher in *Hard Facts,* one of those "ideal and simplified vanishing points toward which lines of sight and projects of every kind converge. From these vanishing points, the many approximate or bungled, actual states of affairs draw order and position. Whatever actually appears within a society can be interpreted as some variant, some anticipation or displacement or ruin, of one of these privileged settings" (9).

The environment, like Stevens's jar or Fisher's "privileged setting," is an epistemological center; it allows us to perceive as unified and logical such recognizably environmentalist discourse as the following, which I selected more or less at random from a collection of essays titled *Worldviews and Ecology:*

> The unprecedented scientific and technological achievement that enables us not only to survey all boundaries of the good earth but even to measure the thickness of the air we breathe is certainly an established fact. Yet, a more compelling actuality is the realization of how precious and precarious this lifeboat of ours is in the midst of the turbulent ocean of galaxies. This realization, heightened by a poetic sensitivity and infused by a religious sense of awe, impels us to recognize as professionals as well as concerned citizens of the world that we ourselves now belong to the category of the endangered species. This poignant recognition is deduced from the obvious fact that we have mercilessly polluted our own habitat.[2]

Were this sort of statement not by now so familiar, one might be perplexed by its cacophony and breadth. Its metaphors are mixed, its "good earth" being figured variously as a surveyed surface, a "lifeboat," and a "habitat," while its register and tone swing from the mundane to the belletristic, partaking of the disparate lexicons of geography, biology, atmospheric science, politics, ethics, and theology. How is it that such polyphonic text can strike us as authoritative and not merely dissonant? Certainly its persuasiveness is enhanced by the urgency of its genre (the jeremiad) and by its appeals to established forms of authority. Surely, too, part of what makes such prose intelligible and attractive is its repeated use of the possessive, the reassurance it offers that the planet is "ours." But it is the discursive mediation of the environment itself, as an apparently stable and self-evident center, that makes such prose "sound right," that prevents it from seeming as opaque as the fictional Chinese encyclopedia quoted by Foucault in *The Order of Things*, that keeps us today from sensing what at some earlier time might have struck us as possessing "the exotic charm of another system of thought," perhaps prompted us even to shake our heads at "the stark impossibility of thinking *that*."[3]

It is most fundamentally this interdisciplinarity, this intersection and interlocking of discourses—and of the often divergent ways of knowing the world for which individually they speak—that creates the epistemological space within which environmentalism may refer intelligibly to its object. I thus use the term *literary environmentalism* to refer neither to nature writing nor to consciously engaged environmental politics—nor to the surface relations between them—but more broadly to the creation of this space and its accompanying sense of ownership. And the specifically *American* literary environmentalism of this book's title refers to the discursive processes of constructing the United States environment as part of the National Symbolic—by studying it, by describing it, and most fundamentally by naming it and hence *possessing* it in a new and more powerful way.

The material and historical contexts within which these processes take place do not completely determine the environment, but they nonetheless prevent it from being, in the words of Edward Said, "a free field of thought and action" (3). Nor can literary environmentalism be seen as a self-evidently pure and "good" resistance to an external and "bad" force that "exploits" the environment. For however it may represent itself and its history, environmentalism has not always operated in isolation from or strictly in opposition to power. Just as often it has been an establishment and consolidation of power—an alignment, as we have only begun to see, with many of the forces it claims in the broadest terms to oppose. Necessarily, environmentalism seeks constantly to buttress the speaking and acting authority—and the performed *identity*—of its agents by establishing links, whether between those agents as individuals, between individuals and institutions (both new and preexisting), or between one institution and another. Out of this peopling and institutionalizing of environmentalism, this expansion and refinement of its matrix, comes the elaboration of its discourse, the incorporation of the otherwise unrelated ways of classifying, measuring, and describing so evident in the example quoted above.

Literary environmentalism is not simply the written record of a political movement, then, nor is it solely the production of that movement's most inspirational and now canonical texts. It is rather the textual manifestation of a larger cultural practice, of an ensemble of interlocking ideas, people, and institutions, of what is today a sprawling formation within which environmental discourse attains its intellectual, popular, and legal authority—a formation within which the environment has been invented and naturalized. Literary environmentalism is thus akin to Orientalism as formulated by Said. It is a "created body of theory and practice" (Said 6), the "corporate institution" empowered to deal with the environment "by making statements about it, authorizing views of it, describing it," all as part of the process of "ruling over it" (3). Of the infinite potential modes for exercising power, literary environmentalism can be seen as a particular "style for dominating, restructuring, and having authority" (3) over the territories and lives for which the environment is invoked as a representation and which it inevitably misnames.[4]

Literary Environmentalism and Subjectivity

Genealogical analyses of discourse are not concerned solely with elucidating the construction of their disciplinary objects; they seek also to "trace the systems of power which have come to constitute human being in our world." They turn us inevitably "to the question of how the subject is produced within social discourses and institutions," so that genealogy's ultimate concerns are "the discourses of subjectivity within the modern and postmodern worlds" (Bové 62). If only covertly, American environmental discourse has quite often been a discourse of national subjectivity. Consider George Catlin's famous call, issued in 1832, for the establishment of a national wilderness park: "[W]hat a splendid contemplation . . . when one . . . imagines them as they *might* in future be seen, (by some great protecting policy of government) preserved in their pristine beauty and wildness, in a *magnificent park,* where the world could see for ages to come, the native Indian in his classic attire, galloping his wild horse, with sinewy bow, and shield and lance, amid the fleeting herds of elks and buffaloes. What a beautiful and thrilling specimen for America to preserve and hold up to the view of her refined citizens and the world, in future ages! A *nation's Park,* containing man and beast, in all the wild and freshness of their nature's beauty!" (261–62). This prescient environmental vision appears at first to be about preserving wilderness. Contemporary readers, however, cannot help but notice its treatment of Indians as somehow an integral part of that wilderness, as not quite identical with it but easily conflatable with it, as if the one cannot be imagined without the other. One also senses that what is to be preserved is not so much the wilderness itself as a "specimen," something that will prove forever exemplary to the future citizens of the republic, particularly to those with the leisure and the inclination to rough it, Catlin style—that is, to white men of the middle and upper classes.

Wilderness is exemplary, then—but exemplary of what? What can wild country teach men like Catlin? Roderick Nash addresses this question in his influential *Wilderness and the American Mind* (1967), which opens with the observation that while "wilderness" is a term "heavily freighted with meaning of a personal, symbolic, and changing kind," it is "notoriously difficult to define."[5] Wilderness cannot be defined simply by enumerating its components; indeed, "the number of attributes of wild country" seems to be "almost as great as the number of observers." This subjective quality, which precludes any "universally acceptable definition," stems from the fact that "while the word is a noun it acts like an adjective. There is no specific material object that is wilderness. The term designates a quality (as the '-ness' suggests) that produces a certain mood or feeling in an individual and, as a consequence, may be assigned by that person to a specific place" (1). In a way that will prove characteristic of "environment" generally, "wilderness" points as much to an action and a speaker as to any physical reality. It is said to produce a certain mood or feeling, but this action of "bewildering" cannot reasonably be said to originate with the landscape. Instead it reflects a mood of the speaker—initially induced, as we shall see, by an inability to reliably *read* the landscape—that is projected back onto the environment. "Wilderness" misnames an anxiety as a geography.

For America's Puritans, uncertainty and lack were the moods that traditionally characterized wilderness. To be *bewildered* was to find oneself, like Hawthorne's Young Goodman Brown, without the means to choose between a confusing array of "conflicting situations, objects, or statements"; the danger of bewilderment was the possibility that, lacking proper guidance, one might stray (O.E. *wilder*) from the proper path. "[C]onceived as a region where a person was likely to get into a disordered, confused, or 'wild' condition," writes Nash, the key image was "that of a man in an alien environment where the civilization that normally orders and controls his life is absent" (2). This early conception thus already implies a link between wilderness and power, for its defining attribute is precisely the absence of that pervasive complex of signs and institutions that order and control and establish norms—of disciplinary power more or less as outlined by Foucault.

People native to and living in the wilderness, to the extent that they were perceived as disordered and uncontrolled, were themselves considered wild. And to the extent that they threatened to disorder the lives of the "civilized" Europeans with whom they came in contact, they were functionally equivalent to the wilderness and readily conflatable with it in precisely the manner displayed by Catlin. The close conceptual link between "wild" landscapes and "wild" people, that is, was not one of simple equivalence—early environmentalists like Catlin did not think of Indians simply as wildlife—but rather stemmed from their functional alignment in the Euro-American dialectic of wilderness and civilization.

Twentieth-century writers have continued to ascribe parallel roles to Native Americans and wilderness. In 1965, for example, Roy Harvey Pearce examined "what it meant for civilized men to believe that in the savage . . . there was manifest all that they had long grown away from" (ix). Such men, he concluded, "could survive only if they believed in themselves," and up until the middle of the nineteenth century "that belief was most often defined negatively—in terms of the savage Indians who, as stubborn obstacles to progress, forced Americans to consider and reconsider what it was to be civilized and what it took to build a civilization. Studying the savage, trying to civilize him, destroying him, in the end they had only studied themselves, strengthened their own civilization, and given those who were coming after them an enlarged certitude . . . in the progress of American civilization over all obstacles" (ix). This is the Indian as savage, as one term in a dialectic through which the Euro-American might define (notably) *him*self as civilized. But the wilderness could perform exactly the same function, as Nash made clear just a few years later: "Wilderness was the basic ingredient of American civilization. From the raw materials of the physical wilderness Americans built a civilization; with the idea or symbol of wilderness they sought to give that civilization identity and meaning" (xv).

Pearce and Nash both distinguish between, on the one hand, "real" Indians and their "real" lands, and, on the other hand, the abjected Other, the scripted actor in a psychohistorical drama of American identity. In wildness is not so much the preservation of the *world*, as Thoreau so famously put it, as of the *self*. And any tangible, prediscursive "realities" of native peoples and landscapes are more or less irrelevant in this process, are perhaps even obstacles, to be overcome not with guns and plows but with words, through the discursive construction of an Other with the required attributes—of a savage and a wilderness intertwined into a savage wilderness. Like the Orient and the Oriental within Orientalism, this wilderness came to be viewed as both a source of civilization and as that civilization's "cultural contestant." In Said's words, it became "one of its deepest and most recurring images of the Other," the "contrasting image" against which it may define itself (1–2), "a sort of surrogate and even underground self" by means of which "it gained in strength and identity" (3).

By the time Catlin issued his call for a "nation's Park," the wilderness and the Indian were parting ways in Euro-American thought. Only one was destined for *preservation;* the other was to be relegated to the *reservation.* The wilderness that had begun as a negative term demarcating the positive attributes of civilization was becoming less a resistant and dangerous opponent than a possession, an attribute, a source of pride that could be subsumed *into* civilization and, once secured there, take on a positivity of its own. It could be fashioned into an object whose proper appreciation was a mark of the civilized individual and whose preservation was the mark of a refined civilization.

This reconfiguration can readily be situated in the early history of the nation. Jay Fliegelman has shown how American men in particular sought to justify their overthrow of the patriarchal authority represented by the British Crown— and to prevent a similar challenge to their own authority as American patriarchs (5, 225–26). In addition, Nash has noted how, following the revolution, "[i]t was widely assumed that America's primary task was the justification of its newly won freedom" (67); the new nation's cultural apologists therefore "sought something uniquely 'American,' yet valuable enough to transform embarrassed provincials into proud and confident citizens." The problem was that the "nation's short history, weak traditions, and minor literary and artistic achievements seemed negligible compared to those of Europe." The solution lay in the fact that "wilderness had no counterpart in the Old World": "nationalists argued that . . . wilderness was actually an American asset. Of course, pride continued to stem from the *conquest* of wild country, but by the middle decades of the nineteenth century wilderness was recognized as a cultural and moral resource and a basis for national self-esteem" (67). The wilderness would also prove an effective vehicle for reconstituting the manhood of the new American patriarch. But in either case, whether the project involved nationality or masculinity, a certain problem was posed by the founding and stabilizing of an identity upon processes of destruction that, as white Americans were coming to realize, could not go on forever. Catlin's early environmentalism offered a neat solution: a wilderness that no longer had to be opposed but could be assimilated and deployed *by its very preservation,* and whose deployment could be made all the more effective by a discursive inflation of its value. This task, as we shall see, would require the sparely described, almost blank wilderness of a Puritan like Mary Rowlandson to be replaced by the romantic, richly textured, and endlessly *readable* landscapes of a James Fenimore Cooper.

Awareness and Ideology

Contemporary environmentalism, in its various guises, remains very much a discourse of subjectivity, as much about people's identities and forms of consciousness as it is about the environment. In *The Practice of the Wild,* for example, Gary Snyder insists that "the wild" "must be admitted from within, as a quality *intrinsic to who we are*" (181, my emphasis). Karl Kroeber argues in *Ecological Literary Criticism* that the romantic poets believed generally "that nature and human consciousness were splendidly adapted to each other" (12); they considered consciousness to be "most effective when most harmoniously attuned to the activities of its nurturing environment" (17), and this romantic concept is still alive today. Mitchell Thomashow explores these links from a more practical standpoint in *Ecological Identity,* which calls for its environmentally aware readers to use "environmental values to construct a personal identity" (xi). At times Thomashow's book links "ecological literacy" and "ecological identity" in ways that explicitly suggest the discursive construction of an emergent self—what I have been calling an "environmentality" or "ecologicality" of the modern subject. Ecological identity, Thomashow writes, is an "orientation and sensibility" that "involves a reconstruction of personal identity, so that people begin to see how their actions, values, and ideals are framed according to their perceptions of nature. . . . Ecological identity refers to how people perceive themselves in reference to nature, as living and breathing beings connected to the rhythms of the earth, the biogeochemical cycles, the grand and complex diversity of ecological systems" (xiii). An unabashedly political construct, ecological identity "is intrinsic to contemporary environmentalism" (xiv), grounding modes of "ecological identity work" whose aim is to "forge a concept of ecological citizenship" (xvii). This image of the "ecological citizen" deftly reconfigures the old conceit of Nature's Nation and rearticulates it through the individual consciousness, as ecological identity becomes no less than "a lens through which the experiences of everyday life take on new meaning" (17). (Much the same, of course, could be said of such other discursively constructed "-alities" as sexuality and nationality.)

Perhaps the best exploration to date of the relation between environmental discourse and American identity is Scott Slovic's *Seeking Awareness in American Nature Writing*. Our best nature writers, Slovic argues, "are not merely, or even primarily, analysts of nature or appreciators of nature—rather, they are students of the human mind, literary psychologists" preoccupied "with the psychological phenomenon of 'awareness'" (3). Such students of the mind are fascinated by the natural environment—the wilderness in particular—because they can enlist it (though not always explicitly) as the constitutive Other of the Self: "Both nature and writing . . . demand and contribute to an author's awareness of self and non-self. By confronting face-to-face the separate realm of nature, by becoming aware of its otherness, the writer implicitly becomes more deeply aware of his or her own dimensions. . . . It is only by testing the boundaries of self against an outside medium (such as nature) that many nature writers manage to realize who they are" (4). This anthropocentric project of self-discovery appears at first to be circular: if such writers have no idea of their own boundaries prior to their encounters with external nature, how can they recognize nature as a "separate realm" in the first place? The truth, of course, is that they already have some sense of "who they are" when they begin their wilderness quests. In the period with which this book is concerned, writers already knew themselves distinct from nature, initially by virtue of their race and sex, and later by virtue of their nationality—as white men and women (men in particular, as women continued to be thought of as the more "natural" sex) and, increasingly, as builders and representatives of a distinctively American "civilization." These senses deeply color the construction of both the writers' own subjectivities and the environment they came to privilege.

Slovic argues that nature writing is "a 'literature of hope' in its assumption that the elevation of consciousness may lead to wholesome political change" (18). Certainly environmentalism will get nowhere in the absence of an informed consciousness. But insight can also be blindness, and there is always the danger that such an "elevation" of consciousness will abet the false awareness known as ideology. Whenever literary environmentalism's fixation on and reification of nature impoverishes social consciousness, it functions ideologically, working at the most fundamental level to impede rather than facilitate "wholesome political change."[6] In such cases ecological discourse winds up functioning for the environmentalist much as Roland Barthes showed the famous *Blue Guides* to function for the bourgeois vacationer, as "'an agent of blindness' that focuses the traveller's attention on a limited range of landscape features, thereby 'overpowering' or even 'masking' the 'real' spectacle of human life and history" that as often as not is responsible for producing those features (Duncan and Duncan 20). And this sort of blindness is not likely to be dispelled by an ecocriticism that treats nature writing as purely communicative rather than constitutive—solely as "a process of verbalizing personal experience"—and that treats nature itself as a preexisting given rather than a discursively constructed artifact. As a number of environmentalists themselves have argued, such a treatment has too often led environmentalists to frame ecological problems as natural and scientific rather than social and political, as inhering in nature rather than in society, so that they may be "fixed" only through the sort of technological manipulations that created the problems in the first place (Grove-White 19).

Environmentalism is such an overt politics that it is hard to see the subtler ways in which it functions as a covert politics, through its discursive construction of a subjectivity and its insistence on the ultimate "reality" of its object—particularly that most "real" manifestation of nature, the wilderness. Thomashow foregrounds this problem when he writes of how it "occurred" to him, in a sort of epiphany, "that ecological identity work can occur *even in a supermarket*" (177, my emphasis). Let us focus for a moment on the sense of surprise registered by the word *even*, which suggests that Thomashow is taking for granted the preeminence of wilderness as the site of ecological identity work. But why shouldn't such work proceed just as insightfully in a supermarket? After all, the supermarket is a complex and instructive nexus of energy flows, as pedagogically sound a window into ecological relationships as a pristine forest or wetland. And doesn't genuine environmental reform depend as much or even more upon changing our social behavior in the market as on understanding the natural state of the wilderness? Why is it that the supermarket's considerable ecological significance is so inobvious that it must "occur" to the environmental identity advocate in what seems like a flash of insight?

What the surprised tone registers here is the mystifying function of "nature." Thomashow notes correctly that "[e]cological identity work requires the ability to overcome both internal and external distractions" (179), but clearly we must not dismiss as "distractions" the very social complexities that any genuinely ecological consciousness ought to keep in view. Otherwise, ecological identity work will operate unwittingly to provide an escape from such complexity (much as the wilderness has traditionally served as an escape from the city), rendering ecologicality itself profoundly anti-ecological. I hope to counter this possibility by consciously critiquing "nature" and destabilizing ecologicality—in part by adopting a Barthesian ecocritical procedure in which the subject's " 'natural attitude' towards the environment is shattered as the apparent innocence of landscapes is shown to have profound ideological implications" (Duncan and Duncan 18).

Postnaturality and Wilderness Performativity

"As we cultivate ecological identity," Thomashow claims, we "are no longer satisfied to live in forgetfulness and denial" (205). Yet in one of the otherwise most thoughtful of the recent exegeses on the problematics of "nature," the American wilderness has itself been constructed as a site of forgetfulness and denial. I am referring to Bill McKibben's widely praised *The End of Nature*, published as a book in 1989 after being serialized in the *New Yorker*. McKibben's treatment of what he terms our "postnatural" predicament demonstrates how "ecological awareness" may function as ideological blindness, and how wilderness, of whose ultimate "reality" we are supposed to be so acutely aware, is not only an invention but a willful *performance*.

McKibben insists that we live today in a postnatural world. Noting that such contemporary phenomena as global warming and acid rain have left no place on the planet untouched by their effects, he argues that nature as we have known it—processes and relationships as they operate independent of human intervention—is disappearing. I suggest that nature cannot be said to be "ending" in the sense McKibben has in mind; rather, his own analysis indicates that we have never quite known nature to exist in that sense at all. He is right, however, to note that the very perception of nature's disappearance has occasioned a rethinking of the term. And because the occasion for such a rethinking presents us with so much opportunity and so much danger, it is unfortunate that *The End of Nature* is suffused with that elegiac tone informing so many of its predecessors—books bearing titles like *The Death of . . .* or *The Last of . . .* and lamenting the disappearance of the wilderness, the frontier, the Indian, and so on. Oblivious to this romantic provenance, *The End of Nature* struggles to articulate postnaturality in the language of a traditional literary environmentalism. The result is a set of contradications that are both symptomatic and instructive.

These contradictions are partly rooted in the old conflict between idealism and nominalism, rehearsed by McKibben as a tension between an objectivist faith in the "reality" of nature and a postmodern view of nature as discursive construct. In one place he writes, as if he adhered to a constructivist position: "When I say 'nature,' I mean a certain set of human ideas about the world and our place in it" (8). In this formulation nature is a pure abstraction, and hence no more threatened than the idea of a unicorn. Elsewhere, however, he writes that "nature is as much an idea *as a fact*" (71, my emphasis), leading us to believe that his is in fact a sort of halfway Platonism, in which it is impossible to speak of the ideal without simultaneously grounding it in the material. Thus we read that regardless of the pervasiveness of DDT, "one could, and can, always imagine that *somewhere* a place existed free of its taint"; that despite such pollution, a region can be thought of as "still wilderness, still pristine in our minds," so that we can "still plausibly imagine wild nature" (56–57). Nature is thus "fragile in reality" yet can remain "durable in our imaginations" (58)—as long as the act of imagining it remains "plausible."

Such talk privileges form but never leaves materiality far behind, and the term that mediates the resulting philosophical tension is *wilderness*. Wilderness epitomizes that mode of nature that partakes of both a formal purity and a tactile, undeniable materiality: in wildness is not so much the preservation of the world as the "plausible" intersection of the real with the ideal. What grounds the name of nature in this model is not some indestructible Form but its tangible physical embodiment: nature pure but physical, something increasingly rare, but when found, readily experienced in its otherness, and seemingly incontrovertible—something, perhaps, like the "unhandselled" materiality that so profoundly shook Henry Thoreau during his famous ascent of Mount Katahdin.

So closely linked are the idea of wilderness and its ground that the one cannot survive without the other. The thing and the idea of the thing are for McKibben the warp and weft of nature's fabric. Thus, even as he holds that the "idea of wilderness . . . can survive most of our 'normal' destruction of nature," and that "[w]ildness can survive in our minds once the land has been discovered and mapped and even chewed up," he nonetheless insists that "now the basis of that faith has been lost." The fabric is not simply wearing thin but is starting to unravel, and the very *idea* of nature "will not survive the new global pollution" (58). Whereas before, environmental disturbances had always seemed local, leaving certain areas untouched and pristine, the new environmental threats are ubiquitous. "By changing the weather," for example, "we make every spot on earth man-made and artificial" (58). And "[p]olitics—our particular way of life, our ideas about how we should live—now blows its smoke over every inch of the globe" (60). In this view, the continued existence of "real" wilderness is necessary precisely in order to reify the idea of nature: "As long as some places remained free and wild, the idea of the free and wild could live" (66).

Wilderness is important here not "in itself" but for its discursive efficacy, its ability to allow an "idea" to "live." In practice, however—in a familiar paradox—the idea of wilderness has always been weakest when "real" wilderness has abounded, and strongest when it has been perceived to be on the brink of disappearance. The best and most celebratory wilderness literature has always evoked in its readers a deep (and politically motivating) sense of loss. Furthermore, in ways I hope to make clear in the chapters that follow, the reification of "wild" nature has always proceeded by means of (and has already been preceded by) cultural practices that are themselves the very antithesis of "wild," activities that are in fact acts of "civilized" social norming. Today more than ever we experience the "wild" through activities that are highly regulated and normed—hiking through famous wilderness areas, for example, or watching wildlife documentaries, or reading canonical nature writing, or participating in National Park Service interpretive programs.

On the one hand, then, McKibben sees nature as a "set of human ideas." On the other hand, "the death of those ideas begins with concrete changes in the reality around us" (8)—as if these "ideas" of nature reflect some other, more "natural" nature ("first nature," unmediated nature, a nature beyond the language that describes it and conjures it). A certain correspondence is implied here between reality and idea, and it is again not nature "itself" but that correspondence that is under attack: "More and more frequently these changes will clash with our perceptions," until finally "our sense of nature as eternal and separate" will be "washed away, and we will see all too clearly what we have done" (8). Here McKibben presumably means we will see the full profundity of the environmental destruction we have wrought. But he could just as easily mean that we will see "all too clearly" what we never really had; we will be compelled to acknowledge the falsity of our cherished "sense of nature as eternal and separate." We will no longer be able to construct "wild" nature as we once did, which is to say, by means of "[o]ur ability to shut the destroyed areas from our minds, to see beauty around man's degradation" (57): "If the ground is dusty and trodden, we look at the sky; if the sky is smoggy, we travel someplace where it's clear; if we can't travel to someplace where it's clear, we *imagine* ourselves in Alaska or Australia or some place where it is, and that works nearly as well" (58). In this model, the "escape" to the natural functions as an aid to forgetting the omnipresence of the cultural, the ubiquity of our own footprints. And through-out the history of the United States, McKibben argues, that escape has always been available—until recently, that is.

Such an escape is decidedly ideological, an element in a more general process not so much of experiencing natural realities as of repressing social realities. McKibben makes this clear when he writes of the Adirondack lake in which he and his wife like to swim. "A few summer homes cluster at one end" of this lake, "but mostly it is surrounded by wild state land" (49). "During the week we swim across and back, a trip of maybe forty minutes—plenty of time to forget everything but the feel of the water around your body and the rippling, muscu-lar joy of a hard kick and the pull of your arms. But on the weekends, more and more often, someone will bring a boat out for waterskiing, and make pass after pass up and down the lake. And then the whole experience changes, changes entirely." This lamentable change, McKibben makes clear, is not so much physi-cal as it is mental. As important as any concrete damage to the environment is the motorboat's intrusion into an otherwise carefully guarded *psychic* territory: "Instead of being able to forget everything but yourself, and even yourself ex-cept for the muscles and the skin, you must be alert, looking up every dozen strokes to see where the boat is, thinking about what you will do if it comes near. It is not so much the danger. . . . It's not even so much the blue smoke that hangs low over the water. It's that the motorboat gets in your mind. You're forced to think, not feel—to think of human society and of people" (49). De-spite the presence of the summer homes, McKibben can experience this limi-nal setting as wild—and hence imagine himself as the Great White Dude—so long as he can perform this crucial *forgetting* "of human society and of people." But the lake ceases to be wild whenever its cultural aspects interfere too much with the willed process of repression, when that culture "gets into" McKibben's mind and disrupts an affective mode of perception that, I will argue later, car-ries its own ideological baggage.

This sort of self-willed repression is characteristic of an entire historiography of wilderness, a historiography to which McKibben clearly subscribes, most no-tably in his lengthy discussion of the journal of that early wilderness enthusi-ast, George Catlin. McKibben quotes selectively from this journal, editing into existence a vision of pure wilderness by cutting away any hint of "human soci-ety and of people"—in this case Native American society and people—within that wilderness. In an act of the imagination comparable to his forgetting of the summer homes at his Adirondack lake, McKibben singles out a long passage, a description of a valley that was, according to Catlin, "far more beautiful than could be imagined by mortal man." In McKibben's words, it was one of those increasingly rare "visions of the world as it existed outside human history." This vision "sticks" in his "mind as a baseline, a reminder of where we began." It is a vision whose escape out of history is an escape into myth, and the author makes no bones about its Edenic appeal: "If this passage had a little number at the start of each sentence, it could be Genesis" (52).

Of course, McKibben can imagine this valley as Eden only if he can imagine Catlin as Adam, and Catlin can be Adam only if he is the first human on the scene. McKibben must thus read Catlin rather perversely, in a way that erases the presence of the many humans who were not only omnipresent in the area but were the very reason Catlin had gone West to begin with. This Native American presence frames Catlin's depiction of the "wild" valley with a power and import that McKibben's editorial scalpel conveniently excises. Here is a sample of that elided narrative frame: "The Indians, also, I found, had loved [this valley] once, and left it; for here and there were their solitary and deserted graves, which told, though briefly, of former chants and sports; and perhaps, of wars and deaths, that have once rung and echoed through this silent vale" (105). To be sure, Catlin himself minimizes the native presence in his Eden, if only by relegating it to the past. Describing in such glowing terms a landscape in which Native Americans have *only* a past, he constructs a landscape in which white Americans may have an uncontested future, a beautiful "prospect" in both senses of the term (Pratt 125).

But Catlin cannot, in a book that is after all *about* Indians, banish that presence entirely; the completion of the job requires some additional editorial work. For Catlin this process of effacement has only just begun, so that the abjected native presence remains perilously close to the surface. The shallow Indian grave yet "speaks" to him, and the sound of all those chants, sports, and wars— all that prior humanity and culture, all that disruptive noise and smoke—has clearly *gotten into his mind,* as McKibben might say. Thus we are not at all surprised to find Catlin prefacing his description of wilderness-as-Eden by relating the following strange occurrence. He is camping out in the beautiful valley, sleeping under the stars, when in "the middle of the night I waked, whilst I was lying on my back, and on half opening my eyes, I was instantly shocked to the soul, by the huge figure (as I thought) of an Indian, standing over me, and in the very instant of taking my scalp!" Catlin is momentarily "paralysed" by a "chill of horror" (103)—and then realizes that he is looking up at his horse. One need not be Freud to see here the return of the repressed, of that which must always be repressed in constructing the Edenic American wilderness, in conceiving of an occupied territory as a scene of origin.

McKibben invokes Catlin's wilderness as if it were a "real" wilderness, an example of the sort of "first nature" that might ground his own imaginative construction of wilderness in the postnatural New England of the late twentieth century. Yet clearly Catlin, too, had *made* a wilderness, and via precisely the kind of willful repression McKibben would use to make a wilderness of his Adirondack lake. In the best postmodern fashion, the "original" turns out to be itself a copy; "nature" turns out to be itself an artifact, and it is this realization—rather than the ubiquity of pollution or the global nature of climatic change—that constitutes postnaturality. Postnaturality is not about our sense that there is no longer any escape from culture into nature—such a feeling, after all, is hardly new. The term more sensibly should refer to our just-dawning sense that such an escape *never was* available. Furthermore, we come to this awareness only by placing History once again before Nature, by reading the environmental narrative not, as McKibben does, as the "discovery" of wilderness but as the performance of an identity and the conquest of an already occupied territory.

Chapter Three

Acts of Environment

> The image of being surrounded is a fundamental psychic picture
> in America.
> —Philip Fisher, *Hard Facts*

The discussion thus far has repeatedly suggested the contingency of environmentalism's object: the environment. The environment is never freely constructed but rather is shaped by the needs that prompt its invocation and the processes involved in its representation. The environment is first of all a word, an element in a discourse, and thus "populated," as Bakhtin has it, "with the intentions of others" (294). It is also a narrated fiction, and thus shares formal properties common to all narrative. Finally, as a product of the imagination the environment is both limited and enabled by socially responsive psychological processes, the varied workings of anxiety and desire. In this chapter I will problematize the environment further by briefly taking up these matters of etymology, typology, and psychosociology—all preparatory to reading John Underhill's promotional pamphlet, *Newes from America* (1638), and Mary Rowlandson's *The Narrative of the Captivity* (1682) as paradigmatic exercises of literary environmentalism at formative moments in American history.

Etymology

A root verb plus a suffix, *environment* once quite straightforwardly denoted "the action of environing": *environ*ment (*OED*). But with the obsolescence of the verb *to environ,* meaning to "encircle" or "surround," this active sense has been lost, so that we no longer hear it the way we do in nouns such as *judge*ment and *govern*ment—words that still resonate with the senses of the judges who judge and the governors who govern, and that immediately recall the legal and political structures that empower those judges and governors.

Even when we use such terms as mere nouns, and despite the work of ideology to cast them as natural and inevitable, we still sense in them their constructedness, their historicity and politicization. Judgments and governments are easily seen to be products of human will and activity, backed up perhaps by social consent but also, in the final analysis, by the specter of violence.

Our sense of *environment*, by contrast, is not of an action but a thing, not a fiction that has been made but a fact that has been discovered. Thanks to a nominalizing process that effaces both act and actor, we no longer speak of what *environs* us, but of what our environment *is*. This is not a trivial distinction, for restoring to environment its sense of originary action allows us to inquire into not only what environs us but how it came to do so, in whose interests, and by means of what agency—crucial questions all.

If, as the *Oxford English Dictionary* suggests, environment originates in action, what is the nature of the act, and who is the actor? Put another way, is there a concrete noun that can be cast as both agent and grammatical subject in a simple sentence directly describing this originary, performative sort of environment? The OED gives little help in disentangling today's environment-as-noun from the earlier environment-as-verb, circularly defining the former as "that which environs." This circle is not broken when the dictionary attempts a definition by enumeration, defining the environment as "the objects or region surrounding anything," for this simply yokes the noun to a substitute verb, *surround*, which though not obsolete is more or less synonymous with *environ*. This deferral merely disguises the problem of the definition's circularity. It seems clear that whatever the concrete entities enumerated by the dictionary, they do not constitute environment-as-noun until and unless they perform environment-as-action. We are no closer than before to knowing what the environment *is* in the absence of such action—or, to put it in two different but related ways, what ontological immanence or absolute presence it might possess allowing us to utter it as a noun plain and simple.

The way out of this circle is to uncover the agency at work in acts of environment. We must shift our attention from the merely grammatical subject—the elusive environment-as-noun—to something whose agency is as real in fact as we assume the environment to be in speech. We need to focus on the speaker who is environed, on precisely that element which, suggestively enough, is left out of the dictionary definition. Bearing in mind the political valence of the question, the identity politics implied by its plural pronoun, we need to stop asking what the environment *is*, stop trying to enumerate its defining elements, and ask instead, How is it that these enumerated elements have come to environ *us*? The answer lies in the *presumption of the presence of,* and ultimately in the *act of entry by,* the speakers who can sensibly say, *"our* environment." It is not any action on the part of our surroundings that has made them *our* surroundings, but the onset of and the continuation of our being here: a matter not of ontology but of history. The originary and defining environment-as-action, to which environment-as-noun always points and from which, however remote, it is logically inseparable, points in turn to specifiable acts of entry and occupation. It is these that account for our being environed, and hence of "having" an "environment" that in a shorthand way at once anthropocentric, self-effacing, and depoliticizing "we" can deploy as a noun.

Yet we speak of the environment, of environment-as-noun, as some sort of genuine (as opposed to merely grammatical) agent that environs us—native, conqueror, and immigrant alike—as if we all shared the same history of environment-as-action. Why this strange construction in which human actors with agency are grammatically cast as passive and undifferentiated objects? As noted above, when people first enter a region they have not previously known and begin to speak of it as *their* surroundings, the region itself has done nothing in particular to metamorphose from terra incognita to environment. What precipitates environment is *entry.* Environment corresponds to, is the inverted expression of, a simultaneous and logically complementary *penetration*—a word I use now consciously to draw a contrast between environmental and sexual discourses. As numerous feminist critics have pointed out, consensual coitus can be thought of not only as a penetration but also as, say, an *incorporation* (as above, the two actions can be thought of as logically complementary), yet the hegemonic term is nonetheless *penetration,* privileged precisely because it foregrounds a dominating, masculine sexual agency. Use of a term such as *incorporation,* with its ascription of sexual agency to the female, is proscribed by a phallic code that effaces female sexuality generally.[1] In its complementarity to originary acts of penetration, environment is clearly analogous to incorporation. Yet within environmental discourse, penetration is not foregrounded but *effaced;* agency is ascribed exclusively to what is in fact its inescapably passive correlate. Given that early environmental discourse seems otherwise unmistakably phallic, such a construction seems odd indeed, until we notice its rhetorical effect of purging environmental discourse of a discomfiting history of colonialist and capitalist "penetrations"—discovery and exploration, conquest and commodification, the now-nameable environment-as-action or "rape of the land"—which precipitated the Euro-American environment in the first place. In the performative sense I have been trying to develop here, that history may now be viewed *as* the environment. This is the "environment" of my ecocriticism, an environment of actions and intentions rather than an abstraction that not only lacks agency and presence, but whose very conjuring is a mystification.

Narratology

The OED defines the environment—in its contemporary usage in the discourse of environmentalism, that is, as environment-as-noun—as the "sum total" of "that which environs; the objects or region surrounding anything." Having dealt earlier with the implications of the environment's putative *totality*, let us here focus on the definitional primacy of the *externality* implied in the traditional definition, on the way the very idea of environment helps divide the world into insides and outsides. The terms here suggest a way of theorizing "the environment" as it is represented in and as it performs in the narratives of literary environmentalism, specifically, in terms of Jurij Lotman's theory of narrative plot typology. According to Lotman, the mythic narrative features at root just two types of characters, "those who are mobile, who enjoy freedom with respect to plot-space, who can change their place in the structure of the artistic world and cross the frontier, the basic topological feature of this space, and those who are immobile, who represent, in fact, a function of this space. . . . [A] certain plot space is divided by a single boundary into an external and an internal sphere, and a single character has the opportunity to cross that boundary" (167). On the most fundamental narrative level there are, as Donna Haraway puts it in adumbrating this passage, only two characters: "the hero and the limit of his action or the space through which he moves" (234). Haraway deliberately uses "he" in this formulation because the narrative hero is the "creator of differences," the one who differentiates his interior from his exterior and as such is "structurally male." The female is "both the space for and the resistance to" such marking (234). She is "an element of plot-space," in the words now of Teresa de Lauretis, "a topos, a resistance, matrix and matter" (44).

Although Lotman writes specifically of myth, de Lauretis of Hollywood cinema, and Haraway of the deep structure of scientific thought and research, it is not hard to recognize in this pregendered "matrix and matter" the environment as it is generally represented: ahistorical, ontologically stable, utterly objectified, and, like any other feminized object in patriarchal discourse, "fixed in the position of icon, spectacle, the one looked at, in which the subject sees the objectification of *his* action and subjectivity" (Haraway 234). The "fixing" of the environment in this position may be thought of as a sort of environmental exploitation in its own right—not the obvious sort of physical destruction that might appear to motivate the environmental narrative, but a more fundamental conceptual appropriation, by the very locating of its boundaries and identification of its properties, of environment as raw cultural material. Like "Woman," this material is not only endlessly reconstructed, but also has as one of its primary attractions its endless *availability* for such reconstruction. It is a sort of renewable resource for constructing the masculine subject on both the individual and the national levels, through the shifting and proliferating narrative strategies of literary environmentalism.

Psychosociology

Environment's implicit differentiation between that which surrounds and that which is surrounded, between self and other, is a process not solely semantic and narrative, but also psychosocial. Annette Kolodny has examined "America's oldest and most cherished fantasy": "the land as woman, the total female principle of gratification—enclosing [*environing*] the individual in an environment of receptivity, repose, and painless and integral satisfaction" (*Lay* 4). Her work critiques the demarcation of a universalized masculine self from the environment in terms that illuminate the present volume, most particularly by contextualizing the psychological and linking it directly to both the social and the literary. In the seventeenth century, such quasi-environmental images as "Eden, Paradise, the Golden Age, and the idyllic garden" were recast in response to contingent social realities, "subsumed in the image of an America promising material ease without labor or hardship, as opposed to the grinding poverty of previous European existence" (*Lay* 6). The New World promised the European "a resurrection of the lost state of innocence that the adult abandons when he joins the world of competitive self-assertion; and all this possible because, at the deepest psychological level, the move to America was experienced as the daily reality of what has become its single dominating metaphor: regression from the cares of adult life and a return to the primal warmth of womb or breast in a feminine landscape. And when America finally produced a pastoral literature of her own, that literature hailed the essential femininity of the terrain in a way European pastoral had never dared, and, from the first, took its metaphors as literal truths" (*Lay* 6). Material history here becomes psychologically grounded metaphor, which then underwrites a naturalized gendered "reality." This fantasy of a feminine landscape is motivated not solely "by personal psychology" but also "by social context" (Kolodny, *Land* xii). What Kolodny terms "regression" here is shaped not only by some universal desire to escape from adulthood but also by a fully contextual wish to escape from the rigors of an early capitalism—with its "grinding poverty" for the worker and its social and spiritual impoverishment for worker and capitalist alike—into a fantasized precapitalist Eden. But of course there could be no such escape; Kolodny stresses that the dynamics of an expansionist colonialism ensured that "the suppressed infantile desires unleashed in the promise of a primal garden were inevitably frustrated," "thwarted by the equally pressing need to turn nature into wealth. In a capital-accumulating economy, this demanded, on the one hand, competition . . . and, on the other, a willingness to violate the very generosity that had once promised an end to such patterns." [2]

The specifically psychological component of Kolodny's model is worth elaborating in some detail, perhaps most usefully—not least because literary environmentalism comes to rely so much upon the gendered discourses of science—in terms of the object-relations approach taken by Evelyn Fox Keller in her analysis of the scientific construction of nature. For the infant, Keller writes, "[b]oundaries have not yet been drawn to distinguish the child's internal from external environment" (81). At this early time, the external environment consists "primarily" of the mother, who is "experienced as an extension of the child," until, via the experiential stages outlined by Jean Piaget, the child "learns to distinguish between self and other, between subject and object." This ability to perceive self as separate from environment in turn "allows for the recognition of an external reality to which the child can relate—at first magically, and ultimately objectively." (Here I am using *environment* as Keller uses it, to refer to the "not-me" of the developing subject rather than to the environment of environmentalist discourse.)

This process, "fraught with intense emotional conflict," is often described as "development" but in fact does not lead unambiguously from an inferior state to a superior one. Keller stresses that "the emergence of the mother as a separate being" awakens in the child a "painful recognition of his/her own separate existence. Anxiety is unleashed, and longing is born." That longing is countered, however, by "a growing enjoyment of autonomy, which itself comes to feel threatened by the lure of an earlier state" (81). Maturity in this model is not achieved by attaining the highest possible level of autonomy, but by successfully negotiating the contradictory forces of autonomy and desire, by becoming "sufficiently secure to permit momentary relaxation of the boundary" between self and other (82). This is the final, but difficult, step "of reintroducing ambiguity into one's relation to the world" (82–83).

Within patriarchy, this ambiguity—this "blurring of the boundary between subject and object"—inevitably "tend[s] to be associated with the feminine" (87). Keller quotes Hans Loewald: "Against the threatening possibility of remaining in or sinking back into the structureless unity from which the ego emerged, stands the powerful paternal force. . . . While the primary narcissistic identity with the mother forever constitutes the deepest unconscious origin and structural layer of ego and reality . . . this primary identity is also the source of the deepest dread, which promotes, in identification with the father, the ego's progressive differentiation and structuralization of reality" (86–87). Thus, in addition to the familiar gendering of the environment itself as feminine, this model predicts a gendering of the ways of relating to that environment. For the masculine subject especially, the already difficult step of "reintroducing ambiguity into one's relation to the world" is made more difficult to the extent that it requires a voluntary assumption of gender ambiguity in a society that compels gender clarity. Relating to nature becomes a matter of gender politics.

In the early stages of development, the difficulty of moving from unity to autonomy is eased by an intermediary between self and other that the British psychoanalyst D. W. Winnicott terms the "transitional object." (Winnicott's example is the baby's blanket.) As a signifier, this transitional object is unmotivated; that is, it does not intrinsically correspond to the mother, but does so only because such a meaning has somehow been assigned to it, as a trope in the fluid signifying system of the maturing child. Although the blanket itself is eventually given up, it is neither forgotten nor repressed, as Winnicott stresses, but rather "loses meaning" (5). It simply ceases to signify, as other objects displace it in a mediative system that changes but continues unabated because the need for mediation never disappears. The "transitional phenomena," in this model, "become . . . spread out over the whole intermediate territory between 'inner psychic reality' and 'the external world as perceived by two persons in common,' that is to say, over the whole cultural field" (5).

At least part of the tremendous power of the "natural" environment to signify within the cultural field owes to its continued use, as trope rather than "real" object, to negotiate the tense boundary between interdependence and autonomy.

That it will, as the "natural" portion of Winnicott's cultural field, be strongly gendered is not surprising, since (regardless of the specific shape it takes as signifier) its raison d'être, its collective and earliest signified, remains the mother. However, this environment-as-transitional-object is no more the "reality" of the world whose welfare is ostensibly environmentalism's concern than the blanket is the infant's mother.

How can any of this help us read *environment* in a specific historical and textual instance? The discussion thus far suggests that literary environmentalism will represent nominal environments via the effacement of performed environments, specifically, via the misnaming of penetration *as* environment. Such representations will collapse time and action into space and place, reducing the complexities and politics of the historical to the comparative simplicity and apparent neutrality of the geographical. In the process, they will also mark off a feminized narrative space within which a masculinized subject can recognize, to repeat Haraway's formulation, "*his* action and subjectivity." (That is, they will help to constitute "man in the landscape," to appropriate Paul Shepard's phrase.) Finally, as displaced object of desire, as that whose delimitation both produces the self and threatens to subsume it, this putatively agentive and feminine space will be ambiguously constructed, something the subject is drawn toward yet also fears.

John Underhill's colonial pamphlet *Newes from America* illustrates these processes well. As a description of the Pequot War *and* the Connecticut landscape, it exemplifies the collapsing of an antecedent environment-as-action onto environment-as-noun, revealing the origins of a landscape trope that will be accessed over and over again in American literary environmentalism—a trope neatly linking issues of possession and representation to constructions of whiteness and masculinity.

Warre-like Proceedings and Speciall Places

We know today—indeed, it was known in 1876—that George Armstrong Custer and his men were not ambushed at the Little Bighorn. They were, however, quite literally and fatally *environed*, and I think Whitman's use of the term in his "Death-Sonnet for Custer" is instructive, invoking as it does the older and explicitly military sense of environment even as it silences the activity of history into the passivity of landscape—into the "wild ravines" and "lonesome stretches" that would eventually be canonized in the national park system. The enduring fascination with Custer's "fatal environment," as Richard Slotkin argues, owes not only to the way it rattled an apparently smug nation, but also to the notion of a powerful Native American people whose renewed "aggression" could rationalize the continuing seizure of their lands. Although by far the best known, the Custer myth was not the first to accomplish this self-serving transformation of history into landscape-text. The pattern was already apparent more than two centuries earlier, in the Pequot War of 1637.

Originating in British colonists' desire for Pequot territory in what is now Connecticut, this conflict's casus belli was a series of reciprocal kidnappings, murders, and skirmishes involving English and Dutch colonists as well as Pequot, Niantic, and Narragansett Indians—although it was specifically against the Pequots that the General Court of Massachusetts declared war. An expeditionary force consisting of approximately a hundred Englishmen and a backup force of Mohegans and Narragansetts, led by John Mason and John Underhill, was quickly assembled. This expedition sailed out of Saybrook and cruised eastward along the coast toward the Pequots' fortified village on the Mystic River. Instead of attacking directly, the colonial force sailed right on by to the east, "deluding" the Pequot warriors in a way that "bred in them a securitie" (Underhill 36). The Puritan force then turned northward into Narragansett Bay, landed secretly, and marched south and west overland—in order, as Mason writes, to "come upon their Backs" (2) and storm the lightly guarded fort where several hundred Pequot women, children, and other noncombatants had been sequestered. Completely fooled by these tactics, the Pequot guards were still asleep when the Englishmen attacked at dawn, Mason at one entrance of the fort and Underhill at the other. Waking amidst the slaughter, the Indians recovered quickly and began to drive the Puritans back. Mason and Underhill, at opposite entrances to the village, then set fire to the wigwams and retreated outside, watching as the fires, "both meeting in the centre of the fort, blazed most terribly, and burnt all in the space of halfe an houre . . . many were burnt in the Fort, both men, women, and children" (Underhill 39). The fort had held at least four hundred people, and Underhill notes that "so many soules lie gasping on the ground so thicke in some places, that you could hardly passe along" (39–40). Those who did manage to escape the fire were picked off by the soldiers waiting outside, and by Underhill's estimate, not more than five got out alive. All but broken after this massacre, the remaining Connecticut Pequots were quickly dispersed, captured, or killed, and English colonists immediately began occupying their newly conquered territory.[3]

For a "civilized" author writing for a "civilized" audience, the chronicling of such savage events posed an obvious problem. As Underhill sums it up: "It may bee demanded, Why should you be so furious? (as some have said) should not Christians have more mercy and compassion?" (40). Both Mason and Underhill, in their separate accounts of the war, respond with a similar rhetorical strategy, a crude displacement of agency and responsibility well calculated to satisfy a Puritan audience: "God was above them," writes Mason of the Pequots, "making them as a fiery Oven. . . . Thus did the Lord judge among the Heathen, filling the Place with dead Bodies!" (9–10). The massacre was not the Puritans' own work, but "the LORD's DOINGS" (14). Both authors repeatedly cast themselves and their men as passive, mere "feeble instruments" in the hands of God, in contrast to the fictional agency of the victims, whose putative actions are deemed to justify both the magnitude and the indiscriminateness of the slaughter: "[W]hen a people is growne to such a height of bloude, and sinne against God and man, and all confederates in the action, there hee hath no respect to persons, but harrowes them, and sawes them, and puts them to the sword, and the most terriblest death that may bee: sometimes the Scripture declareth women and children must perish with their parents" (Underhill 40). Such rhetoric displaces agency onto an undifferentiated Other ("all confederates in the action") while mystifying any worldly motives for the massacre. The discourse bonds action with thing in an obfuscating manner characteristic of much literary environmentalism. The Puritans, writes Mason, "got not the Land in Possession by their own Sword," but rather because the "LORD was pleased to smite our Enemies . . . and to give us their Land" (front.; 21). Underhill makes the same linkage, promising the reader in the very first sentence of his own account that he will "performe these two things, first give a true narration, of the warre-like proceedings that hath been in New England these two years past," and second, "discover to the Reader divers places in New England, that would afford speciall accommodations to such persons as will Plant upon them." He immediately reiterates: in the "Relation of our warre-like proceedings" he will "interweave the speciall places fit for New Plantations, with their description" (1). He will entangle "proceedings" and "places," action and noun, the two strands whose interweaving it was our purpose, in the etymological discussion above, to disentangle. With events and their narration thus beginning to be subsumed into place and its description, Underhill writes precisely of "the scenic Connecticut countryside" (Nelson 12)—of the "scene" of history and aesthetic attraction, of "scenery" in the dual sense that still reverberates confusedly in the discourse of environment.

The Dangers that Hedge It About

Underhill's text is particularly instructive in the way it conflates event and place in an explicitly feminized landscape that vividly encodes its narrative and psychological groundings. This is most evident in the map included in *Newes from America,* immediately after the title page, as a sort of preface to the words following it. The map depicts the Pequot fort at Mystic as two semicircles of sharply pointed palisades, within which can be seen curved rows depicting the natives' "houses" and "streets." The semicircles are slightly offset, creating two gaps marked by the words "Hear entters Captayne Underhill" and "Hear entters Captayne Mason." This drawing's obvious sexual symbolism has been ably analyzed by Anne Kibbey, who was the first to note both that the "illustration of the Puritan men attacking the Pequot fort is also a drawing of a vagina" and that the massacre itself "was the culminating fusion of sexuality and violence," closely linked to the concurrent persecution of Ann Hutchinson (110). What remains to be discussed is the way the figure's houses and palisades have been drawn to resemble teeth, which is to say, the use the figure makes of the *vagina dentata* motif.

Found in one form or another in the mythology of many cultures,[4] this image, with its recasting of penetration as an aggressive incorporation, its projection of male sexual aggression onto a castrating female sexual "appetite," bears psychological and cultural overtones significant to our understanding of gender, violence, and the American environment. Kibbey argues that Underhill's drawing signifies in a fashion that is "subverbal" and "dissociated from language" (110), expressing not only its manifest content but also the very degree of its repression, the degree to which it is verbally *in*expressible. I suggest here that the content itself, the particular metanarrative inscribed by this image upon the paradigmatic environment of Mystic, is a version of the myth of the culture hero known as Toothbreaker. One version of this story describes how "[t]he first men in the world were unable to have sexual relationship[s] with their wives until the culture hero broke the teeth of the women's vaginas."[5] Whether it is the persecuted Anne Hutchinson or the pictorially feminized Pequot Indians, violence and misogyny—the woman *palizado,* or *beaten,* as Underhill ambiguously labels her on the map—are claimed as prerequisites to securing the Puritan faith in the New World. Underhill, his mission at Mystic being to secure the conditions for a new establishment of Puritan culture, casts himself as Toothbreaker: "Hear entters Captayne Underhill," the sexual pun being not just about penetration but what is perceived as the foundational act of begetting culture upon nature, an act performed by the self-defining masculine subject upon a feminine environment.

Parallelling this narrative model is a psychological model, outlined by the psychoanalyst and critic Marie Bonaparte in her reading of Edgar Allan Poe's novel *Berenice*. The folklorist Ekkehart Malotki notes that Bonaparte, "elaborating a remark by Freud" in light of Poe's peculiar anxieties, stresses "the equation of mouth and vagina and considers the notion of the *vagina dentata* and its accompanying threat as 'a factor with roots deep in infantile experience.' At first it was the infant who displayed aggressive, i.e., occasionally biting behavior towards his mother's breast. Later it is the adult who, due to a sense of guilt stemming from his infantile behavior, feels threatened by a mother who intends to castrate him." *Vagina dentata* imagery is thus "interpreted as a projection of the unconscious anxiety of castration and is associated with male impotence" (Malotki 206). Bonaparte characterizes Poe's sexuality as an irreducible complex of love and hate, "both sadistic destruction and necrophilia" (218), as a splitting between action and object, violence toward and yearning for the same thing, destruction and nostalgia—certainly familiar pairings in both environmentalist and colonialist discourse.

Whether in the "subverbal" language of Underhill's map or the displaced anxieties of Poe's character Egaeus, "the danger of sexuality, the punishment that threatens all who yield," finds expression in an obsession with teeth, specifically in "the notion of the female vagina being furnished with teeth, and thus a source of danger in being able to bite and castrate. . . . [W]hen Egaeus yields to the morbid impulse to draw Berenice's teeth, he yields both to the yearning for the mother's organ and to be revenged upon it, since the dangers that hedge it about make him sexually avoid all women as too menacing. His act is therefore a sort of retributive castration inflicted on the mother whom he loves, and yet hates" (qtd. in Malotki 218). This oedipality finds its echo in the feminized landscape whose penetration and occupation are keenly desired but threatened by "the dangers that hedge it about." The writing of the colonial environment as feminine landscape—and of the self as masculine conqueror—requires maintaining this love and this hatred in some psychologically tenable relation, whether crudely, as in Underhill's tale of "warre-like proceedings" and "speciall places," or with the greater sophistication of later environmental narratives. As we shall see, however, the writing of environment can proceed rather differently in different historical circumstances, particularly when the wilderness hero is a woman who resists the environmental narrative's masculinizing pull.

This Wilderness Condition: Mary Rowlandson's Narrative

Immediately after setting foot on the soil of "New England," William Bradford described that contested territory as "a hidious and desolate wildernes," drawing in his account upon the biblical narrative of the Forty Years' Wandering and the conquest of Canaan, invoking one invasion to authorize another. Spinning out this conceit in his *History of Plymouth Plantation,* Bradford laments that his own people could not "as it were, goe up to the tope of Pisgah, to vew from this willdernes a more goodly cuntrie." Not only was there no such mountain near Plymouth, there was no such "goodly cuntrie" to see from it. There was nothing, Bradford makes clear, but wilderness. More accurately, that "nothing" *was* the wilderness, for the term as he uses it refers not to any palpable reality, but quite pointedly to an absence. This wilderness is perfunctorily described as full of "wild beasts and willd men," but when Bradford's description shifts from such stock generalities to the concrete and specific, it necessarily reverts to the negative: "they had now no freinds to wellcome them, nor inns to entertaine or refresh their weatherbeaten bodys, no houses or much less townes to repair too" (96). It is the same emptiness that John Eliot would describe as the "wilderness where nothing appeareth but hard labor and wants" (qtd. in Nash 26), a place devoid of materiality and signification whose only positive feature is its provocation of human action: "labor" engendered by "wants," the latter term being readable as both absence *and* wish, as the machinery of desire.

This is also the wilderness of that early American frontier classic, Mary Rowlandson's 1682 *Narrative of the Captivity.* It is a wilderness that Rowlandson at first posits almost exclusively by circumlocution, in the unmistakable language of lack:

[M]y thoughts ran upon my losses and sad bereaved condition. All was gone, my husband gone . . . my children gone, my relations and friends gone, our house and home and all our comforts within doors, and without, all was gone (except my life) and I knew not but the next moment that might go too. (326)

We had husband and father, and children, and sisters, and friends, and relations, and house, and home, and many comforts of this life: but now we may say, as Job, "*Naked I came out of my mother's womb, and naked shall I return.*" (336)

Although figured as uterine space, this wilderness has no creative ability of its own. It is rather the site of loss, where Rowlandson has "no Christian friend near" (327), where she loses her child—which loss, rather than any positive characteristic of her physical surroundings, renders her in "this wilderness condition" (329). It is never the sort of landscape that subsequent travelers might recognize by her descriptions of it; it is precisely "the wilderness where there was nothing to be seen" (359).

The terror of this defining blankness can be more fully appreciated in terms of the American Separatists' habit of grounding both personal experience and social order in a pervasive textuality, in the belief that there was nothing, as Adrienne Rich puts it, "so trivial that it could not speak a divine message." The high stakes and uncertainty of salvation made the Puritans eager and anxious readers of their surroundings, a people for whom even the "piecemeal thoughts of a woman stirring her pot" were "clues to her 'justification' in Christ" (x). Such introspection played a key role in Puritan ideology and governance even during the best of times; in the aftermath of a tremendous public trauma such as King Philip's War, it was partly through acts of revision, a reassignment of meanings in this saturating social text, that "Puritanism could once again govern, by virtue of explanatory cogency, the entire range of human experience" (Breitwieser 8).

There was nothing in this Puritan universe that did not, or at least could not, signify. But by virtue of what interpretive code? Like any reader confronted with a seemingly unreadable text, Rowlandson faced a hermeneutic challenge, that of creating and justifying an interpretive stance and practice. Rich quotes Anne Bradstreet on the importance and difficulty of such a mission: "[A]dmit this be the true God whom we worship, and that be his word, yet why may not the Popish religion be the right? They have the same God, the same Christ, the same word: they only interpret it one way, we another" (xi). For the seventeenth-century Puritan, the difficulty here was not just individual and idiosyncratic, but communal and doctrinal. It was not merely the justification of the individual in Christ that was at stake, that demanded closure; the justification of the "wilderness errand" itself would founder on polysemy and hence demanded a particular and authoritative interpretation. For "if Archbishop Laud and the Hierarchists back in England were right," as Rich puts it, "what was one doing . . . on that stretch of intemperate coast?" (xi). What, indeed, *was* one doing there? For the captive Mary Rowlandson, frightened, hungry, freezing, and bereaved, that question would have taken on the greatest urgency, and she would by habit have attempted to read her surroundings, her wilderness environment, in search of an answer. As she herself writes, her "earnest and unfeigned desire" was for a "token" or "sign" (329–30)—but that was precisely what the wilderness, by definition, could not provide.

It was when confronted with this sort of "vast blankness," writes Roderick Nash of the New England coast's earliest colonists, that "courage failed and imagination multiplied fears" (26). And it is indeed the imagination that populates the otherwise empty Puritan wilderness, that makes it teem, if not with tangible rivers and mountains and trees, at least with innumerable "troubles" and "difficulties" and "afflictions" (Rowlandson 305). That imagination makes the wilderness nearly as allegorical as the landscapes of *Pilgrim's Progress* or the *Inferno*—in Rowlandson's words, a "lively resemblance of Hell" (326), the "valley of the shadow of death" (363), a "horrible pit" (364)—makes it an inscription of an imported cultural landscape onto the "real" landscape of New England. More particularly, Rowlandson's narrative, like Underhill's, can be read as an inscription of the psychosexual dynamics of *environment* as manifested at a particular historical moment, in this case King Philip's War.

Rowlandson's narrative differs in at least two crucial ways from Underhill's. Later in this chapter I will discuss her refusal or inability to seamlessly adopt the masculine subject position typically created in the writing of environment. Here I want to stress the fact that whereas the Pequot War was naked white aggression, the events of 1675–1676 constituted a genuine and substantial native resistance—in fact, the most effective of the entire colonial period. Philip's Wampanoags, the Narragansetts, and other allied tribes attacked some ninety white settlements, completely destroying twelve of them and killing several thousand colonists. In proportion to the European population of the time, it was the worst war in Anglo-American history, claiming the lives of one in sixteen colonial combatants and severely disrupting commerce and trade. To many back in England the war called into question the viability of the colonial endeavor itself.[6]

The defeat of the Indians in 1676 helped allay such doubts. But the psychological specter of *environment*, which this war more than any other in American history may be said to have embodied, would continue to haunt representations of the event. John Underhill employed the trope of the toothed vagina to project white penetration and aggression onto a feminized and potentially castrating Indian environment, cartographically figured as *vagina dentata*. Puritan accounts of King Philip's War had their own way of characterizing the native threat in terms of an improper and unrestrained female sexuality that threatened masculine power, as in this description of how King Philip cemented his "conspiracy": "[H]is first Errand is to a *Squaw Sachem* (i.e. a Woman Prince, or Queen) who is the Widow of a Brother to King Philip, deceased, he promising her great rewards if she would joyn with him in this Conspiracy, (for she is as Potent a Prince as any round about her, and hath as much Corn, Land, and Men, at her Command) she willingly consented, and was much more forward in the Design, and had greater Success than King *Philip* himself" (*Present State* [1]). This misogynist figure of an Indian queen—named only by the "unnatural" conjunction of her sex and her power ("Squaw Sachem," "Woman Prince")—at once feminizes and dehumanizes the resisting native. It is utterly "vain," we read elsewhere, "to expect any thing but the most barbarous usages from such a people amongst whom the most milde and gentle sex delight in cruelties, and have utterly abandoned at once the two proper Virtues of Womankinde, Pity and Modesty." The castration anxiety underlying this construct is at times explicit. What Underhill's map merely implied is in this account physically performed: "[T]wo men coming from *Malbury* to *Sudbury*, were set upon in the Woods by a Great Number of *Indian Women*, armed with clubs, pieces of Swords, and the like, who by their numbers having over-mastered the two poor Travellers, that had nothing but small sticks to defend themselves with, beat out their brains, and cut off their privy members, which they carried away with them in triumph" (*New and Further* 4).

The motif of the *vagina dentata* thus reappears in the guise of *penis captivus*, suggesting that we read *The Narrative of the Captivity* in terms of the loss and retrieval of the phallus—the loss and retrieval of Mrs. Rowlandson as she functioned for her husband in New England society. As Luce Irigaray reminds us in *This Sex Which Is Not One*, "Women are marked phallicly by their fathers, husbands, procurers," so that women within patriarchy become "the locus of a more or less competitive exchange between men," including, notably, "the competition for the possession of mother earth" (32). Because Rowlandson had been the daughter of the village's wealthiest resident and largest landholder, she empowered her comparatively penurious husband not only sexually but also socially and economically. What were held captive, among other things, were the status and economic power he had gained through her. As Cotton Mather describes the situation, "Mr. *Rowlandson* (the faithful Pastor of the Church there) had his House, Goods, Books, all burned; his Wife and all his Children led away Captive before the Enemy. Himself (as God would have it) was not at home, whence his own person was delivered, which otherwise (without a Miracle) would have been endangered" (qtd. in Howe 92). Mary Rowlandson's captivity here becomes just one loss among others suffered by her husband. This loss in turn stands in for that unnamed loss that would have presumably been inflicted upon his own person had he been present, with the bodily imagery of an endangered "person" subtly but continually figuring captivity of the wife as potential castration of the husband.

Predictably, then, the captive narrator functions to "shelter the masculine covenant" (Howe 97). This function becomes clearer after the Third Remove, when Rowlandson comes into possession of a plundered Bible. This is a crucial turning point in the story, and I would suggest that part of the suspense now centers on the return of not just Rowlandson but of the Bible as well. It becomes in part a narrative of the captivity of the sacred word, and it is this primal word, circulating where previously there was none, that begins the transformation of what had been "an unmarked Christianography" (99) into the sort of legible wilderness we will find in *The Last of the Mohicans*.

In this view, Rowlandson functions not as a writing subject but as bearer of the phallus, a writer by proxy, shepherding the Logos through an as-yet-uncoded space. She begins her sojourn in a wilderness like that described by Bradford, a wilderness that is no positive landscape at all but rather a *condition* of loss and bewilderment. It is a place where she literally does not know how to respond or what to do, even with her most basic emotions: "Although I had met with so much affliction, and my heart was many times ready to break, yet could I not shed one tear in their sight: but rather had been all this while in a maze, and like one astonished" (336). Trapped where there are no signs, Rowlandson longs for one; her "earnest and unfeigned desire," as we have seen, is for nothing more than a "token," a "sign" (329–330). But how can wilderness be made to signify?

It is the Bible that now, like Stevens's jar in the wilds of Tennessee, begins to systematize and encode the space around it. Once Rowlandson is able to advert to this text, she can alleviate her bewilderment and name what she sees around her. Her account up to this point has offered absolutely no description of the landscape as a presence, but that landscape now becomes, in lockstep with a mediating and authorizing scriptural gloss, the object of a recognizable description: "[Q]uickly we came to wade over the river, and passed some tiresome and wearisome hills. One hill was so steep that I was fain to creep up upon my knees, and to hold by the twiggs and bushes to keep myself from falling backward. My head also was so light that I usually reeled as I went, but I hope all these wearisome steps that I have taken are but a forewarning to me of heavenly rest. 'I know, O Lord, that thy judgements are right, and that Thou in faithfulness hast afflicted me,' Psalm 119:75" (340). For virtually every description of this nascent geography, Rowlandson evokes a biblical landscape to match. To read and describe the landscape, she must simultaneously read her Bible, in which the real landscape is to be found—the real landscape of which the merely physical landscape through which she travels is but a type, a comparatively inconsequential manifestation:

> We began this remove with wading over Baquag river: the water was up to the knees, and the stream very swift, and so cold that I thought it would have cut me in sunder. . . . [B]ut in my distress the Lord gave me experience of the truth, and goodness of that promise, Isaiah 43:2. *When thou passest through the waters, I will be with thee, and through the rivers, they shall not overflow thee.* (348)

> At last, after many weary steps, I saw Wachusett hills, but many miles off. Then we came to a great swamp, through which we travelled, up to the knees, in mud and water. . . . I thought I should have sunk down at last, and never gat out; but I may say, as in Psalm 94:18, *When my foot slipped, thy mercy, O Lord, held me up.* (350–351)

Here, perhaps more clearly than with Underhill's text, we see the beginning of a literary-environmental interpretation, the enlistment of the physical landscape in a legitimating master narrative—an initial writing of a landscape that the Euro-American would be able to *read* in order to justify her presence within it. And while from a modern standpoint it may seem difficult to view *The Narrative of the Captivity* as "nature writing" or "environmental literature," it is nonetheless important to our understanding of those genres because it so clearly thematizes the gendered and historically responsive practices of literary environmentalism.

The Wilderness Where There Was Nothing to Be Seen

Rowlandson's early characterization of wilderness as absence sounds like nothing so much as the Western discourse of "Woman," that fictional sex which, as Luce Irigaray puts it, "is not one," which "has nothing to show" and whose "sexual organ represents *the horror of nothing to see*" (26). Wilderness and Woman are both classically predicated on their own negation, on a refusal to "see" them as anything but what they are not. In the first instance this is accomplished by means of a profoundly anti-ecological vision of a disorderly nature and an ethnocentric dismissal of native culture *qua* culture; in the second, via androcentric hierarchies in which "[f]emale sexuality has always been conceptualized on the basis of masculine parameters" (23). Also negated in each case is an entire realm of speech and writing. Rowlandson repeatedly posits wilderness as the site of a sort of unspeech, an unintelligible "din," the "noise and hooping" (330) of a feminized native Other. Shifting and confusing, as unreadable as the wilderness in which it is found and of which it is just another "bewildering" component, this is the speech of those who are "unstable" and "mad" (352), the complete antithesis of a trustworthy speech. "So like were these barbarous creatures to him who was a liar from the beginning" (344), Rowlandson writes of the native people she encountered during her captivity, that "there is not one of them that makes the least conscience of speaking the truth" (342).

Thus figured as predating the Fall and the onset of the Law—"a liar *from the beginning*"—this is a surviving (hence also a resisting) speech, one that has not yet, to make explicit the analogy I have been drawing with *écriture féminine* by citing the words of Hélène Cixous, been "called in by the cops of the signifier." Rowlandson's typologizing wilderness discourse functions to bring this wild din "into the line of order," assigning each of its elements "to a precise place in the chain that's always formed for a privileged signifier," piecing it "to the string which leads back, if not to the Name-of-the-Father" then, in a "twist" that would seem to apply to the activity of the Bible-toting female captive, "to the place of the phallic-mother" (Cixous 892).

In thus encoding what had previously been defined as uncoded and indescribable, Rowlandson is not so much objectively describing the wilderness as she is beginning to replace it with something else, with a new discursive formation that will be called (and still is called) by the same name, but whose effects will prove entirely different. As a crucial term in the dialectic of civilization and savagery, wilderness is to be subjected to what Cixous terms the "phallologocentric sublation" (885), canceled but also preserved and elevated within a larger synthesis. Wilderness as the disorienting, chaotic, and inexplicable is to be sublated into a reified hueristic, an unabashedly *explanatory* construct.[7]

In this new discourse, wilderness becomes less and less Other and more and more at "one with the phallocentric tradition" (Cixous 879). It is in this sense no longer "wilderness" at all, and the ease with which it can continue to pass under the same name may owe in part to the deployment of the phallic mother to reinscribe it—just another instance, perhaps, of the phallocracy deploying women "to mobilize their immense strength against themselves," to be the "executants" of men's "virile needs" (878). Rowlandson is enlisted as the mystifying agent of a new literary environmentalism, as the nominal speaker through which patriarchy apostrophizes the wilderness with a version of Cixous's facetious admonition: "Hold still, we're going to do your portrait, so that you can begin looking like it right away" (892).

If Rowlandson's emerging literary-environmental discourse is in this way sublative, writing and elevating wilderness only by simultaneously negating and misnaming it, how can it be thought of as the discursive vehicle for a future wilderness preservation? What kind of preservation can possibly be predicated on such a cancellation? Environmentalism would indeed later preserve landscapes physically more or less unaltered, but only by means of an incessant and increasingly institutionalized teaching and stabilizing of what those landscapes *mean*, a radical alteration of the destabilizing character that would once have *defined* those lands as wilderness.

Is there an alternative to this preservation that is simultaneously an erasure? Is there a possibility for a preservation that would mean more than simply keeping an expanse of land untrammeled, a praxis that would include such preservation but also exceed it, challenging rather than reinforcing the codes that negate the earlier notion of the "wild"? Taking my cue from Cixous's reference to the unconscious as "that other limitless country," "the place where the repressed manage to survive" (880), I suggest that such a praxis would take seriously the old idea of wilderness as both a geographical place and a psychic and cultural condition while refusing the earlier characterizing of wilderness as a lack. It would be analogous to an *écriture féminine*, a writing that "unthinks" the negating phallogocentric order (882), that breaks the codes that otherwise reign in the wild and make it speak for something else. It would preserve wilderness as radical difference rather than alienating it from its own wildness and fashioning it into a reassuring outlier of civilization. Reconstructed in a discourse that is, in Irigaray's words, "somewhat mad from the standpoint of reason" and "inaudible for whoever listens . . . with ready-made grids, with a fully elaborated code in hand" (29), this wilderness might be as foreign to a modern environmentalist as today's "global ecology" would have been to a seventeenth-century Puritan.

In the particular case of Mary Rowlandson, this other wilderness writing would be the expression of a thoroughly disoriented body rather than a putatively satisfied soul, a writing from a wilderness bodily *experienced* as difference. For Rowlandson, certainly, the conditions for such a revisionary writing were in place, with the tremendous emotional disruption of her losses and captivity recalling what Cixous speaks of as the moment when a feminine writing becomes possible: "that radical mutation of things brought on by a material upheaval when every structure is for a moment thrown off balance and an ephemeral wildness sweeps order away" (879).

Rowlandson's wilderness experience must have palpably outstripped the discourse in which she was constrained to relate it. Mitchell Breitwieser has remarked on the ubiquitous and irreducible excess in her narrative, noting how, in "a kind of ideological misfire," thoughts "come forward that do not reduce entirely to exemplary status" (8). Instead, Rowlandson repeatedly struggles with memories that resist such reduction and thereby permit occasional glimpses of "interdicted subjective presences otherwise almost completely absent from the seventeenth-century New England archive" (Breitwieser 9). Refusing or unable to ignore completely what "experience did to comprehension" (12), Rowlandson is unable to write seamlessly from the usual literary-environmental subject position—that of the white male for whom interpreting the wilderness serves both to consolidate possession and reify masculinity.

This "ideological misfire" occurs partly for reasons of gender. But history, too, is a factor. There was, for example, the political necessity, always present but heightened following King Philip's War, of reassuring those who doubted the wisdom of the colonial enterprise. Counterposed to this was the contemporary theological necessity of producing and maintaining that state of acute anxiety over salvation so central to New England Puritanism. The first of these necessities demanded a certain closure in the interpretation of the local history and geography, while the second thrived in a textual atmosphere of polysemy and deferral in which one could read those places and events incessantly but could never be *sure* of their meaning, any more than one could be sure of one's own election in Christ. It is difficult enough for texts to smooth over the gap between intention and realization; in Rowlandson's narrative, the intentions themselves operate at cross-purposes. Her text repeatedly arrives at impasses created by the dichotomies that structure it—oppositions between anxiety and reassurance, deferral and closure, the personal and the political, the individual and the communal, alienation and integration, experience and ideology, and grieving and exemplification.

Thus as Rowlandson (and, most likely, her male editors) tries to fit her wilderness experience into the dominant discourse, she finds that discourse's language, with its conflicting conventions, to be woefully inadequate. She encounters irreducible dichotomies that repeatedly drive her narrative into a mode of *dé-pense*, of unthinking a totalizing and communalizing framework of representation unable to do justice to her specific experience and her psychological need. The result is a double edge at times incredibly moving:

> I can remember the time, when I used to sleep quietly without workings in my thoughts, whole nights together, but now it is other ways with me. When all are fast about me, and no eye open, but His who ever waketh, my thoughts are upon things past. . . . I remember in the night season, how the other day I was in the midst of thousands of enemies, and nothing but death before me: it is then hard work to persuade myself, that ever I should be satisfied with bread again. But now we are fed with the finest of the wheat, and, as I may say, with honey out of the rock: instead of the husk, we have the fatted calf: the thoughts of these things in the particulars of them, and of the love and goodness of God towards us, make it true of me, what David said of himself, Psalms 6.6. *I watered my couch with my tears.* Oh! the wonderful power of God that mine eyes have seen, affording matter enough for my thoughts to run in, that when others are sleeping mine are weeping. (365)

Audible in this passage are resistances and refusals that keep open the possibility of a "wildness" the narrative functions more generally to foreclose. It foregrounds, first of all, Rowlandson's continuing alienation rather than her integration into the community: while the others are sleeping, she is weeping.

Mentioning "God's goodness to *us*" but stressing what is "true of *me*," it relativizes even as it universalizes, refusing to subordinate personal experience to political exemplification.

In a mode that is decidedly "unthinking," Rowlandson posits in this passage a temporal frame that juxtaposes the elements of experience and exemplification, yoking them together in ways that highlight their irreducibility. She does not assign her bewilderment and pain to some distant past, which would allow her to deploy the immediate present as a separate and more mature site of reassurance and comfort. Instead she replaces that logical temporality with an emotional synchrony in which a season is compressed into a night and the events of years past can be said to have occurred just "the other day." This living past does not *prefigure* the present but rather actively contests it; Rowlandson thus insists that "it is," not "was," "hard work" to wring any assurances out of her experience.

Because it sustains the sort of anxiety that fueled Christian zeal, this acuteness of memory can be viewed as having a certain theological efficacy. But it also alienates Rowlandson from her peers and prevents any communal agreement on the meaning of her experiences. This aspect of the text, this disruption of the drive toward closure and stabilization, is foregrounded where one might least expect it to be—in the psalm Rowlandson chooses to quote in the passage above. This allusion might seem an appeal of the same sort that putatively grounds Rowlandson's descriptions of the New England wilderness, a finalizing referral to biblical authority. But the psalm itself expresses not so much David's suffering, and the meaning of that suffering, as it does his *bewilderment*, his inability to understand his suffering and make it exemplify. Not merely his "bones," as he puts it, but also his "soul" is "sore vexed" (*Psalms* 6:2–3). It is not his physical suffering but precisely this vexation of the soul from which he asks deliverance, and no such resolution is in sight: "[B]ut thou, O Lord, how long?" (6:3). The psalm's topic is not suffering and alleviation but deferral, and it is no accident that while David insists "[t]he Lord hath heard my supplication" and "will receive my prayer" (6:9), he nowhere gives an indication that God has answered that prayer. It is significant that at such a moment of personal crisis Rowlandson refers her readers to a psalm whose subjects are precisely bewilderment and the longing for and deferral of closure.

At certain key points, Rowlandson refuses even the stark dichotomy of presence and absence in terms of which the wilderness had at first been constructed. Commenting on "the extreme vanity of this world," she notes that "one hour I have been in health, and wealth, *wanting nothing:* but the next hour in sickness and wounds, and death, *having nothing* but sorrow and affliction" (365, my emphases). She juxtaposes apparently inassimilable opposites: one hour it is presence, the next it is absence that structures her existence. But the two terms themselves are not wholly distinct, and Rowlandson underscores their interpenetration, characterizing "presence," the putatively positive and self-sufficient term, by means of a double negative, "*wanting* nothing"—lacking lack, as it were, but also, as she soon makes clear, *desiring* lack. Reciprocally, the negative term is formulated as a sort of positive, as a *having* of nothing. Rowlandson moves immediately to exploit the ambiguity of "wanting" as both lack and desire: "Before I knew what affliction meant, I was ready sometimes to wish for it. When I lived in prosperity . . . and yet seeing many, whom I preferred before myself, under many trials and afflictions, in sickness, weakness, poverty, losses, crosses, and cares of this world, I should be sometimes jealous lest I should not have my portion in this life. . . . But now I see the Lord had his time to scourge and chasten me. The portion of some is to have their afflictions by drops, now one drop and then another; but the dregs of the cup, the wine of astonishment, like a sweeping rain that leaveth no food, did the Lord prepare to be my portion. Affliction I wanted, and affliction I had, full measure (I thought) pressed down and running over" (365–366). In a mixing of categories that leaves all ultimately confused, absence becomes a "sweeping" plenitude, a "full measure" "running over," and so on. Such paradoxes create an impasse the text highlights but refuses to resolve. At the end of the narrative, where we might expect an attempt at closure, we find instead this reopening, this preference for the disorienting "wine of astonishment" over the sobering milk of exemplification. Rowlandson preserves her experience of wilderness in a *dé-pense,* a refusal of the writing by which that wilderness is more generally sublated. Faintly audible in this refusal is a language with which the American wilderness might have been written, and with which it might yet be rewritten.

Chapter Four

Performing Wilderness

"Words built the world and words can destroy the world. . . ."
"Well, you take the words; I'll take the rifle. That's the only word I
need. R-i-f-l-e."
—Ishmael Reed, *Flight to Canada*

In *Hard Facts: Setting and Form in the American Novel,* Philip
Fisher examines how James Fenimore Cooper's wilderness romances helped
reinvent "the categories of man and thing" that were so fiercely contested in the
early national period. Elaborating on D. H. Lawrence's and Leslie Fiedler's
influential analyses of the American wilderness as a stage for white male self-
actualization, Fisher stresses that the Leatherstocking novels naturalized their
constructions with the help of a "moral and perceptual practice" through which
Cooper skillfully guided his early readers—a practice that "includes repetition"
(4) and amounts to what I will treat as the performance of a new nature capable
of grounding a new subjectivity. One goal of this chapter is to take Fisher's
argument a step further by exploring how Cooper's most popular wilderness
novel, *The Last of the Mohicans,* not only rehearses but in fact *thematizes* such
performativity.

The Last of the Mohicans demonstrates particularly well the complexities of
the "double articulation of subjectivity and landscape" because it constructs the
natural environment not merely as a stage for the enactment of identity, but
also as a transparently readable book, as a "natural" text capable of hailing its
readers without any cultural mediation. Despite that putative transparency,
however, the novel contradictorily figures Natty Bumppo as the indispensable
interpreter of that text, the intermediary without whom nature ceases to signify.
Nature in this scheme is located variously in the wilderness (as the uncivilized
nonhuman) and in the Indian (as the uncivilized human); in exemplary literary-
environmental fashion, *Mohicans* deploys these loci as "cultural contestants"

enabling the demarcation of a white and male American civilization. Such an articulation requires the stability of a set of interrelated binary oppositions— male/female, white/nonwhite, civilized/savage. But even as it depends upon these categories, the novel also interrogates them, repeatedly inviting readers to wonder, for example, if Cora Munro is "really" "white," or if the noble Uncas is "really" a "savage." The difficulty in answering such questions unambiguously produces a sense of what Marjorie Garber has termed "category crisis" (16), a crisis that could be averted only by grounding the novel's binaries in the seemingly unassailable ur-binary, nature/culture. By novel's end, however, the boundary separating even these terms proves dangerously permeable, deepening rather than ameliorating the sense of category crisis and forcing the conclusion that the wilderness itself is not natural but performative—a possibility signified by the novel's repeated instances of cross-species transvestism.

In its attempt to ground an American culture in American nature, *The Last of the Mohicans* strives to stabilize its writing of wild bodies: the body of the Indian and the body of the wilderness. In both cases, the novel presents wild bodies as self-originating and transparently legible; what is figured by them is decidedly not the blank wilderness of the early Puritans, but the fully sublated, exemplary wilderness that had proved so attractive to American colonists in the wake of the Enlightenment. As Thomas Paine so famously put it, nature is the eternal handwriting of the deistic God, of "the Creation" that "speaks a universal language"; it is "an ever-existing original, which every man can read" (43)— and, by implication, a universal and indisputable source of authority. Paine delineates sharply, as Natty Bumppo would do later, between merely human writing and the culturally uninflected yet ultimately more instructive writing that is nature. "[D]o we want to know what God is?" asks Paine. "Search not the book called the Scripture, which any human hand might make, but the Scripture called the creation" (44). This is more or less how literary environmentalism still tends to invoke the wilderness—as intrinsic and prediscursive, an original inscription whose legibility is prior to and uncorrupted by any cultural marking.

In this chapter I will examine *The Last of the Mohicans'* self-contradictory notion of bodies that can be held to signify great cultural truths while somehow bearing no trace of a "merely" cultural inscription. In so doing I will treat the environment, as I do throughout this book, as a product of history—as emanating from actions and desires that have little to do with "nature" "itself." To the extent that Cooper's wilderness is held to signify, I view it as the perduring nominalization and naturalization of those actions and desires, just as I have earlier treated *environment* as the nominalization and naturalization of such founding acts as conquest and genocide, and such continuing, reiterative acts as National Park Service interpretation. I want ultimately to align my interrogation of the "wild" body with Judith Butler's critique of the prediscursive *human* body. The question in either case is how such bodies are abstracted from the events that produce and reproduce them as "natural." In *Gender Trouble,* Butler observes that Foucault figured the body "as a surface and the scene of a cultural inscription: 'the body is the inscribed surface of events,'" so that the "task of genealogy . . . is 'to expose a body totally imprinted by history'" (129). Noting, however, the way Foucault referred to "the goal of 'history'" as the "'destruction of the body,'" Butler adds that as "'a volume in perpetual disintegration,' the body is always under siege, suffering destruction by the very terms of history. And history is the creation of values and meanings by a signifying practice that requires the subjection of the body." Wild nature can be examined as just such a body, "described through the language of surface and force" and "weakened through a 'single drama' of domination, inscription, and creation." Butler insists that a sort of "corporeal destruction" is required "to produce the speaking subject" (130); similarly, in order for nature to "speak," to signify itself through an apparently unmediated legibility, it must also be dominated, inscribed, and created—all as it is, paradoxically, *destroyed.* I can think of no better way to introduce such a project than by taking a brief detour to examine the paradoxical career of that great lover and prodigious destroyer of natural bodies, John James Audubon.

Shooting as Writing

Longing for the preservation in words of a wilderness he knew was going to disappear in reality, John James Audubon pinned his hopes at first on the art of his famous contemporary, the novelist Sir Walter Scott. "How many times I have longed for him to come to my beloved country," wrote Audubon in his journal in 1826, "that he might describe, as no one else ever can, the stream, the swamp, the river, the mountain, for the sake of future ages. A century hence they will not be here as I see them, Nature will have been robbed of many brilliant charms, the rivers will have been tormented and turned astray from their primitive courses, the hills will be leveled with the swamps, and perhaps the swamps will have become a mound surmounted by a fortress of a thousand guns. Scarce a magnolia will Louisiana possess, the timid Deer will exist nowhere, fish will no longer abound in the rivers, the Eagle scarce ever alight, and these millions of lovely songsters be driven away or slain by man. Without Sir Walter Scott these beauties must perish unknown to the world" (182). I quote this passage partly to demonstrate the prescience of Audubon's early environmentalist sensibility—his sympathies seem modern enough, even if some of his specific predictions are off the mark—and partly to highlight his anxiety as a writer, his conviction that his own work was somehow inadequate to the task of representing and memorializing the American wilderness. As it turned out, of course, that anxiety was unfounded. Audubon was no Scott, yet he could write well enough, and for generations now his work has been routinely included in anthologies of nature writing.

Audubon had a paradoxical sense of his own environmentalism as both discursive and economic, as both idealist and stubbornly materialist. Remarking in 1835 that America was still inadequately chronicling its vanishing wilderness, he wrote that this was not "because no one in America is able to accomplish such an undertaking." He may still have considered himself inadequate in this regard, but he conceded that authors such as Washington Irving and James Fenimore Cooper had proved themselves quite capable. The problem, rather, was that in spite of the work of such writers, the destruction of nature was proceeding "with such rapidity, as almost to rival the movement of their pen[s]" (Audubon, *Delineations* 5). The image here is of an almost direct transmutation of disappearing things into newly appearing words, of a discursive economic engine that mixes labor ("the movement of their pens") with natural raw material to produce the cultural commodity of text.

It was perhaps inevitable that Audubon would thus associate the representation of nature with its consumption. He had already done a good deal of work in taxidermy—perhaps the most transparently violent form of nature writing—and later in life he would support himself through the sale of his famed paintings, each of which had cost the life of not just one but several birds, sometimes hundreds of them. Throughout his life, that is, Audubon participated in an economy that commodified various aspects of wild nature, in a system in which the representation of nature was indistinguishable from its destruction—a destruction that was clearly not going to be *prevented* (Audubon never saw that as a genuine possibility) but could at least be *compensated for* by the concomitant production of valuable artifacts.

Driven by his own sometimes dire financial circumstances, Audubon almost single-handedly took the emerging literary-environmental economy of his time to a new level. A financial failure earlier in life, he turned his fortunes around with his elephant-folio edition of *Birds of North America*, selling nearly two hundred copies at one thousand dollars per set (Kieran 105). In convincing publishers and patrons of the value of what we recognize today as a forerunner of the large-format, "coffee-table" nature book, Audubon was doing more than helping to inaugurate a practice that still flourishes today. He was also demonstrating that nature, via the mediation of art, could participate in a new and more direct way in culture—not, as in the Puritan conception of wilderness, as the irreducibly Other accessible only via a troubled and sometimes traumatic confrontation, but as an object directly exchangeable for, and thus commensurate with, other objects in the marketplace. This sort of commodification of nature was not unique to Audubon, but in his case it is acutely obvious, if only because he personally participated in the entire process. He observed and shot the birds; he then represented them, via the arts of taxidermy and writing as well as painting; he then sought out and developed a market for those representations; and he finally supervised their material reproduction and distribution. It is in Audubon's case particularly easy to see the literary environmental activity of the artist not as a break from but as continuous with his earlier, more obviously economic activities as a sawmill owner and taxidermist.

Yet, philosophically, Audubon seems to have been more Neoplatonist than materialist. He was so famously prolific with his gun precisely because he wished to make each of his representations true to an ideal type that was not to be found in any single bird but could only be inferred from the collectivity. In so doing, he "'typified' nature," in the words of Donna Haraway; he "made nature true to type," deploying his gun to reduce nature's unruly individual variation to an imagined underlying structure (38). This reliance upon the typifying gun makes particularly manifest the way that the "real" "body" of nature is transmuted and made to participate directly in the cultural order, a realm to which— in a thoroughgoing mystification—it is still held by definition to be opposed.

Elaborating on the "historical mode of signification" that has produced gender, Butler explains the dynamics of this mystification. If "the creation of values . . . requires the destruction of the body," then that very destruction implies that "there must be a body prior to that inscription, stable and self-identical, subject to that sacrificial destruction," so that the very fact of inscription seems to point to and to valorize (for we only "sacrifice" what we value) some prediscursive natural body. Butler observes further that "cultural values emerge as the result of an inscription on the body, understood as a medium, indeed, a blank page; in order for this inscription to signify, however, that medium must itself be destroyed—that is, fully transvaluated into a sublimated domain of values. Within the metaphorics of this notion of cultural values is the figure of history as a relentless writing instrument and the body as the medium that must be destroyed and transfigured in order for 'culture' to emerge" (Butler, *Gender* 130). In Audubon's taxidermy and in the paintings based upon it, the body of nature is quite literally emptied out and made to signify on its surface. In this specific instance the writing instrument that accomplishes this, that destroys the body and recasts it as artifact, is appropriately figured not as the paintbrush or pen but as the gun. Positioned as it is at the beginning of that chain in which a living bird becomes first a stuffed figure and only secondarily a painted image— first a surface and then an image of a surface—it is the gun and not the paintbrush that first mediates between the "real," "prediscursive" body of nature and its destruction and inscription. And inasmuch as destroying a target implies the previous existence of that target, shooting powerfully reifies the notion of a prediscursive natural body.

Sadly Abused by Man

Given Audubon's eventual successes, why would he have felt that without the particular aid of Sir Walter Scott the beauties of the wilderness "must perish unknown to the world"? It is tempting to answer that Audubon saw in Scott a figure who could popularize an environmental movement— someone whose literary skill (like that of John Muir later in the century) could charm and motivate the public, whose fame could popularize the movement, and whose cultural authority could legitimate it. But to say this is to project the goals and strategies of a later environmentalism onto a time when they did not exist. For Audubon, the danger seems to have been not that the wilderness would perish "unknown," but simply, as I suggested above, that there would be little in the way of cultural accomplishment to show for its loss. It would never be exchanged for anything possessing the sort of perpetual circulability traditionally secured only in the marketplace of the high-cultural artifact. In 1826, Audubon might have had little inkling of his own eventual stature; indeed, he would have had little reason to think that "nature writing" would become a form of belles lettres at all. But by that time the cultural ascendancy of fiction, and of the historical novel in particular, was perfectly evident, and Scott was perhaps the most prominent novelist then taking a direct interest in wild landscapes.

It should not be really surprising, then, that Audubon wished particularly for Sir Walter Scott to take on the job of immortalizing the wilderness. Nor should it be surprising that Audubon eventually pronounced James Fenimore Cooper a capable substitute, for Cooper shared with Audubon both an admiration of Scott and an early environmentalist sensibility. In fact, in the intensity of his response to the destruction of the wilderness and in his fictional modeling of a specific stance toward that destruction, he clearly outdid Audubon.[1] Ultimately, however, the literary environmentalism of *The Last of the Mohicans* depends less upon Cooper's love of nature than it does upon his novelistic technique. And the crucial aspect of that technique—the one that links him most directly to Scott, from whom he borrowed it—is his handling of the convention of the picturesque. As Blake Nevius has shown, Cooper learned from Scott how to "combine picturesque action with picturesque scenery" (2). And here the student may be said to have outdone the master, for with Scott, "after a lapse of time we can recall his characters and actions more vividly than his physical settings," while with Cooper, what we tend to remember is not any action but a set of brilliantly evoked wilderness tableaux (4). In thus adapting and intensifying this particular aspect of Scott's technique, Cooper made a decisive move toward literary environmentalism—one of whose primary effects, after all, is to naturalize narratives by writing them as landscapes, and to do so convincingly enough that, as Nevius says, the reader forgets the originary action. Lulled into believing we encounter the landscape "itself," we unwittingly internalize the fictions it encodes.

Arguing in similar terms for the primacy of Cooper's scenery over his plots, John F. Lynen has suggested how and why Cooper's fiction might have taken this turn. Foremost among Cooper's shortcomings as a novelist, according to Lynen, "is the static quality of [his] characters," it being "representative of Cooper's method" that his "personages cannot change or grow" (178). This rules out the usual handling of plot, for in a novel "whose situation remains unchanging, action is most completely a matter of finding things out" (183), and the only "real" plot consists "in the reader's and characters' understanding of facts which remain constant" (176). Instead of developing in the usual sense, that is, changing in response to the action, Cooper's characters are simply "seen in the process of discovering the truths of their situation" (178).

When action and characterization are formulated as a process of discovery, however, how is the reader to find out what the characters are to find out? And how is the author to replicate in the reader the sense that "the truths of *their* situation"—the emphasized pronoun here referring both to characters and to readers—were there to be discovered all along? In order for Cooper to "manage" his novel's "real action," it becomes necessary that "the landscape should contain in its visible elements all the social and psychological truths the story will bring into view." The function of the many narrated adventures is simply to "provide the occasion for beautifully realized tableaux" (183), while the novel's "true action" proceeds somewhere beneath the surface of events, in the form of a constant implication and suggestion. "The process of perception in which Cooper engages the reader through his description of the setting enacts in brief the process by which the narrative will develop" (173), and the key to the action, the truth that is to be discovered, remains "always an inference, always something intuited from the tableau of the presently visible world" (175).

An example of such a tableau and such an inference is the deceptively objective-sounding description of a wilderness landscape offered up by the narrator in the quiet lull that succeeds the gun battle at Glenn's Falls: "The uproar which had lately echoed through the vaults of the forest was gone, leaving the rush of the waters to swell and sink on the currents of the air, in the unmingled sweetness of nature. A fish-hawk, which, secure on the topmost branches of a dead pine, had been a distant spectator of the fray, now stooped from his high and ragged perch, and soared, in wide sweeps, above his prey; while a jay, whose noisy voice had been stilled by the hoarser cries of the savages, ventured again to open his discordant throat, as though once more in undisturbed possession of his wild domains" (81). This scene provokes in the admiring Heyward "a glimmering of hope," a "reviving confidence of success" that will rally him "to renewed exertions." It is thus not only picturesque but also *inspiring*—but inspiring of what, exactly? We know as readers what Heyward cannot know as a character: that while it is indeed the "undisturbed possession" of America's "wild domains" that is at issue, those domains are to be wrested not only from the Indians and the French but also, soon enough, from the British. However faintly, we recognize this passage as patriotic history rewritten as a landscape description. It is a thinly veiled picture of the American colonies following "the uproar" of the French and Indian War itself. The victorious British Crown, which maintains a shadowy presence throughout the novel as one of the "distant monarchs of Europe" (15), appears as the fishhawk, "a distant spectator of the fray," perched triumphantly at the panoptic apex of its newly secured empire. Much of Cooper's American audience would have known that it was that very security—the fact that the colonists no longer needed Britain to defend them against the French and Indian threat—that would help enable their subsequent drive toward independence. No longer "stilled by the hoarser cries of the savages," the "noisy voice" and "discordant" notes of colonial discontent thus make themselves heard immediately in the silence.

Exceeding the plotting function identified by Lynen—which seems little more than mere foreshadowing—such "descriptive" passages narrate and gloss mythic passages in American history, presaging the storytelling of the National Park Service interpreter. For the ranger as for the novelist, the process of managing such "plots" is one of naturalizing key elements of a national ideology and subjectivity. As Lynen stresses, Cooper's "main problem in shaping his narrative" is "to manage the revelations naturally, so that the hidden essentials of the situation seem to rise to the surface of consciousness as if they had always been there and are now in the process of being noticed" (179–80). This is, significantly, a matter of interpellating the reader, for the trick lies in the "action of the reader's mind as he [sic] comes to recognize the social scene through the natural scene," thereby realizing, consciously or otherwise, "that a single order underlies both society and nature" (174).

The inscribing of a particular colonial history into Cooper's wilderness landscape is underwritten by narratives of gender and race that are themselves "discovered" in that landscape. As has proved to be consistently the case with the literary-environmental object, the wilderness of The Last of the Mohicans is constructed by collapsing verb into noun, history into place, narration into description—all via tropes of sexualized violence directed against a feminized and racialized Other. Lying always beyond some "impervious" but nonetheless permeated "boundary" (1), Cooper's wilderness is probed and explored by its masculine heroes until, as the narrator summarizes, there is "no recess of the woods so dark, nor any secret place so lovely, that it might claim exemption from the inroads" of the European (11). Figurations of just this sort of coitus-writ-large, often eerily repeating John Underhill's earlier figuring of the wilderness as a female body to which has been ascribed the pseudoagency of "environing," are frequent in the novel. "After penetrating through the brush," says the narrator of Natty Bumppo, "matted as it was with briars, for a few hundred feet, he entered an open space" (125). Elsewhere we read of a silence in the adventurer's camp "as deep as that which reigned in the vast forest by which it was environed" (15), of an "impenetrable darkness . . . [w]ithin the bosom of the encircling hills" (190). Such imagery replicates in an attenuated fashion the *vagina dentata* trope and castration anxiety so prominent in *Newes from America:* "the forest at length appeared to swallow up the living mass [of armed troops] which had slowly entered its bosom" (15).

Neatly linking tropes of gender and race, Cooper figures his wilderness as a womb whose selective fertility will ensure the continuance of whites but not of Indians. Early in the novel, Heyward's party "enter[s] under the high, but dark arches of the forest" (22), then "penetrate[s] still deeper" (28) to arrive at Glenn's Falls, where Uncas and Chingachgook expose "the much prized secret of the place" (52). That secret, predictably enough, turns out to be a cave that, in sheltering Duncan Heyward and Alice Munro, shelters the symbolic progenitors of a white nation as yet unborn. "Prized" in this context is particularly multivalent, becoming readable not just as "highly valued," but also as "seized," and again as "pried open" (*OED*)—the single term conflating the tropes of both virgin and whore, the much-prized and the much-pried, in a context of violence and warfare that is very much about both the seizing and the future peopling of the wilderness.

Part of the viciousness of this virgin/whore dichotomy—invoked in *The Last of the Mohicans* as it usually is, as a totalizing binarism—is that it leaves no room for conceptualizing rape, the one figure that might most appropriately represent colonial acquisition of native land. The novel's caves do, nonetheless, recall John Underhill's mapping of the violated Indian *palizado* at Mystic. As at Mystic, for example, each of Cooper's caves features an anatomically correct set of openings, front and back. But in Cooper's case the accompanying narrative is thoroughly mystifying, lacking the unabashed honesty of Underhill's account. Indeed, Cooper turns the Pequot story on its head, for now it is a white lineage that is threatened by Indians, via a dual forced entry that otherwise replicates the assault by Mason and Underhill at Mystic: "the cavern was entered at both its extremities" (88).

The genocidal subtext in such scenes is not hard to uncover. The reproductive capability of the future nation survives the Hurons' sexual/military assault; Alice is "delivered" from the cave, captive but alive, just as she is "delivered" a second time from the book's other symbolic womb, the cave at the Huron village (263). Her survival in the second instance stands in contrast to the death of the ailing young Indian woman, whom Heyward, pretending to be "a great medicine" (246), has been charged with curing and who clearly serves as a foil for the young, marriage-bound white woman.[2] (Notably, in this second instance Alice is "born" in a sort of transracial drag, passing herself off as the ill Indian maiden whose very life Alice seems to appropriate even as she performs it— one of the novel's many links between drag, performance, and appropriation.) In a combined racial and sexual politics, the landscape becomes the vehicle for selectively breeding a future for whites but not for Indians, a strategy of natu-ralizing—*landscaping*—genocide as a simple failure to reproduce.

Human Values and Natural Forms

Cooper relies on this sort of literary-environmental poetics in his handling of characterization as well as plot. Lynen notes that Natty Bumppo's static and shallow "wisdom" amounts to little more than "vague Uni-tarian pieties" and quite reasonably asks, "[H]ow can such a bundle of received ideas and attitudes amount to a personality?" (187). The answer is by develop-ing an illusion of genuine character for Natty in the novel's ideological, as op-posed to physical, space, "in the affinity between human values and natural forms." It is thus "the landscape [that] creates him, just as he, in turn, interprets it. . . . [G]uided by Cooper's statements, we unconsciously transfer to Leather-stocking our own responses to the novel's landscape. His behavior as a person acting within the landscape seems to spring from such thoughts and feelings as we ourselves have in merely looking at the scene. Leatherstocking's identity is the product of our novelistically controlled view of nature; he becomes a per-son because his response to nature is validated by our own" (187–88). But our own responses, which supposedly validate Natty's, are themselves conditioned by a long tradition of environmental interpretations, among whose precursors we might place those of Natty himself.

This interdependence points up the dialectical interaction between writer and reader, interpreter and interpretee. Interpretive speech is expected and de-signed to enact or awaken some state—new yet already present—in an inter-locutor; it is necessarily *directed toward* someone, and in *The Last of the Mohicans* that someone is preeminently Duncan Heyward. If it is in Natty that Cooper de-lineates the figure and activity of the environmental interpreter, it is Duncan whom he casts as the prototypical interpretee, the specific American type for whom interpretation is to be performed. We see this clearly following the initial battle at Glenn's Falls. As the narrator explains, the "sudden and almost magi-cal change, from the stirring incidents of the combat, to the stillness that now reigned around him, acted on the heated imagination of Heyward like some exciting dream. While all the images and events he had witnessed remained deeply impressed on his memory, he felt a difficulty in persuading himself of their truth. . . . [E]very sign of the adventurers had been lost, leaving him in total uncertainty" (81). This "magical change," transmuting an active combat into a passive, surrounding stillness, neatly evokes literary environmentalism's mystified encoding of violent history into peaceful environment. Such an environment cannot signify itself, however; it must be interpreted, a process temporarily blocked by the contrived absence of the interpreter, Natty. As Lynen argues, it is precisely this narratorial management of interpretation—of the discovery of the fixed truths of the landscape—that constitutes the novel's true plot.

Heyward is left looking about him in bewilderment and awe, like a Puritan captive searching for a sign from God, or a vacationing suburbanite in a national park waiting for a revelation from the ranger in the green uniform. Scenes such as this establish a particular relationship between Natty and Duncan in their respective roles as interpreter and interpretee, a relation paralleled by that between narrator and reader. Such scenes emphasize in particular the opacity of the landscape to the uninitiated, the utter dependence of the interpretee upon the interpreter. Thus, when Natty leaves the scene at Glenn's Falls, Duncan's problem is cast explicitly as a fundamental problem in knowing, "a difficulty in persuading himself of [the] truth" of things, a problem in interpreting images that have impressed themselves onto his memory but cannot by themselves signify any definite meaning. Not just mediation, but—as Fisher stresses—a constantly *repeated* mediation, is crucial. In its absence, Duncan is immediately left "in total uncertainty"; devoid of the "signs" that have been "lost," the wilderness ceases at once to signify.

It is primarily for Duncan that the book's formative interpretation of the American environment is to be performed—and through him, for its contemporary readers. As Nina Baym has pointed out, it is Duncan, and not Natty, whose presence dominates the novel. He is the only character to appear in every scene; his is the "line of sight [that] organizes the action," even though "some awkward plotting . . . is required to carry this through"; and virtually all of that action is "viewed from his perspective." Heyward functions "as the reader's surrogate, the position from which readers would view the action if they were *in* the action" ("How" 73). He is more than just a surrogate, however, for the novel also figures him as patriarch and progenitor. As the aristocratic southerner and ambitious officer getting an intense education in the harsh realities of wilderness warfare, exhibiting his heroism and fortifying his character in the French and Indian War, he is a sort of youthful George Washington, a fictional father-to-be of his country.[3] As such, his union with the racially pure and properly feminine Alice—and his pointed rejection of the racially "tainted" Cora—assures in advance the racial and gender purity of not only the idealized American citizen but also the future model of the interpretee. Duncan and Alice become prototypes of all those whose character and citizenship are to be perfected, just as Freeman Tilden would have it a century later, through the guidance of environmental interpretation.

The novel's interpretation is in this sense both present and future oriented, shaping not just the character Duncan Heyward but also that character's descendants, Cooper's assumed and idealized American readers. This blurs a certain distinction that might otherwise be set up between a narrator who interprets for the reader and a character (Natty) who interprets for other characters. Instead, interpretation at both levels can finally be seen as directed to readers, the one working to perfect them through a direct address in the present, the other working indirectly, positing readers as hereditarily already hailed, by virtue of their figurative descent from their "father." As Duncan's (implicitly white American male) descendants, "we" are to discover as already existing in "ourselves" the truths that the characters are to discover as already existing in the landscape. Lynen's argument must thus be taken a step further, for it is not merely the novel's characters that are treated as static, but also its readers. The American environmental narrative is discoverable not only in the landscape but also in our own fictive ancestry.

A Singular and Ill-Concealed Disdain

Propounded by an illiterate eccentric with no formal education, with no institutional affiliation, with none of the usual claims to authority beyond his male sex and supposedly white race, the environmental interpretations of someone like Natty Bumppo might strike readers as at least a little suspicious. And to the extent that they are directed to a particular interlocutor in a particular time, place, and situation, they should strike us not as universal but as local and situated. How does *The Last of the Mohicans* work to overcome these handicaps, to establish Natty's authority as a reliable interpreter of the wilderness? Perhaps more important, how do we know there is anything "there" in the wilderness to interpret in the first place?

The Last of the Mohicans must construct its wilderness not only as a commodified value but also as a site of stable meaning. The two are closely interrelated, of course, in all the ways we have in mind when we say that meaning can confer value, or that we value something because it is meaningful. But Cooper's narrator works explicitly to confer a sort of prior and enabling value on the wilderness by establishing its *ability to mean,* by expanding and commenting upon its very legibility. The novel repeatedly assigns specific and ideologically responsive meanings to wild nature—that is, it writes the wilderness. In less frequent but more self-reflexive episodes, it argues for the prior notion of the wilderness as a reliable and stable site of meanings. The novel writes about its writing, theorizing with a sometimes surprising explicitness about its own enabling assumptions.[4]

In the first of these tasks, the novel is spectacularly successful, prodigiously inventive in its encoding of ideology into nature, proving itself perhaps the first great classic of the American literary-environmental canon. In the second, however, it fails. Merely by thematizing the question of the wilderness's textuality it already suggests competing interpretations; in attempting to stabilize that textuality—in arguing, in effect, for the wilderness as Logos—it ultimately only calls into question its own semiotic assumptions and processes.

Figuring the New World wilderness as a stable text, as "God's book," Natty valorizes and masculinizes the old notion of a preexisting, "natural" writing even as he marginalizes and feminizes that of a secondary, "artificial" inscription: "'Book!' repeated Hawk-eye, with singular and ill-concealed disdain; 'do you take me for a whimpering boy, at the apron string of one of your old gals; and this good rifle on my knee for the feather of a goose's wing, my ox's horn for a bottle of ink . . . ? Book! What have such as I, who am a warrior of the wilderness, though a man without a cross, to do with books? I never read but in one, and the words that are written there are too simple and too plain to need much schooling; though I may boast that of forty long and hard working years.'" Natty claims to read only in the Book of Nature, which in its divine transparency can speak immediately and truthfully to all. But this contemptuous and sweeping avowal—a claim made emphatically enough to betray some nervousness—is at once qualified by Natty's offhanded admission of all those years of study. If the Book of Nature is in fact so transparent, just what has he been working so hard at? Evidently, reading even a natural inscription can be laborious; even the transparent seems rather opaque. This casual admission wrecks the otherwise neat binarisms that would at first seem to bound and structure Natty's textual wilderness, reinserting the artificial into the natural, the opaque into the transparent, the human into the divine.

Predictably aligned with Natty's privileging of a natural over an artificial inscription is his privileging of speech over writing, and this avowal also runs immediately aground. In chapter 3, where the proudly phonocentric woodsman expounds upon the "many ways, of which, as an honest man, I can't approve," he ranks the reading and writing of his own culture among them: "It is one of their customs to write in books what they have done and seen, instead of telling them in their villages, where the lie can be given to the face of a cowardly boaster, and the brave soldier can call on his comrades to witness for the truth of his words. In consequence of this bad fashion, a man who is too conscientious to misspend his days among the women, in learning the names of black marks, may never hear of the deeds of his fathers" (31). Perhaps this is in part a mere psychological defense, the blustering of an otherwise proud character inwardly ashamed of his illiteracy. Regardless, it succinctly outlines nearly the whole of the phonocentric pose, positing writing as feminine, mediated, distanced from its referent, and unreliable—as absence and deferral—and speech as masculine, direct, close to its referent, and authoritative—as presence and identity. This seemingly simple formulation is riven by contradictions, however, not the least of which is the way it identifies a putatively superior reliance upon speech with a putatively inferior race. For it is "the pale faces," as Magua puts it in a formulation similar to Natty's own, who do not have true speech; whites "have two words for each thing, while a red skin will make the sound of his voice speak for him" (91). Even more disruptive is Natty's realization that writing sustains his own racial and sexual privilege, that his illiteracy denies him access to that racist and masculinist heritage referenced here as "the deeds of his fathers." As we shall see, a man from a literate culture who so unthinkingly adopts this phonocentric pose jeopardizes both his sexual and his racial identity—things that literary environmentalism works otherwise to consolidate.

Let us now trace the novel's thematizing of its own "nature writing" via a sustained reading of two closely related tropes: that of a divine inscription, which is manifested variously as the inscribed body of the Indian and the inscribed body of wild nature, and that of a fully present speech, figured most powerfully and revealingly by what Natty terms the "speech" of his rifle, Kill-deer. In Mary Rowlandson's narrative it is the Bible whose circulation inaugurates and stabilizes the wilderness's textuality; in *The Last of the Mohicans* it is the phallic rifle, *la longue carabine*, that tropes this fundamental literary-environmental activity.

Deployed in parallel functions, the categories of a present speech and a natural writing are both posited by their binaric opposition to the notion of an artificial inscription, to writing in the popular sense of the word. Significantly, the novel thematizes both categories as *failing* as the locus of a stable and self-evident "nature." Curiously anticipating the postmodern view, *The Last of the Mohicans* winds up locating a radically textualized wilderness neither in speech nor in writing, but in *performances* that enlist the reader in the ongoing cultural production of the natural environment.

What Say Your Old Men?

Natty's phonocentrism can be seen as clumsily enacting the paradoxical way in which books, as Barbara Johnson puts it, "rebel against their own stated intention to say that speech is better than writing" (43), as just another turn on the West's enduring phonocentric obsession. But his pose falters in much more specific and politically charged ways within the colonial context of the novel itself. Natty laments his illiteracy—and the resulting ignorance of the deeds of his fathers—during an overtly political argument with Chingachgook over the justice of England's appropriation of Delaware land; the scene dramatizes a native contestation of a self-serving imperialist narrative even as it points up the role of literary environmentalism in defusing and containing such contestation. Defending the ethics of imperial conquest, Natty maintains that his own people's activities have been no worse than those of the Mohicans. Chingachgook, suspecting that the white people's own histories would undermine that claim, challenges Natty to back up his assertions by citing his own tradition. "You have the story told by your fathers," the Delaware chief points out. "What say your old men?" (30). This certainly appears to be a decisive move, for the story recorded by his fathers is precisely what Natty must now admit he does *not* know. Put to the test by a member of a genuinely speech-centered culture, Natty's own phonocentricity is exposed as a wholly figurative stance without any real contestatory force. As a mere *inability* to read and write, illiteracy is not necessarily the same as the genuine orality and phonocentricity Natty pretends to privilege. The immediate result is that Natty finds his entire position negated, and he is forced into a series of embarrassing admissions—that "there is reason in an Indian" (30), that "every story has its two sides," and that Chingachgook's "traditions" are "true" (31).

Chingachgook, by contrast, *is* able to access the deeds of his fathers, and he immediately takes charge of the conversation, narrating "what my fathers have said, and what the Mohicans have done" (31): a history of his own people that justifies their claim to the territory taken by the whites. The novel cannot risk refuting this counternarrative in any obvious way, for the novel's elegiac tone relies upon a sense of pathos that in turn depends upon the truth of Chingachgook's claims. Instead of being refuted, then, the counternarrative is merely interrupted and contained, first by having the conversation bleed off into a discussion of the cause of the tides (31–32)—a rewriting of politics as natural science—and then, after Chingachgook resumes his narrative, by the timely intervention of Uncas (33).

There is, however, a crucial sense in which Natty *does* manage to access and deploy his own heritage, and in the genuine imperial contestation that this scene only dramatizes, this deployment proves decisive after all. Illiterate though he is, Natty does know at least one thing about his ancestry: he "knows" that he is "genuine white."[5] And he can infer at least one thing more: "that all the Bumppos could shoot; for I have a natural turn with a rifle, which must have been handed down from generation to generation" (31). In contrast to Chingachgook's rich oral heritage, Natty's illiteracy leaves him with only a bare genetic legacy, the "fact" of his race and an inherited skill in shooting, with which to justify his own presence on the land. The novel boils the ethics of conquest down to the notion of a superior race and the fact of superior firepower.

The Murderous Speech of Kill-deer

Pressed by Chingachgook to relate the story told by his fathers, Natty suggests that his rifle can somehow speak for him. But this is hardly the only time the novel invokes shooting as a figure for speech. Elsewhere Natty refers to a gun battle as a "conversation," in which he offers to "let 'kill-deer' take a part" (208); during another battle he requests his comrades to let "nothing [speak] but the rifle" (328) until he signals otherwise. Thus when Chief Tamenund asks, "Which of my prisoners is la Longue Carabine?" and Heyward answers, "Give us arms. . . . Our deeds shall speak for us!" (295), we are invited to read the ensuing shooting contest as a sort of debate, and Natty's superior shooting as a sort of eloquence, a great oration comparable to those delivered in the same scene by Tamenund, Magua, and Cora.

But what sort of words are spoken by a firearm? However one might choose to translate such speech—"I hereby declare you a corpse," perhaps, or in the more specific colonial context of the novel, "I hereby pronounce you a subject of my king"—it obviously does more than merely convey information. The pronouncements of the rifle are not mere constantives, that is, but performatives in the classic sense, speech acts that instantiate by means of their very utterance a genuine change in the status of their interlocutors.

Deconstructed by Chingachgook, Natty's phonocentrism does not simply vanish; rather it is driven underground, as it were, to lodge in this figure of the speaking gun. Resurrecting itself there as a performative speech, it can revive the old dream of a full presence in which word, intention, and result—locution, illocution, and perlocution—are one. The novel seems fascinated by such speech and allegorizes it repeatedly, perhaps most notably in the suspenseful shooting contest of chapter 29, in which the rifle's performativity parallels that of another imperialist speech act, the Spanish *Requerimiento*, or "requirement." Drafted in its "classic form" in 1512, the *Requerimiento* was intended to address the many problems posed by the discovery of the Americas, among the knottiest of which were the questionable ethics of conquest and the possibility that "civilized" men might revert to "savagery" during lengthy sojourns among utterly foreign peoples. In response, the Spanish imperial bureaucracy required its agents to read the *Requerimiento* aloud to native populations upon first contact, reasoning that such a performance would, at that crucial moment, reaffirm the identity of the conqueror and legitimate the subjugation of the native. More precisely, the reading was itself considered the act of subjugation. Under the proper "felicity conditions"—which included the presence of a priest and a notary but not, at least in practice, the presence of the native people being addressed—the reading of these words was a speech act, instantiating the concrete political realities it enunciated. By *declaring* natives to be subjects of the Crown, it was held to *make* them subjects of the Crown.[6]

The speaking gun similarly subjugates the native while stabilizing the identity of the colonial, and not just in the fictional world of *The Last of the Mohicans*. Nearly two centuries earlier, in *Newes from America*, John Underhill had recorded that "wee had an *Indian* with us that was an interpreter, being in English cloathes, and a Gunne in his hands, was spied by the Ilanders [members of the Block Island tribe], which called out to him, what are you an Indian or an English-man: come hither, saith he, and I will tell you, he pulls up his cocke and let fly at one of them, and without question was the death of him" (7). Here without doubt we have a category crisis—an Indian speaking a white man's language, dressed in a white man's clothing, and carrying a white man's weapon. In the midst of this fluidity of identity, Underhill assigns to the gun the full performative power of stabilization, the ability to accurately name the speaker's race, to answer the question, "What are you?" even as it subjugates its native interlocutor: "I will tell/kill you." Notably, the speaker's name is never actually mentioned; Underhill seems less concerned with the name itself than with the *act* of naming.

This image of a man in a cross-racial drag, irrefutably identifying himself in a virtuoso performance—and thereby suggesting the performativity rather than any "natural" fixity of identity—reappears much later as the Leatherstocking, Cooper's "white" man in Indian clothing. Underhill's cross-dressing Indian anticipates how Natty and other characters in *The Last of the Mohicans* will perform—as Indians, as animals, as "nature"—while the interpreter's fatally stabilizing speech anticipates (right down to the seemingly obligatory sexual pun) how the speaking gun is to function in Cooper's novel.

No End to His Loping

In contrast to the sweeping formality of the *Requerimiento*—ritualistic, mediated, embedded in a universalizing hierarchy—the performative speech of the woodsman's rifle seems decidedly informal, personal, direct, and ad hoc.[7] But the two practices *function* in much the same way, and the shooting match in chapter 29 of *The Last of the Mohicans* can be read as a fictional equivalent of the *Requerimiento*. Natty's shooting is performed as part of a first-contact scenario, before an assemblage of native people on the brink of subjugation; it is also, as in the episode from *Newes from America*, prompted by a crisis of identity—by Duncan Heyward's impersonation of Natty. And it is again a violent and patently sexual exchange, in this case between the rifle and the two (notably *domestic* utensils that are its targets—an earthen vessel (297) and a hollow gourd (299).

Natty sees his own identity most securely fixed in his race, in his sense of himself as "genuine white." But at this crucial point in the novel, his identity hinges literally on his inherited skill with the rifle. It is not as a white man that he is most renowned, but as *la longue carabine*, as a great shot, and when Duncan challenges his identity, it seems perfectly logical that a shooting match be proposed as a foolproof way to settle the issue. Natty's final shot does indeed appear to secure his claim: with it his "word" is made "good," and the scene seems rather straightforwardly to emblematize stability in naming and authority in speech—both who has it (the white male) and how it is attained (through the violent negation of the sexual and racial Other). The narrator describes Natty's impressive performance as a grounding of language, an end to deferral: "It decided the question, and effectually established Hawk-eye in the possession of his dangerous reputation" (300). The episode would thus seem to undo the metaphysical damage sustained in Natty's ill-fated argument with Chingachgook back in chapter 3, successfully substituting his inherited shooting ability for his inaccessible written heritage.

But more is at stake here than just Natty's identity. Also at issue is the fixity of identity itself, and it is certainly suggestive that the rifle so frequently *fails* to speak unambiguously. Even in this seemingly straightforward shooting contest, Natty does not reestablish his identity until the univocality of the rifle has first been brought into some doubt. For reasons not made very clear—apparently to express his contempt for Heyward's challenge—Natty lets off his first shot without appearing so much as to aim. He appears to do this casually, but actually, as the narrator soon makes clear, that casualness is quite calculated: Natty intends his shot to be not only more accurate than Heyward's, but also more *expressive*. He hopes to make his rifle's "word" signify on two levels at once, simultaneously establishing his identity and expressing his scorn. To the extent that it does so, however, it is no longer a univocal and transparent speech but an ambiguous speech requiring interpretation. It is paradoxically because Natty's performance is so convincing that his audience is divided on whether to attribute the rifle shot to skill or chance: "The first impression of so strange a scene was engrossing admiration. Then a low, but increasing murmur, ran through the multitude, and finally swelled into sounds, that denoted lively opposition in the sentiments of the spectators. While some openly testified their satisfaction at so unexampled dexterity, by far the larger portion of the tribe were inclined to believe the success of the shot was the result of accident" (298). Rather than pinning down identity and meaning, the rifle's speech simply fuels another round of contestation within an interpretive community. Faced with this deferral, we would do well to ask just what, precisely, we are to take as Natty's "unexampled dexterity": his shooting or his acting?

When Underhill's native marksman fires at his enemy, the narrator assures us that he "without question was the death of him." But in *The Last of the Mohicans* we find no such assurances. In fact, we repeatedly find just the opposite: acts of marksmanship that prove at the most crucial moments to be ambiguous. This is most notably the case with the shooting of Natty's great nemesis, the one target he cannot seem to pin down, the ultimate test of *la longue carabine's* stabilizing power: Magua. It is Magua who seems to epitomize deferral itself, who repeatedly evades the significations alloted him. "[T]here never will be an end to his loping," as Natty puts it, using a word that aptly suggests the perpetual sliding of the signifier, "till 'kill-deer' has said a friendly word to him" (186), and Magua does indeed escape every effort made to name him, at least until the novel's climax.

Even the novel's climactic death scene produces no certain closure, for even there the cause of Magua's death is left unclear. Circumstances certainly *imply* that the Huron is finished off by a "word from 'kill-deer,'" but the question is rather pointedly left open. Just where we might expect certainty, the story foregrounds images of fluidity and indeterminacy, leaving the shooting of even such a great marksman as Natty to fail as the trope of a present speech. "A form stood at the brow of the mountain," says the narrator in the novel's penultimate scene, "on the very edge of the giddy height, with uplifted arms, in an awful attitude of menace." Surely this menacing form must belong to Magua, and "[w]ithout stopping to consider his person, the rifle of Hawkeye was raised" (338). But just before firing Natty realizes he is aiming not at Magua, the novel's personification of evil, but at the "glowing countenance" of the psalmist David Gamut. A second later, the real Magua "lopes" into view and attempts, once again, to dodge the bullet that would name him: "he made a desperate leap, and fell short of his mark; though his hands grasped a shrub on the verge of the height. The form of Hawk-eye had crouched like a beast about to take its spring, and his frame trembled so violently with eagerness, that the muzzle of the half raised rifle played like a leaf fluttering in the wind." One might here repeat the words of Underhill's interpreter and ask of Natty, "What are you, an Indian or an Englishman?" It is again a moment of extreme instability, with the signifiers of racial and sexual identity sliding out of control, leaving the putatively civilized white man "crouched" like a "beast"—bestial in his crouched posture and eagerness for the kill, impotent in his inability to make his half-erect gun "speak."

When Natty finally does fire, the actual utterance is played down, camouflaged in subordinate clauses: "Without exhausting himself with fruitless efforts, the cunning Magua suffered his body to drop to the length of his arms, and found a fragment for his feet to rest upon. Then summoning all his powers, he renewed the attempt, and so far succeeded, as to draw his knees on the edge of the mountain. It was now, when the body of his enemy was most collected together, that the agitated weapon of the scout was drawn to his shoulder. The surrounding rocks, themselves, were not steadier than the piece became for the single instant that it poured out its contents." Thus does the rifle speak—but to what effect? "The arms of the Huron relaxed, and his body fell back a little, while his knees still kept their position. Turning a relentless look on his enemy, he shook his hand in grim defiance. But his hold loosened, and his dark person was seen cutting the air with its head downwards, for a fleeting instant, until it glided past the shrubbery which clung to the mountain, in its rapid flight to destruction" (338). Here the reader cannot say of Magua that the rifle "without question was the death of him." It is hard to be sure that Natty has in fact killed his nemesis; except for the single word "destruction," there is little to suggest that Magua has died at all, and nothing to assure us that Kill-deer was the fatal cause. The narrator juxtaposes Natty's rifle shot with Magua's apparently fatal fall but refuses to link them in any causal relationship—if Magua indeed had to summon "all his powers" just to "draw his knees on the edge of the mountain," he might well have dropped off through sheer exhaustion and not because Natty shot him. We do know for sure that Magua has escaped every *previous* attempt to contain him; why not this one as well? Before passing judgment, we would do well to perform an autopsy—but then, where is the body? The novel's final chapter makes a point of showing us the bodies of Cora and Uncas, and we can say with certainty that Cora was killed by one of Magua's "assistants," and Uncas by Magua himself (337). But the body of Magua is withheld from us.[8] Even if we accept that Magua has died, we still cannot say *how*. By Natty's bullet? By simple exhaustion? There is no way to decide; just where we might expect closure, the novel presents us with an enigma, an imaging of the end of deferral as itself a deferral. During its most crucial performance—the moment when this most powerful figure of a fully present speech might most securely ground its claims—the rifle speaks loudly yet seems strangely silent.[9]

A Natural Inscription?

Early in the novel, spying the antlers of a deer just visible through the dense foliage of the forest, Natty brags to Uncas that he will take the buck "atwixt the eyes, and nearer to the right than to the left." Uncas finds this hard to believe:

It cannot be! . . . all but the tips of his horns are hid!"
"He's a boy!" said the white man, shaking his head while he spoke, and addressing the father. "Does he think when a hunter sees a part of the creatur, he can't tell where the rest of him should be!" (34)

The "marksman's aiming" has here become, in John Lynen's words, an exercise in "mak[ing] the mind conform exactly to the conditions of nature" (188)—and among the conditions implied by this passage is a regular and predictable structure, a system of formal relationships that allows the tips of the horns to locate the rest of the animal. Natty does not claim this ability to access his prey's structure for himself alone, but for any skilled hunter, and his claim is held to be true not just of this particular deer, but of any such creature. The ability is neither idiosyncratic nor contextual, that is, but general: not like *parole* but like *langue*. It is a function of that structure by means of which signs on the surface of nature can indicate the realities underneath. Shooting here tropes the reading— and by implication the very existence—of the divine inscription, of the pre- existing system without which the wilderness cannot be thought of as both natural *and* readable.[10]

But is this structure truly "divine" or "natural"? Can a nature exist that is "pure" or "virgin" and also transparently legible? The novel raises such questions repeatedly but rather pointedly refuses to answer them. In the scene above, for example, Natty makes a constative claim about nature's "legibility" and offers to prove it by hitting the buck in a precisely predicted spot. But before he can be put to the test Chingachgook intervenes, reminding Natty that firing would disclose their location to their enemies. The "typifying" power of the rifle is asserted but not tested. Thus let off the hook, Natty need no longer prove his assertion; instead he merely authorizes it. His response to Uncas's argument is reduced to an ad hominem dismissal—"He's a boy!"—and an attempt to align himself with the authority of the boy's father (who notably refuses to take sides). The shift is from a Neoplatonic claim of an absolute formal structure to the strategic utterances of the sophist, to "mere" rhetoric, a shift reminding us that the antlers themselves, from the moment they are invoked as a signifier, are no longer natural but rhetorical. As such, like any other signifier, they are no longer connected reliably to what Natty must now merely assert as their signified. Natty cannot know that the antlers are not in fact connected to a human being rather than a deer—a distinct possibility in a novel that, as we shall see, repeatedly has its human characters performing in cross-species drag.

In *The Last of the Mohicans*, Natty shoots neither at white people nor at such "good" Indians as the Delawares, but rather at animals and such "bad" Indians as the Hurons. This pattern limns the readable body of the wilderness at which he takes aim, which his rifle, to recall Donna Haraway's phrase, will make "true to type"; it objectifies this body in what for Natty are two not-so-distinct loci: the body of the wild Indian and that of the wild landscape. These bodies are presented as *naturally* inscribed, but key passages in the novel undermine this presentation, suggesting instead that we may think of them, in Judith Butler's terms, as having been *made* to signify on their surfaces.

Throughout the novel, the Indian body is assumed to be as transparently readable as the wilderness of which it is figured as a part. The fact that Cooper's natives are so often pictured as stoic and inexpressive does not contradict this; it is, in fact, *because* native bodies are so transparently readable that their owners must labor to render them opaque, must overlay the natural inscription with an unreliable, intent-laden human writing. This can be a matter of life and death. When an enemy is heard one evening lurking near the adventurers' camp, Chingachgook is held to be in particular danger because he sits in the full light of the fire. Uncas slips away to investigate, secure in the knowledge that "[i]f there are any skulkers out in the darkness, they will never discover, by [Chingachgook's] countenance, that we suspect danger at hand" (193). "[T]he noble fellow," as Natty says admiringly, "knows that a look, or a motion, might disconsart our schemes" (194), and by skillfully regulating what today would be called his "body language," Chingachgook manages not to give the game away.

The novel thematizes the Indian body as signifying surface more explicitly as this episode proceeds. A poorly aimed shot is fired at Chingachgook; a second shot is heard; then Uncas returns with what is presumably the would-be assassin's scalp. These events seem irrelevant to the novel's surface plot; their sole raison d'être seems instead to be the discussion they occasion—a thinly veiled treatise on the notion of a natural inscription, steeped with references to a transparent language. Asked his opinion on the number of attackers, Chingachgook responds with a directness that seemingly obviates any need for elaboration, "holding a single finger up to view, with the English monosyllable—'One'" (195). The repeated singularity suggests a unity of signifier and signified, with the uplifted finger indeed deploying body *as* signifier. (If anything, the spoken "One" seems superfluous.) When Heyward asks the returning Uncas for a report, the young Indian proves even more reticent, yet somehow more expressive. "In place of that eager and garrulous narration, with which a white youth would have endeavoured to communicate" such a triumph, Uncas prefers "to let his deeds speak for themselves" by "quietly expos[ing] the fatal tuft of hair, which he bore as the symbol of victory" (195). Chingachgook then performs a close, indeed a *tactile*, reading of this fragment of a body, placing "his hand on the scalp, and consider[ing] it for a moment with deep attention" before announcing his opinion in another single word: "Oneida!" (195–96).

Lest there be any doubt that what we are reading is a linguistic parable, Natty proceeds to explain to the mystified Duncan that while "to white eyes there is no difference between this bit of skin and that of any other Indian," Chingachgook can read it "with as much ease as if the scalp was the leaf of a book, and each hair a letter" (196). The palpability of the scalp approximates and figures the sort of presence Western metaphysics associates with speech, and Natty attempts to infuse that presence into his own figures of writing and the book. It is notable—but by now should not be surprising—that this parable is occasioned by the *shooting* of the Oneida. It is the rifle that both literally and figuratively renders the Oneida's body readable, preventing the sort of intentional performance that otherwise might obscure its "natural" transparency. Dead men tell no tales; they do not write, but *are read.* It is only the living body that can attempt, as with Chingachgook's studied nonchalance, to write an unreliable human inscription over the natural one.

It would seem that in the Oneida scalp, body and word combine most powerfully in a "plain language." Surely this signifier is closely, naturally, and indissolubly linked to its signified: prime evidence, it might seem, that indeed there can be a natural inscription. But in fact the opposite is true, for the hair does not signify, does not become a *scalp,* until it is *detached;* and from the moment it is thus violently wrested from the body and begins to circulate as a signifier, it is already a figure, a synecdoche like the antlers of the buck. And to say, as Cooper's narrator does, that the scalp signifies not the deceased warrior himself but a *victory* is to make not an identification but rather an association— that is, to mediate through another layer of figuration, metonymy. The seemingly natural and transparent signifier of the scalp is thus thoroughly imbricated in rhetorical procedures, and hardly absolves its readers of the labor and responsibility of interpretation. How can we know, for example, that it was Uncas who actually killed the scalp's former owner? It could have been dropped in the scuffle or obtained in some other way. Such uncertainties are left unresolved by the fact that Uncas's deed takes place offstage; indeed they are foregrounded by Natty himself, who chooses this moment to remind us of Indians "who hang upon the skirts of a war party, to scalp the dead, go in, and make their boast among the squaws of [their] valiant deeds" (195). How are we to know that Uncas did not similarly meddle between signifier and signified? We might appeal here to our knowledge of his good character—except, of course, that it is through scenes such as this one that Uncas's character is established in the first place.

Like the body of the Indian, the "body" of the wilderness is presented (and simultaneously problematized) as part of a natural inscription that preexists any reading of it and is held to be always distinguishable from any merely human writing. Every time the fleeing Magua tries to cover his tracks, for example, altering the signs of his passage by laboriously constructing a human landscape that mimics the "natural" one, Natty and his Indian companions are consistently able to follow the trail. Tracking becomes reading, a matter of tracing out a string of differences, and the fact that the three woodsmen eventually *do* hunt Magua down is not only a vindication of their pathfinding skills but also a reification of the divine inscription, of the notion that there is a preexisting text to be "discovered" in nature.

The emblematic activity here is the close reading of the artful writing of nature. Notably it is the doomed Uncas, "quick of sight and keen of wit" (213), who ultimately proves the best reader; he is able to pick out the trail even when Natty and Chingachgook have lost it.[11] Natty favorably contrasts this pathfinding prowess to the reading ability of "the young white, who gathers his learning from books" (213). Magua's great skill, on the other hand, is writing "realistically," consciously arranging the traces of his passage so that they will be indistinguishable from what is held by his readers to be the preexisting field of natural signifiers. Whenever possible, he traverses "a rock, or a rivulet, or a bit of earth harder than common," any place where his passage will not create recognizable difference, will not alter *significantly* the natural configuration of the wilderness. Nonetheless his pursuers, reading with an extreme skepticism, consistently manage to pick out the human from the natural signifier: whenever Magua's artifice "severed the links of the clue they followed, the true eye of the scout recovered them at a distance, and seldom rendered the delay of a single moment necessary" (214).

At length, however, Magua's nature writing does come close to succeeding. "The trail appeared to suddenly have ended" (214), and even though the foresters "applied themselves to their task in good earnest," their "examination resulted in no discovery" (215). They try again, this time "going over the ground by inches": "Not a leaf was left unturned. The sticks were removed, and the stones lifted—for Indian cunning was known frequently to adopt these objects as covers, labouring with the utmost patience and industry, to conceal each footstep as they proceeded. . . . At length Uncas . . . raked the earth across the turbid little rill from the spring, and diverted its course into another channel. So soon as its narrow bed below the dam was dry, he stooped over it with keen and curious eyes [and] pointed out the impression of a moccasin in the moist alluvion" (215–16). Fleshing out the implications of this clue, the landscape readers quickly establish that David Gamut, with the largest feet in Magua's party, had been made to go first; carrying Cora and Alice, the Hurons had then followed precisely in his footsteps, leaving just the one print concealed by the water. "I can now *read* the whole of it," exclaims Natty, who chooses this moment to make explicit the trope of the wilderness-as-book (216, my emphasis).

The critical practice of the adventurers is to diligently seek out the human signifier. But how can they recognize it when they see it? Only by its difference from the natural signifier, by the difference between the bent twig and the straight one, the moccasin print and the undisturbed mud. As Saussurian linguistics assures us, it is only out of such differences that meaning may arise; more important, we know that in such a system "there are only differences." And while "a difference generally implies positive terms between which the difference is set up," Saussure emphasizes that "in language there are only differences *without positive terms*" (120). The novel's opposition of a natural to a human inscription—as two distinct systems, each with its own independent positivity—is illusory, for the very comparison of the natural and the human, the very observation of their difference, inscribes them in a *single* system of differences. This system can be considered neither "natural" *nor* "cultural," for that very distinction arises within the system and cannot precede it.

Uncas's discovery of this human footprint reprises in miniature that moment so crucial to Western metaphysics: the "emergence" of "man." It is the mythic moment of origin, the "discovery" of that initial difference that allows "culture" to differentiate itself from its foundational Other, "nature." It is the sort of moment replayed in contemporary discourses by such events as an archaeologist discovering an early hominid fossil or a primatologist teaching a chimpanzee to sign. "A cry of exultation immediately announced the success of the young warrior," says the narrator, and "the whole party crowded to the spot," with Natty regarding the moccasin print "with as much admiration as a naturalist would expend on the tusk of a mammoth or the rib of a mastodon" (216).

But why must this moment be reprised here, at this particular juncture of this particular novel? The aim of the close reading is to locate the kidnapped white maidens—particularly Alice, the imperiled future of an American civilization that will fade back into savagery if, as its symbolic progenitor, she is suffered to bear the children of a "natural" race. Haunting the novel, on the one hand, is this specter of miscegenation, whose mere biological possibility challenges the racist notion of fundamentally separate orders of humanity. But in addition there is the gradual erosion of the nature/culture distinction itself, as the adventurers' closer and closer reading of the landscape-text uncovers that distinction's artificiality. In order to sustain a literary-environmental discourse that opposes "civilization" to "wilderness" (and white to red, male to female, and so on), the adventurers must sustain the nature/culture system; to maintain that system they must rescue Alice, whose purity alone can (symbolically) reproduce it; to rescue Alice they must follow her trail; and to trace out her trail they must parse ever finer distinctions between nature and culture. It is Magua, always profoundly troublesome, who threatens to expose this circularity, this lack of any genuine origin. It is Magua who drives them relentlessly toward the vanishing point where difference and meaning seem to disappear, and it is there that the mythic origin of culture must be asserted and celebrated anew.

Along with the human trail, of course, is rediscovered the wilderness through which it leads and against which it is conceptualized. It is only through the recognition of the not-quite-effaced "human" signifier, the trace of Magua's earlier passage and intention, that wilderness-as-natural-inscription once again becomes conceivable. In this sense Natty Bumppo is never in an uninflected or untrammeled "wilderness" at all, nor can he be. The writer of nature—Magua or his equivalent—is always and must always be one step ahead of the "discoverer" of nature. But paradoxically, literary-environmental discourse can continue to treat its object as natural only through the effacement of that prior human marking. Just as environmentalist discourse will generally have to efface the early presence of Native Americans in order to conceive of a "virgin" American wilderness, preservable in a "pure" state, so Natty must hunt down and eliminate Magua and his "polluting" human mark.

Yet without that mark, the wilderness fades into illegibility—another reason, perhaps, why *The Last of the Mohicans* becomes so strangely silent at the moment of Magua's long-anticipated "destruction" (338). Natty has his peripatetic antagonist where he wants him, clinging precariously to the cliff side, ready to drop any moment under the strain, and this moment is, as we have seen, one of intense liminality. Natty has just moments ago mistaken the gentle David Gamut for the evil Magua, while the narrator uncharacteristically figures the white hero not as savvy woodsman but as bloodthirsty animal, "crouched like a beast about to take its spring" while "the muzzle of the half-raised rifle played like a leaf fluttering in the wind" (338). It is difficult, finally, to know what to make of this image of a wavering phallus which confounds the nature/culture boundary rather than clarifying it. Natty does, however, manage to raise his rifle. He shoots, and Magua falls, but we still do not know whether it is a bullet from Kill-deer that brings the Huron down or simple exhaustion. At this most crucial point, has the typifying power of the rifle *again* been merely asserted, without being proved? A glance at Magua's corpse, a reading of his transfigured body, might settle the matter—but that body is never seen.

A Performance Worth Regarding

"Long ago," writes Anne Sexton in "Red Riding Hood," "there was a strange deception / a wolf dressed in frills, / a kind of transvestite." When Marjorie Garber quotes from this poem in her *Vested Interests: Cross-Dressing and Cultural Anxiety* (375), we most readily assume that what is "strange" about the "deception" is the image of a male wolf in female attire, the crossing of the boundaries of sex and gender. Yet is it not also disconcerting to ponder the crossing of *species* boundaries, to view this durable image of the nonhuman dressed up as the human? Cross-species drag and performance can be considered as a form of transvestism in its own right, a confounding of the natural in the accoutrements of the cultural (and vice versa).

According to Garber, transvestism is always an index of broader cultural phenomena, inviting us to contextualize and historicize the texts that foreground it. In particular it points to a "category crisis," a breakdown of previously definitive distinctions, and thereby "puts in question identities previously conceived as stable, unchallengeable, grounded, and 'known.'" Garber considers this sort of disruption to be transvestism's most telling function (13). Paralleling Judith Butler's claims for the performativity of sex and gender, Garber argues for transvestism's "extraordinary power" to call into question not simply perceived original categories but the *idea* of "original" meanings or identities (16). "[T]he compelling force of transvestism in literature and culture," she writes, stems "from its instatement of metaphor itself, not as that for which a literal meaning must be found, but precisely as that without which there would be no such thing as meaning in the first place" (390). Category crisis itself is seen ultimately as "not the exception but rather the ground of culture"; by forcing and negotiating such crisis, transvestism in fact "creates culture" (16). In the case of nature/culture cross-dressing, transvestism would seem to be at its outer limit, creating culture in a state of self-parody.

Shirley Samuels has suggested that in writing *The Last of the Mohicans*, Cooper may have been influenced by a Leni-Lenape origin myth in which "the drawing of human beings into culture is accomplished by the pursuit and consumption of the natural. . . . The emergence of persons is thus linked to the marking of the difference between what's natural and what's cultural: nature worship only becomes possible once the separation between persons and nature has been violently effected." [12] Any blurring of this "violently effected" separation raises the specter of the *sub*mergence of persons, in a sort of "miscegenation between nature and culture" (89), and the latter half of Cooper's novel thematizes just this threat. The motivation for seeking out the two white women is as much to frustrate Magua's sexual claim on Cora as it is to facilitate the courtship of Alice and Duncan. This obsession with racial stability is just one facet of the broader aim of effecting and maintaining separation generally; it is necessarily bound up with the fixing of other threatened categories, such as those of gender and class, that are also seen as natural. Near the conclusion of the novel, for example, the women's father makes a plea for a general equality of gender, class, and race, hoping that, if only in the afterlife, "the time shall not be distant, when we may assemble . . . without distinction of sex, or rank, or colour." But Natty then proceeds not simply to reject this liberal plea but to stabilize "sex, rank, and color" all at once by subsuming them in the archcategory nature: "To tell them this," he says, "would be to tell them that the snows come not in the winter, or that the sun shines fiercest when the trees are stripped of their leaves!" (347).

But despite such conservative pronouncements of a naturally fixed cultural order, the plot shift from chase to rescue in *The Last of the Mohicans* occasions a discursive shift from a foundationalist to a relativist and performative worldview. Earlier, success had hinged upon skillful tracking, on the correct "close reading" of the wild body. Such a strategy was predicated upon a traditional view of Truth and epitomized by the ability of careful reading to expose Magua's artificial inscription—his artifice—by distinguishing it from the seemingly natural inscription of the wilderness. Once the two women have been located, however, the heroes rely almost wholly on artifices of their own, on rhetoric and performance, on the contextualized understanding of signifying practices seen as strategic rather than simply "true" or "false." As the novel approaches its finale, its groundings move away from Natty's notion of a stable nature and toward the fluidity of performance—suggesting that nature is not "natural" at all but *performative.*

Critics have long complained that Cooper's always shaky plotting threatens to break down entirely toward the end of *The Last of the Mohicans,* and that this threat necessitates the absurd substitutions that end up carrying the plot: Heyward's impersonation of a native healer, Natty's performance of a bear, Uncas's decidedly superior performance of that bear, Chingachgook's performance of a beaver, and so on. But it is not just the plot that is breaking down by this point. The crucial silences of the speaking gun and the persistent insinuation of human rhetoric into the putatively natural inscription of the wild body precipitate a sense of category crisis, of a breakdown in the very structures by means of which nature and culture have been separated in the first place. In the wake of these twin failures, the book's drag scenes are not ludicrous at all, but predictable attempts to reinstate the threatened categories via another strategy.

While he is traveling deep in enemy territory, Duncan Heyward is brought up short by what he at first takes to be an Indian village: "The water fell out of this wide basin, in a cataract so regular and gentle, that it appeared rather to be the work of human hands, than fashioned by nature. A hundred earthen dwellings stood on the margin of the lake. . . . Their rounded roofs, admirably moulded for defence against the weather, denoted more of industry and foresight, than the natives were wont to bestow on their regular habitations. . . . [T]he whole village or town, which ever it might be termed, possessed more of method and neatness of execution, than the white men had been accustomed to believe belonged, ordinarily, to the Indian habits" (218–19). Heyward ponders this scene for several minutes, then sees the "suspicious and inexplicable movements" of what he takes to be native people but are really beavers. He next spies a human form which he and Natty both take for an Indian but is really a white man, David Gamut. When all is revealed a moment later, the narrator implicates his readers in these unwitting performances, as usual aligning their point of view with Heyward's: "The reader may better imagine, than we describe, the surprise of Heyward. His lurking Indians were suddenly converted into four-footed beasts; his lake into a beaver pond; his cataract into a dam, constructed by those industrious and ingenious quadrupeds; and a suspected enemy into a true friend" (222). Note that neither Gamut nor the beavers have been consciously performing here. They have not been wearing masks that they suddenly remove so as to reveal the "true" significations of their "natural" surfaces. The "converting" is accomplished rather by the narrator, who disguises his own activity in the passive voice ("were suddenly converted"). Occupying the position of grammatical subject thereby emptied out we find various manifestations of "nature": the lake, the cataract, the putatively "natural" Indians, and the Other more generally: the "enemy." The narrator further effaces his own agency by subordinating his descriptions and manipulations to the imaginations of his readers. Yet the effect—the reader's surprise—is the same as the shock that would have been effected by a consciously performed drag. This little parable of misrecognition "acts" just like a performance yet appears "natural," a mere mistake on Duncan's part.

Even after this naturalized performance has been revealed, however, after the confused categories have supposedly been clarified, there remains a certain residue of confusion. The narrator leaves us not quite sure whether beavers are wild (undomesticated animals) or civilized (intelligent and industrious beings who construct well-ordered communities). The cultural continues to feel strangely natural, even as the wild (cataract and lake) remains oddly artifactual and human (dam and pond).

Later, and notably at this same spot, Chingachgook dons the mask of a beaver and affords the novel's readers a "real" performance of nature. The spectacle this time is not that of a white man taking animals for humans but of an Indian taking a human for an animal. As a party of Huron warriors file past the pond, they pause to allow a member of the party to address this "beaver" as his totemic kinsman; the warrior speaks "as if he were addressing more intelligent beings" (284). Only as the Hurons are leaving do we catch the irony and learn that he *had* been addressing a more intelligent being: "Had any of the Hurons turned to look behind them, they would have seen the animal watching their movements with an interest and sagacity that might easily have been mistaken for reason. Indeed, so very distinct and intelligible were the devices of the quadruped, that even the most experienced observer would have been at a loss to account for its actions, until . . . the party entered the forest, when the whole would have been explained, by seeing the entire animal issue from the lodge, uncasing, by the act, the grave features of Chingachgook from his mask of fur" (285). Unlike Duncan, a novice woodsman, the experienced Hurons should not have been so easily taken in. The narrator makes it sound simple enough: all they had to do was turn around and look. The plot, however, requires that they *not* look—doing so would give away the heroes' battle plan—and so they do not. In this scene the success of Chingachgook's performance is notably not attributable to his skill; his performance is marred by "distinct and intelligible" "devices" that might easily have tipped off an observer. The ability to detect the original beneath the mask—to limn the wilderness by separating the natural from the cultural—is no longer seen as a matter of acuteness of perception, of the sort of "close reading" performed upon the landscape earlier by Uncas and Natty; it has instead become just another narratorial device.

There is a playfulness in the way Cooper highlights his narrator's and his readers' complicity in these performances, but the question they raise is serious enough: How are we to know that *any* object presented to readers as natural or original—right on up to that object viewed as the most natural, that sine qua non of nature, the wilderness—is not itself performed, a performance that a self-effacing narrator chooses not to reveal to us in the same way Cooper's narrator refuses to reveal Chingachgook to the Hurons? It is significant, I think, that this question arises at just the spot where Heyward himself was so badly deceived. If the novel interpellates us as Heyward's symbolic descendants, the legatees of his readerly skills and weaknesses, it seems to be warning us to read the wilderness landscape-text with caution, to keep in mind the possibility that beneath the surface of the signifiers of the wild lies not some wild essence or foundation, but merely the "grave features" of human intention, ensconced in a "mask of fur." [13]

According to Judith Butler, what is parodied in transvestism is not any particular identity, but the very "notion of an original . . . identity" (*Gender* 138). At the Huron camp, Heyward praises Natty's performance of the bear in terms that similarly privilege performance over original, noting that "the animal itself might have been shamed by the representation" (257). Natty responds that he "should be a poor scholar, for one who has studied so long in the wilderness, did I not know how to set forth the movements and natur of such a beast! Had it been now a catamount, or even a full sized painter [panther], I would have embellished a performance, for you, worth regarding! But it is no such marvellous feat to exhibit the feats of so dull a beast; though, for that matter too, a bear may be over acted! Yes, yes; it is not every imitator that knows natur may be outdone easier than she is equalled" (257–58). Reappearing in this parody is the figure of the Book of Nature, of Natty's years of reading the natural inscription. But here, reading is only a sort of heuristic or rehearsal, no longer a pathway to Truth but a prelude to performance. Before, Natty's scholarship had consisted of reading nature, learning to track and to aim, making his mind "conform" to the wilderness, and it culminated in shooting, in proving out the truths inherent in nature's preexisting structure. Here, however, nature study culminates in drag and performance, in the active *creation* of surface significations whose truth or accuracy is contingent, ultimately ascertainable only in the local efficacy of a performance.[14] The emphasis on drag in *The Last of the Mohicans* thus undermines the earlier notion of the wilderness as, to revert to Butler's formulation, "mute, prior to culture, awaiting the inscription-as-incision of the masculine signifier for entrance into language and culture" (*Gender* 147–48). Like the human body, the "body" of "nature" must be seen as "not a 'being,' but a variable boundary . . . a signifying practice within a cultural field."[15]

In chapter 25, the captive Alice Munro is rescued from the cave at the Huron encampment, borne but also born out of the womb of the wilderness. This is the same womb from which her counterpart, the young Indian maiden, in a gruesome reminder of the historical exclusions enabling the birth of "nature's nation," will be carried dead on a bier: also borne, but stillborn. Alice's restoration, like that of her predecessor, Mary Rowlandson, may be viewed as the recovery of an entire posterity, as another fictionalized origin, a (re)birth of a white race and an American civilization that will be reared on the grave of Alice's unfortunate foil. It is also, again as with Rowlandson, a rebirth and reconfiguration of the wilderness through which she has been circulating, which her circulation has marked and rendered knowable in an entirely new way. Her rescuers are Duncan, in the paint and clothing of a Huron tribesman, and Natty, in the skin of a bear—men who are unable, finally, to reach her except through performance, through masquerading as "nature" in their symbolic midwifery. In so doing, they epitomize "history and generation" as these "are acted out on the bodies of women, that is, those who can transmit identity" (Samuels 99–100). To introduce this episode that so tellingly interweaves the themes of nature, culture, gender, and performance, Cooper quotes, appropriately enough, from *A Midsummer Night's Dream*. The allusion neatly foreshadows the chapter's theme of the play within the play, preparing us for the dizzily nested performances to follow. It also succinctly emblematizes what I have taken to be the very "meaning of this masquerade" (256), the performativity of the American wilderness itself. "Have you the *lion's* part *written?*" asks Snug in this epigraph, linking one of our most potent symbols of wildness to the thoroughly human realm of discourse and performance. Answers Quince: "You may do it extempore, for it is nothing but roaring" (255).

Chapter Five

Four Views of Yosemite

> [T]o aestheticize morality is to make it ideologically effective. . . . If
> the aesthetic comes . . . to assume the significance it does, it is be-
> cause the word is shorthand for a whole project of hegemony, the
> massive introjection of abstract reason by the life of the senses.
> What matters is not in the first place art, but this process of re-
> fashioning the human subject from the inside, informing its sub-
> tlest affections and bodily responses with this law that is not a law.
> —Terry Eagleton, *The Ideology of the Aesthetic*

In *My First Summer in the Sierra,* the pioneering environmentalist and deep ecologist John Muir presents himself as a perfectly familiar
American type. Escaping the chaotic din of the lowlands, reveling in his soli-
tude while ascending vast, empty, and seemingly timeless landscapes, he is the
American Adam, a figure wholly removed, it would seem, from human society
and history. Muir's seductive prose enhances this Adamic illusion, helping us
forget that for much of that first summer he was not alone, that in fact his presence in the High Sierra in the late 1860s had been underwritten by the con-
juncture of quite specific historical events—in particular the influx of capital
into post–Civil War California and the diversification of resource extraction en-
terprises that occurred as the gold fields played themselves out.[1]

When *First Summer* is read as pure nature writing, as it generally is, it is easy
to overlook the ways in which its wilderness narrative is structured by economic
concerns. It opens with Muir lamenting that "money was scarce" and then engaging to spend the summer working for one Pat Delaney, a budding capitalist
who owns a flock of sheep he hopes to fatten on Yosemite's high country meadows (1). It closes with a numerical accounting of the summer's profit and loss.
Of the 2,050 sheep "that left the corral in the spring lean and weak," writes
Muir, 2,025 "have returned fat and strong. The losses are: ten killed by bears,

one by a rattlesnake, one that had to be killed after it had broken its leg on a boulder slope, and one that ran away in blind terror on being accidentally separated from the flock—thirteen all told. Of the other twelve doomed never to return, three were sold to ranch men and nine were made into camp mutton." Thus, Muir continues, "ends my forever memorable first High Sierra excursion" (182–83)—and thus ends his wilderness narrative, neatly bracketed by and integrated back into the business enterprise that had originally enabled it.

The book's dramatis personae consist of Muir, Delaney, and an itinerant laborer, a shepherd the author refers to only as Billy. (Muir has been hired primarily to keep an eye on the latter, whom Delaney does not entirely trust with his investment.) Muir repeatedly compares the tall and lanky Delaney to Don Quixote (7), adverting playfully to a feudal iconography even though "the Don" and his hirelings actually comprise the familiar capitalist triad of investor, manager, and laborer—the class structure of an urbanizing nation transported in microcosm into the Yosemite wilderness. That structure is as inherently conflicted in the woods as it is in the city, and not surprisingly Muir's narrative affords occasional glimpses of labor strife. Thus when Delaney is late replenishing the camp's supply of flour for bread, Billy grumbles that "since the boss has failed to feed him he is not rightly bound to feed the sheep. . . . 'Good grub, good sheep. That's what I say'" (51). This crisis is averted when Delaney arrives with fresh supplies, but later, when he and Billy argue over how best to manage the sheep, the proud shepherd abruptly quits (143). Dipping into a labor pool swollen with those dispossessed by the rapidly consolidating American empire, Delaney promptly replaces Billy with "two shepherds, one of them an Indian" (144).

Of course, Muir is less interested in Man and History than he is in Nature, and only rarely do we directly glimpse such social discord in what for the most part is unalloyed wilderness narrative. *First Summer* in fact epitomizes the literary-environmental function of recasting social relations *as* natural relations. In one particularly telling passage, Muir remarks on how little he misses Delaney during his lengthy absences from the sheep camp. Left thus "alone" (he is actually camping with two other men), Muir feels "not a trace of loneliness. . . . On the contrary, I never enjoyed grander company. The whole wilderness seems to be alive and familiar, full of humanity. The very stones seem talkative, sympathetic, brotherly." [2] The society that might otherwise include the two sheep men (notably never named) is here provided by the wilderness itself—a substitution that can be seen as both an early expression of deep ecology and a thoroughgoing mystification. Nature provides Muir with a form of companionship his co-workers cannot, if only because of the way their human presence and economic activity conflict with the process of his Adamic self-construction.

At the same time that wild nature functions as society, Muir's most immediate *real* society—the lower-class Others he supervises—seems to become indistinguishable from nature. He describes at some length, for example, Billy's greasy clothes, which "have become so adhesive" with pine resin and cooking fat that "the pine needles, thin flakes and fibres of bark, hair, mica scales and minute grains of quartz, hornblende, etc., feathers, seed wings, moth and butterfly wings, legs and antennae of innumerable insects, or even whole insects such as the small beetles, moths and mosquitoes, with flower petals, pollen dust and indeed bits of all plants, animals, and minerals of the region adhere to them and are safely imbedded. . . . These precious overalls are never taken off, and nobody knows how old they are, though one may guess by their thickness and concentric structure. Instead of wearing thin they wear thick, and in their stratification have no small geological significance" (90–91). Here the class Other is gratuitously aligned with Nature, the object of the naturalist's observation and theorization. The emphasis on the "geological significance" of the shepherd's single piece of workaday clothing obscures what a more sympathetic observer might have seen as its *sociopolitical* significance, the way it signifies Billy's poverty.[3]

Throughout *First Summer*, the human characters' responses to the wilderness are heavily determined by the class structure they bring into it. For Muir, Yosemite is a pastoral landscape that from the book's beginning reminds him of the days when shepherds were (supposedly) not so alienated from nature. He implicitly contrasts the sensitive and eloquent pastoral shepherd of classical poetry with Delaney and Billy, neither of whom is able to appreciate the natural beauty of, for example, the wild azaleas, whose blossoms elicit admiration from Muir but—because they poison the sheep—condemnation from the other two men. For similar reasons, what Muir considers the natural music of the wilderness is inaudible to Billy: "Of all Nature's voices baa is about all he hears. Even the howls and ki-yis of the coyotes might be blessings if well heard, but he hears them only through a blur of mutton and wool, and they do him no good." What for Muir is a glorious, beckoning wilderness—significantly, as we shall not be surprised to see, an enchanting *book*—is for Billy a highly rationalized patchwork of rocky ground and "green pastures," dangerously spiked with "various poisons" (14–16).

Muir tries to get his companion to see Yosemite as he does, but Billy stead-fastly refuses: "I have been trying to get him to the brink of Yosemite for a view, offering to watch the sheep for a day, while he should enjoy what tourists come from all over the world to see. But though within a mile of the famous valley, he will not go to it even out of mere curiosity. 'What,' says he, 'is Yosemite but a canyon—a lot of rocks—a hole in the ground—a place dangerous about falling into—a d—d good place to keep away from.'" Muir persists, "press[ing] Yosemite upon him like a missionary offering the gospel, but [Billy] would have none of it": "'I should be afraid to look over so high a wall. . . . It would make my head swim. There is nothing worth seeing anywhere, only rocks, and I see plenty of them here. Tourists that spend their money to see rocks and falls are fools, that's all. You can't humbug me. I've been in this country too long for that'" (70). Inexplicable for Billy is the existence of a class of people willing not only to risk their necks to visit such a dangerous place but to spend money to do it. He understands the value of wilderness as forage for the sheep, but not as part of the nascent economic calculus of literary environmentalism, within which landscapes like Yosemite would soon have far more value as social text than as raw natural resource.

Muir's reference to "stone sermons" underscores the emerging impor-tance of this perceived textuality of the wild landscape. The durable trope of the Book of Nature was already one of his favorite and most frequently invoked metaphors—but also one he found troubling. As Barton Levi St. Armand has noted, Muir's most fervent references to this "book" seem merely "dutiful," if not "clichéd and shopworn" (38), as if betraying a lack of genuine confidence in the notion of nature-as-transparently-readable-text. St. Armand points to one of Muir's early journal entries, which reveals what must have been a profound anx-iety for a writer who would later claim so frequently and confidently to read from nature's book: "When a page is written over but once it may be easily read, but if it be written over and over with characters of every size and style, it soon becomes unreadable, although not a single confused meaningless mark or thought may occur among all the written characters to mar its perfection. Our limited powers are similarly perplexed and overtaxed in reading the inexhaust-ible pages of nature, for they are written over and over uncountable times, writ-ten in characters of every size and color, sentences composed of sentences, every part of a character a sentence. There is not a fragment in all of nature, for every relative fragment of one thing is a full harmonious unit in itself. All to-gether form one grand palimpsest of the world" (qtd. in St. Armand 38). At its grandest, it would appear, nature is also at its most overdetermined and opaque. Rather than a transparently legible text, nature is an all-but-illegible palimpsest, so densely charged with meanings as to convey no meaning at all. "[I]n spite of his protestations about unity," Armand notes, Muir was "no longer able to entertain (never mind interpret) the much blotted and erased palimpsest that the Book of Nature has become" by the time he was beginning his wilderness wanderings (38).

It is not hard to see why Billy's refusal to read the "glorious book" of Yosemite—indeed, to admit there was anything there to read in the first place—would have left Muir so sorely vexed. If anything, it would have reminded him of his own suspicions about the legibility of the purported natural text. What if Billy's obstinance and Muir's anxiety were well founded, and rather than a "stone sermon," Yosemite really *was* "only rocks"? That question has a particular significance for the history of literary environmentalism, because long before Muir was to make the now-famous valley the focal point of his radical environmentalism, it had already been enlisted to perform a specific function, had already been written, like many a *literal* sermon, with an eye toward disciplining those of Billy's class. Before Muir enlisted the Yosemite landscape as the primary vehicle for his radical environmentalism, it had already been made the vehicle of a social conservatism.

Just how that came about, and how from the very beginning the process was contested, are the subjects of this chapter, which will examine the works of four authors who preceded Muir in writing the Yosemite landscape canonized as the nation's first wilderness park. Key figures in "the double articulation of subjectivity and landscape," these writers constructed Yosemite Valley as a fully functional component of the National Symbolic, writing an "environment" disciplinary of the sort of "ecologized" American subjectivity that Billy the shepherd refuses to adopt. In a historical context linking a nascent environmentalism to the new literary realism and the corporate capitalism that was then transforming the West, they wrote Yosemite as a fully canonical text capable of performing a broad range of cultural work—but not, however, without arousing discordant voices that would join Billy's in contesting the new environmental narrative.

The early history of Yosemite Valley has been recounted several times, most recently by Rebecca Solnit in *Savage Dreams*, and I will review the story only briefly here.[4] Native Americans of California's Ahwahneechee tribe had lived in and around the valley for centuries, creating a history of their own, which, like the continuing presence of the Ahwahneechee themselves, still disrupts the official historical narrative of the region.[5] That later history, the Euro-American "written record," began late in the fall of 1833, when Joseph Reddeford Walker tried to lead a party of fur trappers across the Sierra Nevada to the Pacific Ocean and got bogged down in the snows of the Sierra Nevada, somewhere along the high mountain divide between the Merced and Tuolumne Rivers. According to the memoir of one member of the Walker party, Zenas Leonard, while searching for a way off this divide he found himself looking down upon cliffs that seemed "to be more than a mile high" and huge waterfalls that seemed to, as he puts it, "precipitate themselves from one lofty precipice to another, until they are exhausted in rain below" (41). This was almost certainly the "first white sighting" of Yosemite Valley. But because Leonard's account was not widely circulated at the time and generated no public interest in the region, historians have generally declined to credit him with the valley's "discovery." In order to "count" within traditional historical discourse, a discovery must be more than a first white sighting; it must also introduce the object into the consciousness of the discovering society—and Leonard's account failed to do that, falling almost immediately into obscurity. At any rate, there is no evidence that the Walker party exercised even the most perfunctory of the discursive privileges of the "first white man to see," that of *naming* what has been seen.

The white men who finally did exercise this Adamic prerogative were members of the Mariposa Battalion, participants in the so-called Mariposa Indian War of 1851–1853. The excuse advanced for this lopsided "war" was the killing of three men at a trading post owned by James Savage, an opportunistic and extraordinarily successful miner, trader, and frontiersman whom Solnit aptly compares to Joseph Conrad's Mr. Kurtz (338). Savage's main concern in the fighting appears to have been to shore up his sagging trading empire, which had been based largely on his personal initiative and authority. The war may, in fact, have begun as little more than "a personal vendetta" (Solnit 272), but Savage managed to convince local officials that this isolated incident at the trading post might spark a mass uprising. He was authorized to form a militia unit, the Mariposa Battalion, and to place himself in charge.

The war itself was neither spectacular nor decisive. While tracking a group of Ahwahneechee families led by Chief Tenaya into Yosemite Valley in March 1851, the battalion found only one Indian among the abandoned villages—an elderly woman unable to flee with the rest. Rather than pursue and engage the tribe, Savage and his men spent the next three days systematically searching the valley floor, torching every dwelling and all the food stores they could find—a scorched-earth policy that would soon bring many of Tenaya's followers, if only temporarily, to the reservation. During this brief initial foray the soldiers decided to christen the valley "Yosemity," apparently in the mistaken belief that this was its native designation. A second Mariposa expedition followed in May, pursuing and capturing Tenaya and several dozen followers who had slipped away from the reservation. In 1852, responding to a report that Ahwahneechee tribesmen had killed two white miners at Bridalveil Meadows, federal troops invaded the valley, where they found and summarily executed five native men. Tenaya, meanwhile, had left the reservation a second time and crossed the mountains to live with a group of Paiutes in eastern California. He was never recaptured, and he died in 1853—not, apparently, doing battle with the whites but as the result of an argument with some Paiutes.[6]

As newspaper accounts of the Mariposa War filtered to the eastern cities, attention shifted from the fighting to the valley's landscape. Public interest in Yosemite grew quickly, and by 1863 the movement was afoot to preserve it as a park. The details of this crucial institutionalization, unfortunately, are still not clearly understood, though it appears not to have resulted from any widespread popular appeal. Senator John Conness of California, who introduced the Yosemite park bill in Congress in the spring of 1864, claimed later that the idea had been presented to him by a small group of "gentlemen . . . of fortune, of taste, and of refinement," but he did not name them. Future park superintendent Frederick Law Olmsted may or may not have been among these "gentlemen"; other likely candidates include Thomas Starr King, who was the author of a popular book on New England's White Mountains and who was then planning a book on the Sierra Nevada; and Israel Ward Raymond, a representative of the Central American Steamship Transit Company (which stood to benefit from increased tourist travel to California). Unlike so much subsequent environmental legislation, this first park bill sparked no public debate and was approved rapidly and quietly in Congress. President Lincoln, preoccupied with Civil War matters, signed it into law in the summer of 1864 (Runte 21).

First View: Lafayette Bunnell and "The Best Prospect Yet"

Little would be known of the Mariposa War, and even less about the Mariposa Battalion's "discovery" of Yosemite, were it not for the participation of Lafayette Bunnell, who recounts the events in his *Discovery of the*

Yosemite and the Indian War of 1851 Which Led to the Event. Bunnell was born in Rochester, New York, in 1824 "and carried to Western wilds in 1833," the same year Zenas Leonard had peered down into the valley from its snowbound perimeter. In the West, as Bunnell rather apologetically notes, his "opportunities for culture were limited"; in particular he "found that the experiences of frontier life" had not provided him with "the best preparations for literary effort" (ix). His Yosemite book was "his first attempt at authorship" and also his last. No one has ever called it a masterpiece.

Why did Bunnell write the book at all? Like Zenas Leonard before him, he was the most literate member of his party and may on that account have felt a special responsibility to chronicle events. He claimed that the many second-hand accounts of the war were "so mutilated or blended with fiction" as to warrant "a renewed and full statement of facts," and he did not deem it "just" that readers "should forget the deeds of [the] men who had subdued her savages, and discovered her most sublime scenery" (ix). On the other hand, he waited nearly thirty years before publishing his own version of those events; it seems likely his real motivation was a desire to link his name and fortunes retroactively to what by then had become a world-famous locale.

Of particular interest for our purposes is *The Discovery of the Yosemite's* literary-environmental structure, its casual and ubiquitous linkage of "subdued savages" and "sublime scenery" and its simultaneous articulation of landscape and subjectivity. Representative in this regard is the book's description of Major Savage's burning of a native food cache—a passage that Bunnell seems to have crafted carefully and that is worth quoting in full. Bunnell has previously informed his readers that the soldiers, before burning the Ahwahneechee villages, had set aside a supply of captured food for their own use. Now that the battalion has completed its work and is preparing to leave, this reserve, too, has been put to the torch. Bunnell, meanwhile, has just returned from a day of "exploring," enjoying the scenery and searching for any remaining food stores; the flames from the burning food stores are "leaping high" as he addresses himself to Savage:

> I briefly, but with some enthusiasm, described my view from the cliff up the
> North Cañon, the Mirror Lake view of Half Dome, the fall of the South
> Cañon and the view of the distant South Dome. I volunteered a suggestion
> that some new tactics would have to be devised before we should be able to
> corral the "Grizzlies" [i.e., the Ahwahneechees] or "smoke them out." The

major looked up from the charred mass of burning acorns, and as he glanced down the smoky valley, said, "This affords the best prospect of any yet discovered; just look!" "Splendid!" I promptly replied, "Yo-sem-i-te must be beautifully grand a few weeks later when the foliage and flowers are at their prime, and the rush of waters has somewhat subsided. Such cliffs and waterfalls I never saw before, and I doubt if they exist in any other place." I was surprised and somewhat irritated by the hearty laugh with which my reply was greeted. The major caught the expression of my eye and shrugged his shoulders as he hastily said "I suppose that is all right, Doctor, about the waterfalls, etc., for there are enough of them here for one locality, as we have all discovered; but my remark was not in reference to the scenery, but the *prospect* of the Indians being starved out, and of their coming in to sue for peace. We have all been more or less wet since we rolled up our blankets this morning, and the fire is very enjoyable, but the prospect that it offers to my mind of *smoking out* the Indians is more agreeable to me than its warmth or all the scenery in creation." (91–92)

The two men's misunderstanding hinges on the meaning of the words *discovered* and *prospect*. What Savage has discovered is not a grand vista of Yosemite Valley, but an imperial strategy, a means for *acquiring* the valley. And by "prospect" he means an attractive vision of the future, in contrast to Bunnell, who takes it to mean the aesthetic beauty of the presently visible landscape. If Savage's position strikes us today as more brutally honest than Bunnell's, it is because for him the temporality of history has not yet disappeared into the timelessness of nature.

This ambiguous term *prospect* in fact has a long history in colonialist travel narrative. Mary Louise Pratt has shown how it invariably implicates such writing in an imperialist teleology, how it points always toward "the goal of expanding the capitalist world system." In the texts that foreground this sort of dual "prospect," "European enterprise is seldom mentioned, but the sight/site as textualized consistently presupposes a global transformation that, whether the I/eye likes it or not, is already understood to be underway. In scanning prospects in the spatial sense—as landscape panoramas—this eye *knows itself* to be looking at prospects in the temporal sense—as possibilities for the future, resources to be developed, landscapes to be peopled or repeopled by Europeans" (125). The distinction between the presently visible landscape and the imagined future occupation and reconfiguration of that landscape tends to become blurred in such writing. Bunnell uses the term *prospect* in its present-tense sense of "scenery," but also enlists the present scene to prefigure a utopian future when the unpleasant and distracting "rush" of events will have subsided and "the foliage and flowers [will be] at their prime." Similarly, Savage's genocidal work is future oriented (the fire will eventually result in the Ahwahneechees' "coming in to sue for peace") but also presently satisfying (its warmth "is very enjoyable"). Such temporal confusion is further complicated in this particular text by the fact that the narrator—speaking in the 1850s—is closely aligned with the author—who writes nearly thirty years later, from within the reconfigured future toward which the text points. Despite this blurring, there is little confusion about which subject position is privileged; Bunnell's contemporary readers would clearly have identified with the sophistication of the narrator rather than the crudity of the fortuitously named Savage.

It is important to note that the narrator does not see the battalion's genocidal activities as any less ethical than Savage does. Bunnell is "irritated" but hardly horrified by the major's laughter; he sees the battalion's activities as more distasteful than unethical. He arrogates to himself a superior sensibility rather than a moral high ground, and in the process what strikes us today as the crucial issue, the immorality of conquest, is deflected from ethics to aesthetics. In this fashion *The Discovery of the Yosemite* exemplifies the more general ideological function of aesthetic discourse. As Terry Eagleton has shown in his analysis of Alexander Baumgarten's *Aesthetica* (1750)—the philosophical treatise that first theorized the modern notion of the aesthetic—such discourse should "be read as symptomatic of an ideological dilemma," of what was then a vexing question: "How can reason, that most immaterial of faculties, grasp the grossly sensuous?" The answer lay in the aesthetic, conceived as a new form of "cognition" that "mediates between the generalities of reason and the particulars of sense" (15). Through such mediation, power becomes "aestheticized," rendered "at one with the body's spontaneous impulses, entwined with sensibility and the affections" (20).

The primary ideological effect of this aestheticizing is to significantly "transform the relations" between "morality and knowledge" (Eagleton 28). The earl of Shaftesbury would make this transformation more explicit, claiming, as Eagleton summarizes, that "there is somewhere within our immediate experience a sense with all the unerring intuition of aesthetic taste, which discloses the moral order to us. Such is the celebrated 'moral sense' of the eighteenth-century moralists, which allows us to experience right and wrong with all the swiftness of the senses" (34). The aesthetic aligns morality with "the springs of sensibility," positing a moral *sense* that "consists in 'a real antipathy or aversion to injustice or wrong, and in a real affection or love towards equity and right, for its own sake, and on account of its natural beauty and worth'" (34). This mapping of the rational onto the sensual—a specific manifestation of literary environmentalism's more general mapping of history onto nature—has a tremendous ideological efficacy because "feelings, unlike propositions, cannot be controverted" (38).

The aesthetic thus comes to serve as an "alternative" to a genuine ethics. But where a genuine ethics would concern itself with reasoning out the morality of actions, the aesthetic routes such concerns into an appreciation of the beauty of what is (above all) *seen*. Bunnell's play on the word *prospect* collapses action-in-time into a timeless "view" capable of subtly valorizing that history. For Shaftesbury, "[b]eauty, truth and goodness are ultimately at one: what is beautiful is harmonious, what is harmonious is true, and what is at once true and beautiful is agreeable and good. . . . 'For what is there on earth *a fairer matter of speculation, a goodlier view or contemplation,* than that of a beautiful, proportion'd, and becoming action?' . . . Truth for this passed-over Platonist is an artistic apprehension of the world's inner design: to understand something is to grasp its proportioned place in the whole" (Eagleton 35, my emphasis). In Bunnell's case, this atemporal, spatialized "whole" functions as a sort of synchronic equivalent to the self-legitimating capitalist teleology whose goal is the acquisition and transformation of the entire American continent. To view the spectacular Yosemite landscape is to affectively apprehend and appreciate Manifest Destiny itself, the larger design within which acts of genocide have their "proportioned place."

In *The Discovery of the Yosemite,* Bunnell invokes the temporal and the atemporal simultaneously, setting up a division of ideological labor in which he *aestheticizes* the battalion's activity while the less sophisticated Savage *rationalizes* it. Savage subordinates the sensual pleasure of the warmth afforded by the burning food stores to the rational prospect of military victory; he rejects feeling in favor of the prospect offered to his "mind," his calculated awareness of the likely historical effect of his actions. He understands the rightness of his actions through reason, albeit a reasoning we today find repugnant. Bunnell understands essentially the same thing, but he understands it as it presents itself to his eye. He no more doubts the rightness of his actions than does Savage, but he apprehends this skewed morality aesthetically, in a mode of understanding that persists to this day.

Bunnell repeatedly stresses his own aesthetic apprehension and just as frequently contrasts those tender feelings with the obliviousness of his less sophisticated companions. Much as Muir would complain later about Billy the shepherd, Bunnell writes that "very few of the volunteers seemed to have any appreciation of the wonderful proportions of the enclosing granite rocks" (90), and he quotes Savage as saying that Yosemite was just "what we supposed it to be before seeing it, a h—— of a place" (92). His aesthetic sensibility serves as the class marker distinguishing him from his crude comrades in arms:

> To obtain a more distinct and *quiet* view, I had left the trail and my horse and wallowed through the snow alone to a projecting granite rock. So interested was I in the scene that I did not observe that my companions had all moved on. (64)

> [T]he coarse jokes of the careless, and the indifference of the practical, sensibly jarred my more devout feelings . . . as if a sacred object had been ruthlessly profaned, or the visible power of Deity disregarded. (68)

> From my ardor in description, and admiration of the scenery, I found myself nicknamed 'Yosemity' by some of the batallion. . . . From this hint I became less *expressive*, when conversing on matters related to the valley. My self-respect caused me to talk less among my comrades generally. (95)

In foregrounding this class dichotomy, Bunnell is both aestheticizing the landscape and hailing his readers into an aestheticized morality. "[R]efashioning the human subject from the inside," to recall Eagleton's words, he interpellates his readers as subjects who can understand the narrated events as justifiable by virtue of the beauty of the landscape those events helped acquire. The reader's only moral obligation is to appreciate "the visible power of Deity"; as appreciation becomes the locus of ethics, any persisting guilt may be displaced along class lines, onto those who are "coarse" and hence "indifferent" to natural beauty.

Second View: Frederick Law Olmsted, Social Engineer

Scholars and environmentalists alike have stressed the fundamental importance of Yosemite Valley's official preservation. To David Brower, the creation of the Yosemite park was "a key starting point for environmentalism in the United States" (46). To Hans Huth it was the "point of departure from which a new idea began to gain momentum," namely the systematic approach to landscape preservation that would culminate in the national park system, an "institution admirably suited to fill the needs of the people" (48). Perhaps as important as the legislation itself was Yosemite's first management report, written in 1865 by the new park's first superintendent, the noted landscape architect Frederick Law Olmsted. "With this single report," according to Laura Wood Roper, "Olmsted formulated a philosophic base for the creation of state and national parks," a base that "made explicit and systematic the political and moral ideas" implicit in Congress's creation of the park and that "not only justified their unexampled action but established it as sound precedent" (Olmsted 13). The report has "since his time become a fundamental policy of the National Park Service" (Todd 145).

Unlike Bunnell, Olmsted found in Yosemite much more than a mere landscape. He thought of himself as "a sort of social engineer," as Roper puts it, "whose function was to civilize men . . . and to raise the general level of American society" (282). He hoped to make Yosemite the cornerstone of a wide-reaching social technology that could, among other things, unite and consolidate a fractured national identity, improve the nation's supposedly worsening physical and mental health, and elevate the public's morals. The valley's ability to accomplish all this cultural work—its perceived ideological efficacy in the articulation of subjectivity and landscape—did not inhere in the landscape itself. It was inscribed there in direct response to such specific historical events as the Civil War, the growth of urbanization and industrialization, and the capitalist restructuring of the West. Far from being "natural," the Yosemite that became the initial object of institutional environmentalism owes its modern "nature" to a complex intersection of aesthetic, sociological, ecological, and other discourses attendant upon those events. Olmsted's view of the valley can best be illustrated by tracing its genealogy through a pair of northeastern urban reforms in which Olmsted was involved: the so-called rural cemetery and New York's Central Park.

The rural cemetery movement began in Boston in the 1820s as the expression of a growing dissatisfaction with life in an increasingly crowded and heterogeneous city. This movement was contemporaneous with the development of the earliest Boston suburbs, and the rural cemetery can in fact be seen as analogous to the suburb, with the relocated grave serving, like the suburban home, "as a haven in a heartless world" (J. Farrell 106, 110). It was also a sanitation reform, one of several civic improvements then under consideration in response to a population explosion that, in the fifty years since the Revolution, had put severe pressure on local environments.

Air and water pollution in particular were felt to be exacerbated by the interment of corpses in overcrowded city cemeteries.[7] As early as 1822, Boston residents had debated (but not approved) a proposal to ban in-city burials. Of course, even had such a measure passed, it could not in itself have solved the problem. New cemeteries would be needed outside the city, but who would create and manage them, and how would they be financed? How large should they be? Who might be interred there? Might the land set aside for them perform social functions other than just burial? In debating such questions, rural cemetery advocates moved beyond their initial concern with sanitation to larger social and political issues. Some wondered "whether vault burial was discriminatory within a democratic society" (Sloane 44), others whether government should have any involvement at all in such matters. It is worth noting that the debate foregrounded and integrated several themes that would find expression not only in the new cemeteries but also in New York's Central Park and then in California's Yosemite park: questions not only of sanitation, but also of democracy, of ecology, of preservation in perpetuity, and of government's role in preserving and managing public lands. The rural cemetery movement would transform what had been almost exclusively a religious topic into a new and far more comprehensive discipline. Removed from the churchyard, burial would be regulated more and more within the discourses of science and aesthetics—particularly as these two discourses came to be combined in the new discipline of landscape architecture, whose early development as a profession was intimately bound up with the rural cemetery movement.

FROM MUMMIFICATION TO MUSEUMIFICATION

In 1825, three years after Boston's proposed ban on in-city burials was defeated, a prominent Cambridge physician, Jacob Bigelow, took up the interment problem again. "[I]mpressed with the impolicy of burials under churches or in churchyards approximating closely to the abodes of the living," as one contemporary put it, Bigelow met at his home with a number of prominent Bostonians and inaugurated the movement that would culminate in 1831 with the dedication of the first of the rural cemeteries: the seventy-two-acre, carefully landscaped Mount Auburn. (Other cities followed Boston's lead, most notably New York, whose Green-Wood Cemetery opened in 1838.) A botanist as well as a physician, Bigelow was a member of the medical faculty at Harvard and a founding member of the Massachusetts Horticultural Society. He was also an enthusiastic admirer of William Cullen Bryant's "graveyard poetry," and it was thus perhaps inevitable that the cemetery movement he founded would realize in concrete practice the popular romantic association of death and burial with picturesque scenery.

In arguing for the utility of his proposal, Bigelow infuses this sort of romantic aestheticism with the new scientific discourses of sanitation, botany, and an early version of ecology. "[S]o inseparably do we connect the feelings of the living with the condition of the dead," he is recorded as saying in his address to the 1825 meeting, that we must "analyze . . . the principles which belong to a correct view of the subject." Foremost among those principles is the complete rejection of any sort of mummification in favor of the rapid and natural decomposition of the corpse. Bigelow secularizes his argument, basing it not on theology but on the observation of "nature": "If we take a comprehensive survey of the progress and mutations of animal and vegetable life, we shall perceive that this necessity of individual destruction is the basis of general safety. The elements which have once moved and circulated in living frames, do not become extinct nor useless after death;—they offer themselves as the materials from which other living frames are to be constructed." This early ecological rhetoric highlights natural cycles and interdependencies and predicts apocalyptic consequences if they are ignored: "The plant which springs from the earth, after attaining its growth and perpetuating its species, falls to the ground, undergoes decomposition, and contributes its remains to the nourishment of plants around it. The myriads of animals which range the woods or inhabit the air, at length die upon the surface of the earth, and if not devoured by other animals, prepare for vegetation the place which receives their remains. . . . Were it not for this law of nature, the soil would soon be exhausted, the earth's surface would become a barren waste, and the whole race of organized beings, for want of sustenance, would become extinct." Only man, "the master of the creation," at his own peril "does not willingly stoop to become a participator" in this "routine of nature" (qtd. in Walter 29–30).

In his address Bigelow condemns the tremendous efforts made in other cultures to preserve the human corpse. Shifting his strategy, he invokes the rhetoric of democracy rather than ecology, noting that the only reasonably successful attempts at embalming "are cases of extraordinary exemption . . . such as can befall but an exceedingly small portion of the human race." The "common fate," by contrast, is to obey "the common laws of inert matter." Mummification is not merely elitist and un-American, he says, it is also *unnatural,* a useless "resistance" to inexorable leveling processes that obliterate social distinctions— processes that must be obeyed if we are not eventually to "gather round us the dead of a hundred generations in a visible and tangible shape." And "what custom," asks Bigelow, "could be more revolting?" (Walter 32–33).

To prevent such an environmental catastrophe—not to mention the *political* catastrophe connoted by the image of the dead masses "revolting"—nature "ordains" that, like everything else in nature, human bodies "should moulder into dust." Bigelow's compactly dialogic argument skillfully blends this secularized Christian voice with the discourses of the noble savage and the democratic discourse of individual dignity. "[T]he sooner this change is accomplished," he continues, "the better." Decomposition should occur "peacefully, silently, separately—in the retired valley or the sequestered wood," because there "the soil continues its primitive exuberance" and "the earth has not become too costly to afford to each occupant at least his length and breadth" (Walter 34). Having repeatedly constructed ecological process as a social, sanitary, and aesthetic good, Bigelow's argument finally makes a seamless segue back into a naturalized Christianity: "This can be fitly done, not in the tumultuous and harassing din of cities,—not in the gloomy and almost unapproachable vaults of charnel-houses,—but amidst the quiet verdure of the field, under the broad and cheerful light of heaven, where the harmonious and ever-changing face of nature reminds us, by its resuscitating influences, that to die is but to live again" (35).

Despite Bigelow's stress on death and decomposition, the longing for immortality has not disappeared; it has merely been redirected. As "consecrated ground" that is to "remain forever, inviolate" (13), it is now the cemetery *landscape* rather than the human body that will be eternally preserved. Green-Wood's charter makes elaborate legal provisions for the cemetery's "permanence," ensuring funds for the site's "perpetual care" and exempting the land "forever" from taxes and assessments that might eventually necessitate its foreclosure and sale (Cleaveland iv). Management at the site itself is preservationist: "ample provision is made" to ensure "the perpetual embellishment and preservation of the grounds" (v), with the cemetery's "noble and varied forest-growth" in particular to be "studiously preserved, except where convenience or necessity require[s] its removal" (vi). The desire for mummification has been displaced from the human body onto the body of nature, in terms that prefigure the land management policies later formulated by Olmsted for Yosemite.

What Bigelow was proposing in 1825 was not just a new form of burial but an entirely new kind of public space. The rural cemetery was to be public and secular, democratic and sanitary, and museumified in a permanently picturesque state. Because such spaces were without precedent in the United States, their creation entailed considerable financial risk. Regardless of whether the new cemetery was a for-profit, nonprofit, or government-run enterprise, there was the nagging question of whether enough lots would be sold to sustain the enterprise. The organizers "were committing their association to centuries of burying the dead," as one historian puts it, "but what if the public would not buy?" (Sloane 45). To hedge their bets, the cemetery founders joined forces in 1829 with the Massachusetts Horticultural Society, which for some time had wished to create an experimental garden on a large scale. It was to be a mutually beneficial arrangement: the cemetery organization would not have to bear the full financial risk of the venture, and the Horticultural Society felt that the combined garden and cemetery "would ultimately offer such an example of landscape gardening as would be creditable to the Society" (46). As it turned out, this arrangement was not so mutually beneficial after all; the Horticultural Society did put up the six thousand dollars for the purchase of the Mount Auburn site, but the planned experimental garden never materialized (Rotundo, "Rural" 235). Nonetheless, the link between the rural cemetery and the science of horticulture—so crucial to the professionalization of landscape architecture—would endure through the end of the century.

Fulfilling early hopes that it would be not merely a "repository of the dead" but also "a place of consolation for the living" (Walter 28), the rural cemetery quickly became a popular recreation site, often attracting hundreds of visitors per day. By mid-century the crowds at New York's Green-Wood Cemetery were estimated to exceed thirty thousand visitors annually; they "strolled the grounds, guidebook in hand," "enjoying the fresh air" and "picnicking along undulating paths" (Jackson and Vergara 19)—much as they would do in Yosemite a generation later.

This popularity made the new cemeteries a logical site for the exercise of a certain cultural work that they had been expected to perform from the very beginning. Jacob Bigelow, for example, had mentioned the "didactic implications of the new landscape aesthetic" realized by the rural cemetery (J. Farrell 100). And one of his contemporaries characterized these spaces as providing the opportunity "to meditate on present plans and future prospects" in a beautiful and inspiring, yet also morally chastening, environment—where, as Wordsworth put it, one may "recognize / In nature the language of the sense, / The anchor of our purest thoughts" (Walter 5, 7). Another observer noted how the new cemeteries prompted "the sentiment of retrospection and reverence which embalms forever the examples of the benefactors of our race" (J. Farrell 108).

"VIRTUOUS HABITS OF PLAY"

Apparently it was William Cullen Bryant who first popularized the idea of a large park for Manhattan (Rosenzweig and Blackmar 24). But it was Andrew Jackson Downing, the prominent landscape architect and protégé of Frederick Law Olmsted, who first saw clearly that such a park could, in its didacticism and its normalizing of tastes, systematically replicate and broaden the disciplinary functions of the rural cemetery. Downing, in fact, conceived of the urban park as essentially a scenic cemetery without the graves, inaugurating an association of park and cemetery that would long endure on the institutional level.[8] Downing joined forces with Bryant, and in 1851 the state legislature approved their proposal for the plan that would become Central Park. Appointed as superintendent of the project was Frederick Law Olmsted, Downing's friend and former pupil. Olmsted admired the writings of both Bryant (whom he knew personally) and Ralph Waldo Emerson; he agreed with the Transcendentalists generally about "the moral value of nature" and had been particularly impressed with Emerson's recently published essay of the same name. Though he was sympathetic to the Jeffersonian vision of a democracy stabilized by a rural citizenry (Todd 48–49), he was himself an inveterate New Yorker who knew perfectly well that the nation's future character was to be increasingly urban. He knew that even the wilderness of the far western frontiers would eventually be exhausted. One way to characterize Olmsted's wide-ranging work is to see it as mediating the tensions between frontier ideal and industrial reality—as an attempt, that is, to sustain a rural democratic vision for what was becoming an urban proletariat.

Central Park was not to be a cemetery, but Olmsted nonetheless envisioned it as a species of sanitary reform. His work during the Civil War as a member of the United States Sanitary Commission (the future Red Cross) had involved sanitation as we think of it today, activities aimed at preventing the spread of infectious diseases (notably, given our topic, through the proper disposal of corpses). But in the mid-nineteenth century the term *sanitation* had a much broader range of connotations. Along with today's familiar usage, as the OED makes clear, it implied an absence of "deleterious influences" of the social as well as the biological sort. Similarly, "sanity" could mean what today we think of as strictly physical health, but it carried in addition a connotation of what today we might term "wholesomeness." Health was considered "as much a moral as a biological condition," while disease "was associated with 'dissipation,'" which included activities like drinking, gambling, and boxing. Olmsted saw in this comprehensive notion of *sanitation* the potential for a full-fledged conservative social reform (Rosenzweig and Blackmar 24).

As a prominent officer in the new American Social Science Association, Olmsted believed that "a social climate was evolving favorable to the promotion of a collective concern for the physical and moral welfare of all Americans" (Todd 33, 35). He and his Central Park supporters considered their proposal a "sanitary" or "health" measure in broadly social terms, and at the root of society was the family, the nexus where the park was to work its magic. Reform advocates believed the park "would provide a site for 'healthy' and 'manly' exercise" and an alternative "to rough male sports or the temptations of 'brightly lighted streets.'" In their place it would "encourage *family* outings and inspire 'home associations'" (Rosenzweig and Blackmar 24–25). "A park," added William Cullen Bryant, linking this reconfigured masculinity to an equally reconfigured capitalism, "might promote 'good morals and good order' by encouraging virtuous habits of play as well as work" (26). Femininity, too, was to be transformed. Many liberal observers believed that women's poor health could be traced to "their general lack of opportunity for physical and mental development." An urban park would provide a particularly valuable chance for "fair pedestrians to [engage in] healthful and natural exercise" and find relief from "the burden of domestic duties" (25). Of course, by setting aside a small portion of the city's public space as a site where women might "properly" appear, park proponents simultaneously legitimated the continuing segregation of the sexes elsewhere.

Like advocates of the rural cemetery, the park's proponents practiced a not-so-subtle class politics of elevating their putative inferiors. Downing, for example, declared that proper landscape architecture could embody "moral rectitude" in "rational enjoyments," and thereby "soften and humanize the rude," while the New York Horticultural Society's backing of the park was driven by its vision of "gardens that would enhance 'cultivation'—in both senses of the word"

(Rosenzweig and Blackmar 29–30). Robert Minturn and his wife, Anna Mary Wendell, two of the project's earliest advocates, also came to see the park in such a light. Throughout the 1830s the Minturns had been well-known philanthropists, friends of the beggars who crowded their door, but Robert's approach to poverty then took a conservative turn. Deciding in 1843 that "personal benevolence was a 'dangerous species of charity,'" he gave his support instead to the New York Association for the Improvement of the Poor, which maintained that the "injudicious dispensation of relief" was the chief cause of increasing poverty. The association's agents would separate out the "incorrigible mendicants" (who were to be packed off to the almshouse or the penitentiary) from the deserving poor (who were to be given limited physical relief and ample advice on remedying the character flaws that had landed them in poverty). Minturn's fellow park advocates may well have agreed with his basic class sympathies, but they tried to convince him "that a park would be a less repressive means of reforming the character of the city's working classes" (26). This easy conceptual shift from the penitentiary to the park suggests how the park was to function, in Althusserian terms, as part of the Ideological State Apparatus, disciplining the poorer classes by policing tastes rather than by using direct force.

Olmsted, along with his partner in the park enterprise, Calvert Vaux, cast this ideological exercise in democratic terms. While designing the park the two gradually moved "from defining pastoral scenery as the aesthetic goal of a public park to a larger social philosophy that claimed, as Vaux put it, to 'translate Democratic ideas into Trees & Dirt'" (Rosenzweig and Blackmar 136). Olmsted in particular expressed an unshakable faith in the elevating powers of his own class. His second annual report on Central Park notes that the purpose of this public space is to provide "healthful recreation for the poor and the rich, the young and the old, the vicious and the virtuous"—one cannot help but note the sympathies betrayed by the equations *poor* = *young* = *vicious*, and *rich* = *old* = *virtuous*—by exerting "a distinctly harmonizing and refining influence upon the most unfortunate and lawless classes of the city" (131, 241). "Rejecting the views of his 'cowardly conservative' opponents, for whom class-based cultural divisions were fixed," Olmsted writes that the working classes might gain "the refinement and taste and the mental & moral capital of gentlemen" by means of the "moral influence" of properly designed parks (qtd. in Rosenzweig and Blackmar 241). However closely Olmsted's class may have guarded its economic capital, it had moral capital to spare, and one reason for making the park as attractive as possible was to redistribute this symbolic wealth as widely as possible. Olmsted wished "to force into contact the good & bad, the gentlemanly and the rowdy" (139) in the public space of the park, where a judiciously naturalized landscape would have a "harmonizing and refining influence upon the most unfortunate and most lawless classes of the city,—an influence favorable to courtesy, self-control, and temperance" (131).

Despite the supposedly inherent abilities of landscape to uplift and refine, however, none of this would happen "naturally." Olmsted believed firmly that the ruling class would have to teach the people how best to use the park. On the one hand, he had long believed that beautiful landscapes could "materially promote Moral and Intellectual Improvement" by "instructing us in the language of Nature," as if nature could speak to us without mediation (qtd. in Todd 49). On the other hand, "[i]n order for the park to exercise its 'harmonizing and refining influence,' the public needed not just firsthand contact with natural beauty"—an unmediated experience of nature—"but also 'efficiently controlled and judiciously managed' supervision and guidance" (Rosenzweig and Blackmar 140). As Olmsted reported to the Central Park commissioners shortly after being hired as superintendent, in language that presages the interpretive programs that would later be formalized by the National Park Service, "[a] large part of the people of New York are ignorant of a park, properly so-called. They will need to be trained to the proper use of it, to be restrained in the abuse of it." By "abuse," Olmsted meant the sort of "careless stupidity" which he felt stemmed from notions that the park was "'like a wood,' with which Americans associated 'the idea of perfect liberty'" (239). Ten years later, before resigning his Central Park superintendency and leaving for California, Olmsted cited the small number of arrests made in Central Park as evidence in favor of his theories, noting in his journal that "[t]he American public is one of the easiest in the world to regulate if any body will take the responsibility of regulating it" (258).

THE POWER OF SCENERY

In 1863, Olmsted resigned his Central Park position and took a job in California managing the Mariposa County mining properties of the former explorer and Republican presidential nominee, John Charles Frémont— land near Yosemite Valley that had once been under the control of James Savage. Olmsted's social connections, his experience with Central Park, and his physical proximity to Yosemite all drew him naturally into the circle of elite Californians then discussing the proposed state park. When Congress passed and President

Lincoln signed the Yosemite bill in 1864, Olmsted was appointed to the commission charged with managing the new grant and quickly became its head.

Up to this time the primary spheres of operation of landscape architecture—the cemetery and the park—had been exclusively urban and suburban. The seamlessness of Olmsted's transition to managing the new *wilderness* park underscores the fundamental parallels in social function underlying both disciplinary cityscape and wilderness landscape, suggesting that this initial institutionalizing of environmentalism had less to do with preserving the Yosemite environment "itself" than with contemporary social concerns. The environmental reform that took the form of the national park was in fact continuous with the reform of the urban cemetery and the city park, reforms that became "environmental" only because of Olmsted's theory of the socializing utility of nature.

In August 1865, during a visit to the valley with the other commissioners, Olmsted wrote the commission's initial report—the first written text to issue from the bureaucracy of the newly institutionalized environmentalism. This report has since come to be regarded as remarkably prescient and foundational, as a sort of environmental Magna Carta that established the "philosophic base" for future park preservation.[9] Subsequent treatments of park history would foreground the overtly environmentalist aspects of this philosophy while largely ignoring its implicit social theory, obscuring the degree to which Olmsted and his fellow commissioners saw environmentalism as a vehicle for implementing broadly social aims.

Drawing on his Central Park experience, Olmsted viewed the valley's preservation as the *creation* of a work of art—as just one of the several great public artworks completed during the Civil War. The report's preamble demonstrates how Olmsted believed art to participate directly and decisively in history:

It is a fact of much significance with reference to the temper and spirit which ruled the loyal people of the United States during the war of the great rebellion, that a livelier susceptibility to the influence of art was apparent, and greater progress in the manifestation of artistic talent was made, than in any similar period in the history of the country.

The great dome of the Capitol was wholly constructed during the war, and the forces of the insurgents watched it rounding upward to completion for nearly a year before they were forced from their entrenchments on the opposite bank of the Potomac; Crawford's great statue of Liberty was poised upon its summit in the year that President Lincoln proclaimed the emancipation of the slaves. Leutze's fresco of the peopling of the Pacific States, the finest work of the painter's art in the Capitol; the noble front of the Treasury building with its long colonnades of massive monoliths; the exquisite hall of the Academy of Arts; the great park of New York, and many other works of which the nation can be proud, were brought to completion during the same period. (13–14)

Even as Union soldiers were asserting the territorial integrity of the nation, its artists were celebrating the ascendancy of federal power (the dome of the Capitol), the power and stability of capitalism (the Treasury Building with its "massive monoliths"), and the triumph of imperialism ("the peopling of the Pacific States"). The image of the "insurgent" Confederate soldier watching the completion of the dome in particular emblematizes Olmsted's belief in art's power over the wayward citizen, its role in social unification—precisely the powers he had attributed earlier to the carefully contrived (yet "natural") landscape of Central Park, which itself formed part of this intrabellum expansion of the National Symbolic. This belief spills over into Olmsted's decriptions of the physical landscape of Yosemite Valley, which he terms "the greatest glory of nature" precisely because of "its *union* of the deepest sublimity with the deepest beauty" (16, my emphasis).

Olmsted's rhetoric underscores his larger concerns with the health of the body politic, a concern that combines economics, psychology, and political science into an emerging environmentalist discourse of what might be called "social sanitation through outdoor recreation." Two specific advantages are to accrue from the Yosemite park. The "first and less important" of these is economic: "the direct and obvious pecuniary advantage which comes to a commonwealth from the fact that it possesses objects which cannot be taken out of its domain." He argues in effect for environmental preservation as a form of sustainable development, as opposed to the sort of resource extraction economy epitomized by the recent gold rush, whose deleterious ecological *and* social effects had become painfully obvious to him while he was managing the Mariposa estate. He describes how the "industrious and frugal people" of Switzerland have utilized their scenery to common advantage, with revenues from tourism having supplied "for many years the larger part of the state revenue . . . without the exportation or abstraction from the country of anything of the slightest value to the people." For California and the United States, he concludes, Yosemite might prove "a similar sort of wealth to the whole community" (17).

More important than mere pecuniary and ecological advantage, however, are "considerations of a political duty of grave importance to which seldom if ever before has proper respect been paid by any government in the world." Olmsted's report couches this argument in terms vaguely psychosociological, insisting upon the "scientific fact that the occasional contemplation of natural scenes of an impressive character, particularly if this contemplation occurs in connection with relief from ordinary cares, change of air and change of habits, is favorable to the health and vigor of men and especially to the health and vigor of their intellect." Without such recreation, men and women are susceptible to "a class of disorders" that include such forms of "mental disability" as "softening of the brain, paralysis, palsy, monomania, or insanity." Less severe but more frequent results of a lack of outdoor recreation are "mental and nervous excitability, moroseness, melancholy or irascibility," all conditions that incapacitate the sufferer "for the proper exercise of the intellectual and moral forces" (17) and, among other things, render the sufferer unfit for productive labor and proper gender performance. Reprising the argument he had made earlier in defense of Central Park, Olmsted writes that outdoor recreation offers its "greatest blessing" to those classes of Americans traditionally excluded from it: the poor more than the rich, and the "agricultural class" more than the urban. "Women," he adds, "suffer more than men" (20).

Despite its emphasis on inclusiveness, Olmsted's vision is hardly a democratic one. Rather it universalizes and normalizes a particular set of tastes and makes of them a foundation not only of aesthetics but also of sanity and morality. Certain "faculties and susceptibilities of the mind" are "called into play by beautiful scenery," and "there can be no doubt that all have this susceptibility." The "power of appreciating natural beauty," so "intimately and mysteriously associated with the moral perceptions and intuitions," is thus natural and universal, "something which the Almighty has implanted in every human being." Yet, this mental susceptibility "is much more dull and confused" in some people than in others. Olmsted's theorizing, in fact, consistently implies an elitist and racist teleology in which Yosemite's preservation marks a milestone not so much of the history of environmentalism as of the history of American taste and culture, a teleology that relegates dissenters to the realm of the uncivilized: "The power of scenery to affect men is, in a large way, proportionate to the degree of their civilization and the degree in which their taste has been cultivated. Among a thousand savages there will be a much smaller number who will show the least sign of being so affected than among a thousand people taken from a civilized community" (20–21). Olmsted concludes that this "is only one of the many channels" in which the "distinction between civilized and savage men is to be generally observed" (21). Landscape appreciation becomes just another axis of difference, closely allied with the axes of race and class, though theoretically distinct from them. The Yosemite landscape will function not merely to sustain the mental health of the civilized individual, but also to define the degree and mode of the individual's civilization, at once aestheticizing and naturalizing existing social hierarchies.

Third View: Clarence King

Clarence King, geologist and writer, founder of the United States Geological Survey and author of the best-seller *Mountaineering in the Sierra Nevada* (1872), arrived in California in 1863, the same year as Frederick Law Olmsted. King had gone west to join the newly formed California Geological Survey, which he felt would offer him field experience to supplement the classroom training he had just completed at Yale's new Sheffield Scientific School. He and Olmsted had been friends back east, and when Olmsted took over the management of the old Mariposa estate, he asked King to help inventory the property's mineral resources. With the geological survey in hiatus, King agreed.

The Mariposa needed the attention of someone like King. The huge, gold-rich estate had been owned since 1847 by the explorer John Frémont, the fomenter of the Bear Flag Revolt that wrested California from Mexico. In spite of Frémont's haphazard management, the Mariposa's mining operations had at first been profitable enough. But by the time Olmsted took over as its superintendent in 1863, both the estate and the general had seen better days. General Frémont had lost effective control of the grant and gone heavily into debt; to make good on the estate's many encumbrances, his creditors joined together as the Mariposa Mining Company and began floating its stock.[10] In less than fifteen years, that is, the Mariposa had slipped from the grasp of the archetypal rugged individualist into the control of Wall Street. It was in this respect the West in microcosm. The events at Mariposa presaged and typified the economic transformations that would occur with greater and greater rapidity in the West of the latter nineteenth century, events widely perceived in terms both mythic and economic as the inexorable passage from a heroic to a prosaic age, from the bold enterprise of the hero to the colorless and systematic exploitation of a northeastern capitalist technocracy.[11]

These events also heralded a revision of masculinity. As Gail Bederman has shown, this was the beginning of a period in which "a number of social, economic, and cultural changes were converging to make the ongoing gender process especially active for the American middle class": "By the last decades of the nineteenth century, middle-class power and authority were being challenged in a variety of ways which middle-class men interpreted—plausibly—as a challenge to their manhood. Ever since the middle class had begun to define itself as a class in the early nineteenth century, ideals of gender and of 'manliness' had been central to middle-class consciousness" (11). Bederman adds that "between 1873 and 1896," years that encompass much of King's career, "severe economic depressions resulted in tens of thousands of bankruptcies and drove home the reality that even a successful, self-denying small businessman might lose everything, unexpectedly and through no fault of his own. Under these conditions, the sons of the middle class faced the real possibility that traditional sources of male power and status would remain closed to them forever—that they would become failures instead of self-made men" (12). In response, American men of the middle class adopted "a new sense of primal manhood very different from Victorian manliness." They came to believe "that true manhood involved a primal virility," and "men who saw themselves in terms of this masculine primitive ethos were drawn to a variety of 'savage' activities" (22)—among which we may surely include "roughing it" generally and King's blustering style of mountaineering in particular. King's multifaceted career was intimately bound up with the complex social and economic changes of his time. In his adventure writing, as William Howarth puts it, he exemplified the "romantic ideal of self-reliant heroism" (King, *Mountaineering* xii) called for by the new masculinity, while his professional activities, by bringing western resources more and more under the sway of corporate investors, just as consistently functioned to foreclose on such heroic, individualistic enterprise.

In 1864, King was already thinking ahead to his greatest professional triumph, the ambitious Fortieth Parallel Survey, which would map and inventory a vast swath of the West and lay out the path for a transcontinental railroad. But his first survey was far more modest: after the creation of the Yosemite park, Olmsted appointed King to determine the boundary of the new grant and produce a map. Amid what he described as the "prosaic labor of running the boundary line" (*Mountaineering* 120), King had plenty of time to admire the scenery, which for him was a mythic western narrative, the visible record of an older and more heroic order. The boundary line ran through the High Sierra country above the valley walls, from which it seemed that the Ice Age glaciers had only recently retreated, leaving behind bare expanses where "[n]ot a tree nor a vestige of life was in sight." It seemed a place where life was just beginning, offering to King a vision of the bleak Eden of the Darwinists he so much admired. Peering down into the valley, now verdant but once filled with primal rivers of ice, he found it impossible "not to imagine a picture of the glacial period" when erosion sculpted Yosemite into its present shape. His description in *Mountaineering in the Sierra Nevada* depicts the scene as it must have appeared in the Pleistocene era:

Granite and ice and snow, silence broken only by the howling tempest and the crash of falling ice or splintered rock, and a sky deep freighted with cloud and storm,—these were the elements of a period which lasted immeasurably long, and only in comparatively the most recent geological times have given way to the present marvellously changed condition. Nature in her present aspects, as well as in the records of her past, here constantly offers the most vivid and terrible contrasts. Can anything be more wonderfully opposite than that period of leaden sky, gray granite, and desolate stretches of white, and the present, when of the old order we have only left the solid framework of granite, and the indelible inscriptions of glacier-work? To-day their burnished pathways are legibly traced with the history of the past. (130–31)

Nature for King is, first, an "indelible inscription," a readable landscape, and, second, "her," the feminine object of the male gaze. "She" is also a mythic history, the record of tumultuous passages, from storm to calm, from savagery to civilization, from wilderness to metropolis—most generally from a primitive but admirably heroic past to a civilized but lamentably prosaic present. Throughout the book, King is most particularly struck by the contrasts between the naked granite expanses of the heights and the luxuriant forest growths below, where "richness of soil and perfection of condition" sometimes actually "prove fatal through overcrowding." The Sierra landscape for King is a map of the human world, a Malthusian narrative full of proto-ecological warnings for the future, its forests "wonderfully like human communities" where "[o]ne may trace in an hour's walk nearly all the laws which govern the physical life of men" (119).

A REALIST AESTHETIC

In 1870, during a respite from the fieldwork of the Fortieth Parallel Survey, King reviewed a pseudoscientific travel narrative, James Orton's *The Andes and the Amazon,* for the *Overland Monthly.* Though his friendship with *Overland* editor Bret Harte had everything to do with King's receiving this assignment, he was nonetheless an appropriate choice for the job, for two reasons. As a working geologist, he was familiar with the new ideas then being introduced by science into the popular imagination. And as a developing writer who had already published a travel piece of his own in the *Overland* and was at work on several more (which would be collected in 1872 in *Mountaineering*), King was grappling with the special problems inherent in writing about little-known lands. These two facets of King's career—the literary and the scientific—were not as disparate as they might at first seem, for both involved the same challenge: writing western landscapes in a manner comprehensible to a largely eastern audience. As both reader and writer, King thought of himself as a "realist"—as a sensitive observer capable of perceiving the way things "really" are and an objective writer whose words faithfully mirrored that reality. I want now to read King—the geologist as well as the adventure writer—as he reads the landscape, and to problematize the seemingly straightforward conception of realistic representation. In particular, I want to show the close relationship between King's realist texts, his work as a scientist, and the ongoing commodification of the landscape itself.

King's critique of *The Andes and the Amazon* focuses on the book's departure from what appears in retrospect to have been a key part of his developing literary aesthetic. In particular, he faults Orton for failing to convey anything new, for occupying "that uninteresting middle condition where he has neither the *naive* sensitiveness of a new traveler, nor the penetration of the practiced observer. No sooner is he mounted upon a mule than he begins to recognize things with a reckless freedom. The ghosts of Humboldt and Darwin flank him upon either side. What they had seen, he sees. Not once does he lift his eyes from the dusty trail, but confines himself to the *role* of a corroborator" (King, "Current" 578). Orton, that is, has failed to elicit any genuinely new sensations in the reader, for whom the book is a mere "corroboration" offering only the chance to "recognize" what has been encountered before—in this case, in the travelogues of Humboldt and Darwin.

King's emphasis on the desensitizing effect of repetition, and especially of "recognition," would seem to make him an early exponent of the sort of formalism later codified by Viktor Shklovsky, for whom "the purpose of art is to impart the sensation of things as they are perceived and not as they are known," "to make objects 'unfamiliar'" (58). But for Shklovsky, making the reader "see" rather than merely "recognize" is a matter of effort, of "art as technique"; the object must be "defamiliarized" in order to remove it from the domain of automatized perception. King is suggesting another means of attaining the same end, a means implicit in his specific concern with narratives of travel and exploration—a genre characterized by special limitations but also special opportunities. In the words of Mary Fuller, such narratives "document a situation of enunciation in which the matter of speech, the topic, the referent, physically existed but was always going to be physically absent from the place of speaking and listening" (46). This conception suggests special problems I will address later; what is important here is that in the genuine exploration narrative, the "matter of speech" *begins* as something unfamiliar to the reader. To represent such material using the technique of some preceding travel writer hardly makes it any newer; if anything, this begins the process of *familiarizing* it. The travel writer thus seems to be particularly susceptible to illusions of mimesis, for the obvious way out of the dilemma is to avoid any evident technique at all, to reproduce the object unadorned in its already unfamiliar reality. For King, this crude realism is the "technique," suggested in his critique of Orton, of the naive traveler who need only read the landscape sensitively and then mirror it faithfully for the reader.

King's account in *Mountaineering in the Sierra Nevada* of a ride to a remote camp suggests that he thought of his own descriptive nature writing as just such a mimetic reproduction, the unforced result of encountering the world as if he were Emerson's "transparent eye-ball": "I was delighted to . . . expose myself, as one uncovers a sensitized photographic plate, to be influenced; for this is a respite from scientific work, when through months you hold yourself accountable for seeing everything, for analyzing, for instituting perpetual comparison. . . . No tongue can tell the relief to simply withdraw scientific observation, and let Nature impress you" (108). The movement from science to literature is for King a shift from the active to the passive, from the masculine to the feminine, from analysis to impression—from the production of knowledge *about* the landscape to the mimetic reproduction *of* the landscape. Though this movement takes him into a literary mode, it is paradoxically a movement *away* from language (it is something about which "no tongue can tell"). What King sees himself moving *toward* is not words about things, but things themselves—particularly, as the reader of *Mountaineering* quickly realizes, things in their most basic and immutable manifestations. This tendency certainly reflects King's concern with what, as a geologist, he viewed as the "hard, materialistic reality" of nature (253). But it is also consonant with a peculiarly American conception of the "real," in which, as Lionel Trilling puts it, "reality is always material reality, hard, resistant, unformed, impenetrable, and unpleasant" (qtd. in Sundquist 16). This conception of a rock-solid reality appealed not only to the geologist in King, but to the writer as well, for "that mind alone is felt to be trustworthy which most resembles this reality by most nearly reproducing the sensations it affords" (17). If mimesis is the key to representing landscape memorably, then mimesis that somehow does justice to a landscape's most fundamental and enduring phenomena is the key to representing it truthfully and convincingly.

Thus it is hardly surprising to find in King's nature writing the recurring tendency, as Ernest Fontana puts it, "to reduce things to their bare essentials, to strip away the superficies of vegetation, animal life . . . and human culture"; in doing so, he seeks in stone a foundation for a more trustworthy language. He seeks "not only . . . accurate knowledge of the unexplored mountains of California, but direct unmediated experience of the absolute, primal world of matter. . . . King's descriptions of the Sierra mountainscapes are attempts to recreate in language an unmediated experience" (25). Certainly King's writing is most energetic in those mountaineering episodes that take place above timberline, above the last settlements and the last vegetation, where he is left alone to contend with the primal simplicity of rock and ice. But the fact that his attempt to reproduce "unmediated experience" has resulted in some highly energetic stories hardly validates their underlying aesthetic. Such an attempt is complicated, for one thing, by conflicting assignments of gender. King sees scientific work as masculine, literary work as feminine; to passively let nature impress one may be a "relief," but it conflicts with the demands of both the new masculinity and the structure of the literary-environmental narrative. As the nature writer becomes feminized (soft, passive, and impressionable), nature becomes masculinized (hard, active, and impenetrable). This queering of the sexual-environmental matrix does not disqualify it as a site for constituting a masculine subject, but it does produce a palpable tension that, as we shall see in the case of King's adventures with Dick Cotter, cannot be completely avoided.

King's attempt to reproduce "unmediated experience" is also, of course, *linguistically* untenable. The fundamental claim underlying his aesthetic—that matter and experience can pass into language with the same directness and fidelity with which landscape passes into image in photography—would almost immediately be called into question by a series of bizarre events in his own career.

Mountaineering in the Sierra Nevada appeared the same year as Mark Twain's *Roughing It,* in 1872, but it was *Mountaineering* that was hailed by the *Overland Monthly* as "the book of the season." The book was well received elsewhere as well, and within two years would sell out five printings (Wilkins, *Mountaineering* v). Its popularity may have owed something to King's involvement in the Great Diamond Swindle of 1872, a scam that had begun two years earlier when two men posing as miners appeared in San Francisco carrying a sack of rough diamonds. The two men—Philip Arnold and John Slack—were secretive at first, dropping just enough hints to start the entire city speculating about their cargo and the mine from which it must have come. The diamonds were appraised, first in San Francisco and later by the Tiffany establishment in New York, and valued at $100,000. Slack allowed San Francisco banker William Ralston to talk him into selling his share of the putative mine—whose whereabouts were still kept secret—for just that amount. Arnold did not sell out until later, when what had turned into a speculative frenzy hit its peak; he received half a million dollars for his share (Wilkins, *Clarence King* 171–82).

In July 1872, Ralston filed incorporation papers for the San Francisco and New York Mining and Commercial Company, which was promptly capitalized at $10 million. To verify the mine's authenticity, Arnold and Slack allowed a visit by company officials and the expert Henry Janin, who was regarded as one of the most competent and incorruptible mining engineers in the country. Janin liked what he saw. "I consider this a wonderful discovery," he wrote in a report that appeared August 10, "and one that will prove extremely profitable. . . . I do not doubt that further prospecting will result in finding diamonds over a greater area than is yet proved to be diamondiferous" ("Diamond Bubble" 379). Janin speculated that the diamond fields, if worked by just twenty miners, could yield as much as $1 million worth of gems per month. This in turn generated widespread speculation that the mine might severely depress the international diamond market, and even shift the center of the gemstone industry from Amsterdam to San Francisco. Janin's pronouncements circulated widely in the newspapers, and by the end of the summer, investors had formed at least twenty-five "wildcat" companies, capitalized at more than $200 million in total, in hopes of cashing in on the boom as soon as the location of the fields should be made public (Wilkins, *Clarence King* 173, 182–83).

Everything was in place for a major rush, which undoubtedly would have taken place had it not been for the intervention of Clarence King. Whenever their survey work brought them into contact with civilization, King and his crew had sought out the latest diamond news, and by the end of the summer they had pieced together enough clues to locate the purported diamond field in a remote, potentially diamondiferous region of eastern Utah within the confines of King's survey. Clearly such a major find in his own bailiwick could not be ignored, and when the summer's fieldwork was completed, King set out quietly to inspect the claim himself, arriving at the site in November. There he found footprints; following them to where they converged with other tracks, he found mining notices posted on trees. A quick search of the area turned up several rubies and a few diamonds, and at first he was as much a believer as Janin. Further inspection, however, began to reveal disturbing evidence, and by the end of the second day King was convinced the ground had been salted and the claim was a fraud (Wilkins, *Clarence King* 177–79). When Ralston and Janin were informed, they returned to the site with King, who had little trouble convincing them that they had been deceived. The story went public, and King was lauded not only for saving investors millions of dollars, but also for preserving the reputation of California's fledgling financial establishment. He was the toast of the nation, and his name graced front pages from San Francisco to London. Not coincidentally, sales of his recently released book surged (Wilkins, *Mountaineering* vi).

The entire episode can be read as a linguistic parable: the swindlers' clever manipulation of the investors and the media engendered an intertext made up of newspaper stories, investment prospectuses, the report of the mining engineer, and, of course, the carefully written but putatively natural landscape of the diamond field. Such a text was not without precedent, its linguistic underpinnings being in fact typical of the "El Dorado" narratives so common in the literature of the Americas. A similar situation—Walter Ralegh's claims in his 1596 *Discoverie of Guiana* concerning a fabulous South American gold mine— has been analyzed in an instructive way by Mary Fuller and is worth examining briefly here for the parallels it offers to the diamond swindle.

The apologia worked up by King James's court to justify Ralegh's execution subjects the latter's claims concerning the existence of what he variously called Manoa or El Dorado to a close analysis. "James's accusations amount to an intensely skeptical critique of Ralegh's language," writes Fuller. "He claims that

Ralegh's writing is a screen not for *things* but for palpable intentions; that the things of which he writes are imaginary, and that their objective properties . . . are constructs responsive to the wish and will of the writer." To defend his text against such skepticism, Ralegh had resorted to physical evidence in the form of gold ore, a "handfull of the mine," which he hoped would ground his claim somewhere beyond the untrustworthy realm of language. Though he doubtless did not think of it in quite these terms, he hoped to demonstrate that at the end of the chain of signifiers making up the legend of Manoa there was something incontrovertible, a material object that was not itself the product of any linguistic operation. In so doing, Fuller notes, he was attempting to make use of "resources not available to the mere poet: speaking of gold, he puts a piece of ore in the refiner's hand" (44).

But material reality—in Ralegh's case, a "handfull of the mine"—proves insufficient to validate such claims. How, for one thing—even if one assumes the existence of El Dorado—was the reader in London to know that the ore had actually come from there? The supposedly "mute" testimony of objects turns out to be not univocal but ambiguous, and hence to require spoken or written corroboration; instead of providing the hoped-for escape from words, the material routes the reader back into the circuit of language. In the case of the discovery narrative—much as we saw with Natty Bumppo's repeated attempts to ground the sign in "nature"—not even *things* turn out to be free of the influences that engender the figurative drift of language. As Fuller notes, the objects Ralegh produced "as underpinnings for representations" turned out to be "fully implicated with rhetorical procedures: substitutions of parts for whole, transportations, ellipses. . . . [I]n the particular case of Ralegh, the part-for-whole synecdoche of *handfull* for mine masks a previous figure of metonymy—in fact, a congeries of previous figures" (45). Ralegh's critics had good reason to question the validity of his synecdoche, of his rhetorical substitution of a handful of ore—which might have come from anywhere—for an actual gold mine in Guiana. Clearly, the synecdoche cannot be valid unless the felicity of the underlying metonymy, the "naturalness" of the association of the transported ore with a specific mine, can be established. This Ralegh could not do with certainty because, as he admitted, he had never personally been to El Dorado; he claimed only to have come near it (54).

In the end, the *material* Ralegh had hoped would serve as irrefutable testimony for his own claims—and more generally for the underpinnings of the investor confidence necessary to early colonialism—turned out to be vulnerable to the same sort of skeptical analysis to which his *words* had been subjected. In a final effort to validate his claim, he returned to Guiana in search of the mine itself, an expedition that became "literally a search for the referent, a place to which [could] be attached the proper names *Manoa* and *El Dorado*," and which, unfortunately for the soon-to-be-executed Ralegh, proved fruitless (51).

The text engendered by the diamond swindle has much in common with other El Dorado stories. There was, for example, a great deal of money at stake—as a number of nervous investors were all too aware—and the remote, still-secret location of the mine precluded the usual means of verification. It thus shared what Fuller calls the "peculiar constraints" of the discovery narrative, of "a writing situation . . . in which the issue of truth, veracity, was particularly at stake and also particularly difficult to check" (45). More important, its authority rested ultimately on an appeal to the material—in this case, to the gems displayed in San Francisco by Arnold and Slack, and the stones turned up by Janin in situ in the field.

King was not a linguist but a geologist, and his on-site investigation of the swindlers' text focused not on its words but on the material representations underpinning them. His procedure, which recalls the virtuoso tracking activities of the heroes in chapter 21 of *The Last of the Mohicans,* amounts to a "close reading" of the material: "[W]e . . . lay down upon our faces, and got out our magnifying-glasses and went to work, systematically examining the position of the stones and their relation to the natural gravels. The first point which excited my suspicion was the finding of a diamond on a small point, or knob of rock . . . in a position from which one heavy wind, or the storms of a single winter, must inevitably have dislodged it" (Deposition). The questions King must answer— How did this object come to be here? Is its occurrence natural or the result of human intervention? Are these formations such as would naturally be associated with a diamond field?—are essentially questions about rhetorical procedures, about the transportations and substitutions undergone by the object/ signifiers supporting the swindlers' truth claims.

His suspicion aroused by what appears to be an unnatural transportation, one that has left a diamond sitting where the elements would not have allowed it to remain for long, King continues the investigation. His plan for "testing the whole question" consists "of a system of outside prospects conducted over the whole mesa, carried out by digging a bushel or two of earth, averaging it, sifting it in sieves, and then washing both the saved gravel and the refuse dirt at the stream; of an examination of the trails and tracks of all the party; a following of their work from beginning to end; . . . a scrutiny of the rock itself, and of the so-called Ruby Gulch. . . . The result . . . was that we found no single ruby or diamond anywhere off the neighbourhood of the rock or off the line of the original Arnold survey." At issue here is the appropriateness of a metonymy. The swindlers' claims rely on the purportedly natural association of the gemstones to the gravels in which they are found, but King's investigation demonstrates that the gems are actually more closely associated with the hoaxers themselves: "I fixed upon the trail of Arnold and Janin, recognizing Mr. Janin by his slender foot. . . . Along the line of their outward march, here and there in the vicinity of survey stakes, we found an occasional ruby, but 10 ft. off their line of travel never one." The final touch in King's analysis of the swindlers' text is his examination of the ant mounds found at the site. Because ants bring small stones from lower levels of the earth up to the surface, prospectors use anthills the way a psychoanalyst uses a dream or a slip of the tongue—to gain information about a formation's underlying structure. King's examination reveals "artificial holes broken horizontally with some stick or small implement through the natural crust of the mound, holes easily distinguished from the natural avenues made by the insects themselves; when traced to the end each artificial hole held one or two rubies." The purported association of the stones in the anthills with the underlying levels of the putative mine, another metonymical underpinning for the part-for-whole synecdoche of the gems displayed in San Francisco, is again invalidated. Not only are the holes made by men clearly distinguishable from those made by ants but, as King so tellingly adds near the end of his deposition, in every case "about the salted ant-hills were the old storm-worn footprints of a man" (Deposition).

It later came out that Arnold and Slack had actually purchased the gems in Amsterdam and London (Wilkins, *Mountaineering* 184). If we agree with Fuller that a thing "carried from a place in which it is proper to one in which it is not proper" has already "undergone the process which makes words figurative or metaphorical" (49), then King's deposition amounts to a demonstration that what was claimed to be natural was all along rhetorical, the result of human agency—a construct, to recall Fuller's words, "responsive to the wish and will of the writer." The swindlers' salted landscape-text is comparable to the "lying trail" written by that other troublesome figure, Cooper's Magua, the one destabilizing the grounds of an expanding corporate capitalism just as the other destabilized the grounds of a European colonialism.

In an exaggerated way, King's exposure of the diamond swindle demonstrates how decidedly unnatural intentions insinuate their way into seemingly "natural" or "realistic" representations. It reminds us of the persistence of rhetorical mediation between language and the things it claims to represent—in particular, of the suspect character of King's own mimetic aesthetic. Yet King seems never to have applied the lesson to his own texts; if anything, his trust in the authority and objectivity of his language grew stronger following the diamond incident. He seems to have seen in his analysis of the swindlers' text not a warning about the subtlety and persistence of mediation, but a vindication of science as a way of discovering and outwitting it.

This heightened confidence in his own language is evident in a long passage describing his 1873 ascent of Mount Whitney that was added to the 1874 edition of *Mountaineering in the Sierra Nevada*. Following the climb, looking back at the peak from below, King reflects on the persistence of "mythologizing" in our appreciation of landscape—a mode he feels has typified descriptions of mountains ranging from the Aryan myth of the "white elephant" Dhavalagiri to Ruskin's "Mountain Gloom" and "Mountain Glory" chapters in *Modern Painters* (252). Contrasted with this mode is the scientific approach, as exemplified by the Alpine writings of the geologist John Tyndall. "To follow a chapter of Ruskin's," King writes, "with one of Tyndall's is to bridge forty centuries and realize the full contrast of archaic and modern thought" (253).

King acknowledges the power and attraction of the Ruskinian mode, but leaves no doubt as to which of the two is to be privileged. As he muses on "the geologic history and hard, materialistic reality" of the mountain, his reverie is interrupted by an archaic figure, a Paiute Indian elder, who tells him that "the peak was an old, old man who watched this valley and cared for the Indians, but who shook the country with earthquakes to punish the whites for injustice to his tribe. . . . I watched the spare, bronzed face, upon which was written the burden of a hundred dark and gloomy superstitions; and as he trudged away across the sands, I could but feel the liberating power of modern culture which unfetters us from the more than iron bands of self-made myths. . . . I saw the great peak only as it really is, a splendid mass of granite, 14,887 feet high, ice-chiselled and storm-tinted, a great monolith left standing amid the ruins of a bygone geological empire" (253). The familiar dichotomy between myth and reality is here widened by King, who demotes myth to mere "superstition" as he imputes a "liberating power" to modern culture—which for him, as for so many others of his generation, is epitomized by science. His alignment of science with "reality" implies the replacement of the Indian's myth with a projection of his own, but King does not make obvious what is really at stake here: the displacement of one ideology by another. The Indian's myth, his interpretation of the meaning of natural phenomena, is openly political, for it hopes to facilitate the restoration of his people's lost power. But whereas the content of the Indian's myth is explicit, the politics with which King replaces it is disguised; couched in the language of science, it appears natural and objective to any reader who valorizes such language.

This movement is very deft. The appearance is not of two ideologies in contention, but of an obvious "myth"—clearly a construct, openly political—being replaced by an innocent description, a mimetic, "unmediated" representation of just that sort of hard reality that, as Trilling reminds us, was well calculated to instill trust in the minds of King's American readers. King promises to show us the mountain "as it really is," and indeed the facts he proceeds to give us are reasonably accurate. But by offering them as a replacement for the Indian's myth—which is not a fact but a truth, a statement about the meaning of fact— he collapses a crucial distinction. This sort of conflation is common in "objective" or "realistic" discourse; in such usage, "*fact* and *truth* are the same, *fact* and *meaning of fact* are the same. All you have to do is invoke the magic word, reality" (Westbrook 13). King uses the word *really* here in just this way: as the magic word that allows him to pass off mere facts as their own meanings, to mythologize under the cover of simply reproducing the "real" in language. But to say that a mountain is 14,887 feet high is not merely to state a fact; it is also—if only in the implication that the fact is worth foregrounding for the reader—to suggest an interpretation. Of what value, after all, is this particular fact? To the Paiute elder—who might not dispute its *accuracy*—such a precise figure as "14,887 feet" has no *meaning*, for it has no relation to his ideology, to his culture or its prospects. But it is meaningful to King precisely because it establishes a usefully precise datum in the immense grid he is imposing on the landscape, a mapping whose primary purpose is to allow the region to be more efficiently controlled and exploited by his own culture.

That this is the context in which this particular detail begins to have meaning is made clear by the metaphorical passage immediately following it, in which the mountain, clearly a perdurable symbol of American hegemony, towers above the "ruins" of the Indian's culture, whose time has passed just as surely as a former geological epoch. To write that the mountain has undergone erosion is to report a fact of geology. But to do so using metaphors grafted onto nature from the realms of sculpture and painting—"ice-chiselled and storm-tinted"—is to assign a meaning to this fact, to suggest that there is a shaping hand, a conscious design, at work in nature. For King, that design could be no other than the belief that the nation's westward expansion, so greatly facilitated by his surveys, had divine sanction. In the same vein, by identifying the Paiute's culture with inevitable geological processes, King naturalizes that culture's disappearance; his realistic description legitimates power by representing as natural what is really the result of human agency.

HOW I LOVED COTTER: MYSTIFYING THE FRONTIER

In *The Legacy of Conquest,* Patricia Limerick stresses that in order to "be moved from national resource to commodity to profit, the West's holdings clearly had to be transformed by an investment of capital and labor," adding that this is "the elemental fact obscured by the myths and romances" of the American frontier (97). King's writings illustrate this point repeatedly. "The mountains of our great vacant interior," he writes in a typical example, "are not barren, but full of wealth; the deserts are not all desert; the vast plains will produce something better than buffalo, namely beef; there is water for irrigation, and land fit to receive it. *All that is needed is to explore and declare* the nature of the national domain" (qtd. in Raymond 631; my emphasis). Of course King knows the West is not "vacant" at all; if the tales in *Mountaineering* are any indication, virtually everywhere he turned in it he found Indians, Mexicans, and newly arrived whites already in possession. But the rhetoric of discovery, as Mary Louise Pratt has demonstrated, habitually effaces such human presence, producing an "attenuated" prose in which agency resides not with human beings but with the land itself (123). Thus for King it is neither labor nor investment but *the land itself* that will produce wealth in the West, just as it is the land that will legitimate its own appropriation. Such writing bespeaks the confidence of a maturing capitalism that sees no real obstacles between the discovery of raw resources and their transformation into wealth: "all that is needed" is to know what is there and to "declare" it one's own. And the ideological effect of such writing, as Limerick suggests, is to obscure the realities of western transformation, to write out of existence the unequal social structures organizing frontier economies. The West appears Edenic not only in its absence of previous human occupants, but in the absence of fixed social classes.[12]

That King founded his aesthetic, as he thought, in a "realistic" rejection of mythmaking is ironic, given that today *Mountaineering* reads so patently as part of the nation's myth of a "classless frontier." If this seems so in King's descriptions of landscape, it is even more evident in his narrative passages, particularly in the two chapters detailing the ascent of Mount Tyndall. King's official report on this exploit is quite prosaic (Wilkins, *Clarence King* 68), but the account in *Mountaineering* is full of bravado and hairbreadth escapes and has obviously benefited considerably in the retelling. This embellishment aims, of course, to thrill the reader and to enhance the writer's masculinity; it also embodies the idea, popularized twenty years later by Frederick Jackson Turner, of the democratizing effects of the frontier. This myth creeps up on the reader gradually in those passages, scattered throughout *Mountaineering,* where the raw exigencies of western life bring members of disparate races and classes into intimate contact—the backwoods settlement where all eat together in the only inn, or the mountain storm that brings everyone together in the warmth of the same campfire. With the exception of its pronounced homosociality, it is essentially the sort of interclass conviviality Frederick Law Olmsted hoped to induce with Central Park.

Like Olmsted, King moved in the highest society. In New York he frequented William Cullen Bryant's Century Club; in Washington he was a close friend of the likes of Henry Adams and John Hay. On the high mountains of the Sierra Nevada, in contrast, King frequently found himself teaming up with the only other member of the survey crew willing to take the risks of extreme mountaineering: the mule skinner, Dick Cotter. These two men would rarely have crossed paths back east; out west, however, as they pass through one alpine adventure after another, the social barriers between them appear to fall away. This process reaches its climax on the perilous ascent of Mount Tyndall, just when their shared hardships become most extreme—when night overtakes the climbers on a narrow shelf of rock, forcing them to bivouac with neither fuel nor shelter in temperatures fast falling toward zero. Such extreme circumstances produce a degree of intimacy and cooperation impossible within the strictures of the metropolitan class structure. "How I loved Cotter," King wrote of the long, freezing night in which they nearly perished. "How I hugged him and got warm, while our backs gradually petrified, till we whirled over and thawed them out together!" (51). Here we see the natural exigency of frontier existence keyed to its highest pitch; survival not only allows but seems to dictate an interclass and intrasex intimacy that would elsewhere be proscribed.[13]

For the remainder of the climb, King and Cotter appear to work together as equals. Cotter more and more frequently takes the lead when King is at a loss as to how to proceed, and when the terrain steepens, they rope themselves together so that, should the worst happen, they will "share a common fate" (58). At one point, King is forced to tie his silk handkerchief, a signifier of his superior status, around a spike of rock as an anchor (57); its abandonment later on the climb symbolizes the rugged wilderness landscape "filtering out" distinctions of class.

Cotter and King reach the top of the peak two days later. The apparent class integration that has developed during the climb will resume during their long trek homeward, but for a moment on the summit, we are reminded that it is only a myth after all. "I rang my hammer upon the topmost rock," King writes of this moment of triumph. "We grasped hands, and I reverently named the grand peak MOUNT TYNDALL" (64). The pronouns here are noteworthy: the two men share equally in the event by shaking hands, but to King alone is reserved the right of naming the peak. This prerogative is his, of course, by virtue of his rank in the survey hierarchy, in the class structure that, despite the narrative's intimations to the contrary, he has transported intact into the heart of the "democratizing" wilderness.

This brief slip is for King what the unnaturally placed diamond was for Arnold and Slack: an unintentional revelation that the "realistic" text is not a faithful reproduction of some objective "reality," but instead a construct, "responsive to the wish and will of the writer." The social function of this construct becomes clearer when we realize that it appeared just as King's detailed surveys were making the West *less* democratic—when, by facilitating the orderly development of the region by absentee corporate financiers, they were precluding the individualistic entrepreneurship of the American democratic myth. To see the myth in this way is to see its similarity to that told by the old Indian, for whom mythologizing was a means of perpetuating a vision in spite of disturbing evidence that it would never again be a reality. It is also, perhaps, to see what may well be the only consistent thread running through the widely varied activities of King's career: his reading and writing of the West in ways that served an ideology of capitalist expansion. When that ideology called for accurate maps to facilitate development, King was there to provide them with his transit and barometer. When it called for a secure and predictable investment climate, King was there again—this time to deconstruct a swindle that threatened to panic the market. Finally, as the influx of capital began the economic reorganization that would eventually replace the mythic frontier hero—the lone prospector, the resourceful forty-niner, even the death-defying, mountain-climbing geologist—with the likes of Kennecott Copper and Peabody Coal, King was there again; not to deconstruct this time, but to construct a landscape that seemed the very embodiment of boundless opportunity, that maintained in image the illusion of what was even then being foreclosed in reality.

Fourth View: Theresa Yelverton's *Tale of the Yo-semite*

Published in 1872, Theresa Yelverton's *Zanita: A Tale of the Yo-Semite* tells the story of strong-willed Zanita—the first "white" child born in the famous valley. She is portrayed as incorrigibly "wild," and the plot turns on her parents' and stepparents' attempts to "civilize" her. Most of the novel's characters have real-life counterparts in Yosemite residents and visitors Yelverton met during her stay there in 1870. Zanita's parents, Placida and Oswald Naunton, are modeled closely on James and Elvira Hutchings, two of the valley's earliest would-be homesteaders. Zanita and her sister Rosalind, nicknamed Cozy, are based on the Hutchings's daughters, Florence and Gertrude (called Cosie in real life). The energetic, wilderness-loving Kenmuir, as his name suggests, is based on John Muir. John Brown resembles Joseph LeConte, a geologist at the University of California campus at Berkeley and a frequent visitor to the valley. John's wife, Sylvia, bears some resemblance to Yelverton herself, though the Browns' durable union is nothing like the author's disastrous real-life marriage to the rakish William Charles Yelverton, son of Ireland's Viscount Avonmore.[14]

The novel's narrator, Sylvia Brown, having proceeded in advance of her geologist husband on their summer vacation, stumbles upon the Nauntons' secluded domestic sanctuary when young Kenmuir guides her into the valley. Placida and Oswald Naunton, in contrast to their tomboyish daughter, seem the very soul of Victorian propriety: the husband is strong, gentle, and understanding; the wife is beautiful, worshipful, and wan. As a couple they seem perfectly matched and appear at first to have an ideal marriage. The story's rising action begins when Placida dies of consumption and Sylvia agrees to take

Zanita into her home in Oakland. In what is characterized as less a moral duty than a scientific experiment, a "study of human nature" (104), Sylvia attempts to transform the wild child into a proper young lady.

In this she at first appears to be successful. With the help of the nuns of the Ursuline order, who are portrayed as studied disciplinarians and astute pedagogues (102), the unruly child grows up to be a cultured and beautiful young woman. Soon, alas, she finds herself attracted to Egremont, a dashing and mysterious Englishman who refuses to divulge his past (he is either a genuine but grievously wronged nobleman or a bold impostor). Fearing an elopement, Sylvia decides to sequester Zanita at the Naunton homestead back in Yosemite; Egremont anticipates the strategy and arrives there first. The two lovers continue meeting, but Egremont gradually falls in love with the conventionally ladylike Cozy. When Zanita finds out, her newfound discipline cannot prevent the grisly disaster that ensues. Egremont is found dead among the rocks, having fallen several thousand feet from Glacier Point, and Zanita's corpse turns up in Mirror Lake, having fallen from the overhanging brow of Half Dome. Oswald speculates that Egremont must have taken his own life after killing Zanita, but others suspect just the opposite. (Both Zanita's fall and the subsequent uncertainty over its cause are reminiscent of Magua's demise in *The Last of the Mohicans*.) The novel ends with the marriage, some years later, of Kenmuir and Cozy.

Early critics dismissed *Zanita* in the contemptuous terms long reserved for the sentimental novel of the nineteenth century. One reviewer called it "ephemeral," a good example of what "a lively imagination can do with unreal people . . . and improbable incident" ("Zanita," *Nation* 326), while another thought it "a very unnatural and utterly meaningless story" that does not pretend to have a plot" ("Zanita," *Times* 3). Following this chilly reception, the book fell into obscurity until 1991, when it was reprinted in conjunction with the one hundredth birthday of Yosemite National Park. Taking issue with Yelverton's contemporary critics—and taking my cue from David Robertson's pioneering reevaluation (48–49)—I argue that *Zanita* is actually an entertaining novel which, far from being ephemeral and meaningless, engaged significant contemporary issues. It is, however, decidedly *unnatural*, in ways its contemporary readership did not and perhaps could not have appreciated. Before examining just how this is so, I want to situate the novel within two marginalized traditions—one literary, the other environmentalist.

It is not hard to see why *Zanita* has until recently remained opaque to literary critics. With its comparatively ungendered landscape and its female protagonist, its language and plot are both at odds with the patriarchal norms that have shaped the canon of American literature. As Nina Baym has pointed out, an "entrammeling society" and a "promising landscape" are crucial elements in the typical frontier novel, and they are almost inevitably "depicted in unmistakably feminine terms" that "limit [their] applicability to women" ("Melodramas" 133). Society appears as domineering mother, nature as enticing bride—a combination capable of propelling a heterosexual male protagonist very nicely through a story (and through a wilderness) but incapable of functioning the same way for a sentimental novel's female protagonist. One result is the wholesale absence of women's frontier novels from the early American canon (124). Critics such as Baym have since suggested alternative critical norms that not only acknowledge the concerns of early women readers but also reflect the serious cultural debates within which novels such as *Zanita* were written.

Jane Tompkins, for example, sees such texts not as deficiently enacting a traditional male fantasy but "as doing a certain kind of cultural work within a specific historic situation" (200). *Zanita* is in this respect like that more famous "women's novel," *Uncle Tom's Cabin,* which, Tompkins reminds us, is not a simplistic outpouring of sentiment but a complex retelling of "the culture's central religious myth—the story of the crucifixion—in terms of the nation's greatest political conflict—slavery—and of its most cherished social beliefs— the sanctity of motherhood and the family" (xii). Similarly, *Zanita* can be read as retelling another cherished myth—the belief that the nation derived a special character from its civilization of the wilderness (and the much newer belief that America might preserve that character by preserving the wilderness). It does so in terms of contemporary political debates over both feminism and a nascent environmentalism, and also in terms of a set of social beliefs—in this case, the importance of socializing "difficult" children such as Zanita. Read in this way, *Zanita* is positioned at the intersection of four different discourses: the discourse of family and children that, at least in the United States, had been traditionally female or "sentimental"; the discourse on savagery and civilization that from the beginning had been constitutive of an "American" identity; the ongoing discourse of women's rights that would witness the 1872 arrest of suffrage activist Susan B. Anthony; and the discourse of environmentalism that was just then emerging in the influential writings of John Muir and would lead to the establishment in 1872 of Yellowstone National Park.

In writing of the history of American environmentalism, it has become something of a cliché to note that the root of the word *ecology* is the Greek *oikos,* or home, and that ecology is thus the study of "our home," the environment. It has not been at all common, however, to mention that within capitalist patriarchy, "home" has much more literally meant the sphere relegated to women for their "proper" thought and activity—so that for nearly a century women's literature was seen as synonymous with *domestic* fiction—or that the traditionally feminine discipline of *home* economics started out as human *ecology.* These links are not coincidental, yet until recently every serious history of environmentalism gave the impression that women were absent from the movement for its entire first century, up until Rachel Carson published *Silent Spring* in 1961. In a movement with literary roots reaching back to the early nineteenth century, Carson is typically presented as the first woman to write seriously about environmental issues.

Oikos has in fact come to name the study of relationships in two traditionally masculine disciplines. First there was *economics,* which concentrated on extra-domestic exchanges among men, discounting the unpaid work done by women in their homes; then there was *ecology,* which studied relationships within nature to "discover" how nature operates "on its own." As the form of nature most purified of the human mark, ecology's sine qua non was "wilderness," which would be legally defined, in the famous wording of the 1964 Wilderness Act, as a place where *man* "is a visitor who does not remain"—certainly a very interesting place, but not anyone's home.

Ecology, like economics, thus belied its etymological origins through a willful repression of the feminine and the literally (as opposed to metaphorically) domestic. There is another strand of environmentalism, however, grounded in the Latin root for "home," *domus.* On the frontiers of the nineteenth-century United States, this marginalized *domes*tic environmental tradition was not concerned so much with preserving the wilderness as with more practical considerations of making a healthy home and community there. Its focus was not on nature as an autonomous, objectified realm but on such practical questions as, Now that we're here, how do we go about putting in the garden, raising the children, and doing the laundry—all without unnecessarily marring the beauty of the place? Some of the concerns of this domestic approach to frontier writing are faintly observable in Mary Rowlandson's concerns with food preparation, domestic exchange, and the welfare of her surviving children in *The Narrative of the Captivity*. But they become much more recognizably feminist and environmentalist in the nineteenth century with the advent of frontier narratives written by women settlers, such as Caroline Kirkland, who also happened to be professional writers.[15]

While wittily describing her experiences on the Michigan frontier of the early nineteenth century, Kirkland argues in *A New Home—Who'll Follow?* (1839) that frontier life poses special difficulties for women. She concedes that men also must work hard at pioneering, but insists that the transition to frontier life affords them particular opportunities and advantages: "Woman's little world is overclouded for lack of the old familiar means and appliances. The husband goes to his work with the same axe or hoe which fitted his hands in the old woods and fields, he tills the same soil, or perhaps a far richer and more hopeful one—he gazes on the same book of nature which he has read from his infancy, and sees only a fresher and more glowing page; and he returns to his home with the sun, strong in heart and full of self-congratulation on the favorable change in his lot. But he finds the home-bird drooping and disconsolate. *She* has been looking in vain for the reflection of any of the cherished features of her own dear fire-side. She has found a thousand deficiencies which her rougher mate can scarce be taught to feel as evils" (262). In one of the book's typical passages, Kirkland is visited by two new arrivals, Mr. and Mrs. Rivers. The latter is visibly wilting at the prospect of living in a sparsely appointed log cabin; Mr. Rivers, however, oblivious to his wife's very real fears, dominates the conversation, making "innumerable inquiries, touching the hunting and fishing facilities of the country around" and insisting that "the country was a living death without them." Kirkland concludes of this scene that the husband's "indifference" to his wife's feelings "spoke volumes of domestic history" (119). The passage subtly suggests that, for women, frontier life portends a sort of "living death" under *any* circumstances.

Kirkland notes further that where frontier women quickly develop a sense of "hostess-ship toward the new comer," men do not. "I speak only of women," she writes of this sense of cooperation and mutual responsibility, for "men look upon each one, newly arrived, merely as an additional business-automaton—a somebody more with whom to try the race of enterprise, i.e., money-making" (118–19). Anticipating the famous Turner thesis but giving it a feminist twist,

Kirkland sees frontier life as bringing men into isolation and competition while women create democratic cooperative structures. Similarly, it is frontier women who first develop what would today be called an environmentalist sensibility. Because they "feel sensibly the deficiencies of the 'salvage' state" (263), women are most motivated to relieve them. "By and bye a few apple-trees are set out; sweet briars grace the door yard, and lilacs, and currant-bushes; all by female effort—at least I have never yet happened to see it otherwise where these improvements have been made at all. They are not all accomplished by her own hand indeed, but hers is the moving spirit" (264). Hand in hand with such environmental improvement went an early form of environmental preservation. Observing how rapidly construction was ruining the "grand esplanade" of her own frontier community near Detroit, for example, Kirkland pleads "that the fine oaks which now graced it might be spared"—and then complains bitterly that "these very trees were the first" to be sacrificed in the new development (24).

While the profit motive thus undermines environmental values, Kirkland makes it clear that the same motive also undermines domestic values. She understands how what today would be called capitalist patriarchy, through its simultaneous marginalization of women and nature, deforms both the natural *and* the social environments. Thus she notes how "the habit of selling out so frequently" renders the "*home*-feeling" "almost a nonentity in Michigan. The man who holds himself ready to accept the first advantageous offer, will not be very solicitous to provide those minor accommodations, which, though essential to domestic comfort, will not add to the moneyed value of his farm, which he considers merely an article of trade" (44). Kirkland is particularly critical of those settlers "who have left small farms in the eastward States, and come to Michigan with the hope of acquiring property at a more rapid rate. They have sold off, perhaps at considerable pecuniary disadvantage the home of their early married life; sacrificed the convenient furniture which had become necessary to daily comfort, and only awake when it is too late, to the fact that it kills old vines to tear them from their clinging-places." Caught up in a system that brings middle-class domestic values into conflict with a rapidly expanding capitalism, such settlers "are much to be pitied"—"the women especially" (261).

It should now be clear that broadening our conception of what can count as "the environment" makes it possible to construct an alternative tradition of environmentalism in which the appearance of the woman environmentalist need not wait until the sudden and seemingly anomalous arrival of Rachel Carson in 1961. Such an alternative would not only enrich what remains a rather impoverished notion of environmentalism's history; it would also provide a perspective from which to better understand a literary tradition that has celebrated and preserved the works of, say, a Henry Thoreau or a John Muir but not those of a Caroline Kirkland or a Theresa Yelverton.

The traditional history of environmentalism can be said to move centripetally. It typically begins with the emotional response of male explorers and scientists to vast, remote tracts of the wild outdoors. Only gradually does it move inward to concern itself with issues closer to community and home, a development that culminates in the 1960s with the realization that America was poisoning the very food, air, and water it was bringing into its domestic spaces (in fact, into its very bodies). The alternative environmentalism I am pointing to here, by contrast, unfolds centrifugally. In this tradition ecology *begins* in the home and moves outward to a concern with the community and finally the wilderness. In this alternative tradition—whose contemporary luminaries include women ranging from Lois Gibbs to Terry Tempest Williams—the links between *eco*logy, home *eco*nomics, and *dom*estic fiction are not coincidental at all, but quite logical.

The differences between these two environmentalisms are at once semantic and disciplinary. They turn upon a long-running contestation over just what the term *oikos* might mean, on what can count as the *object* of environmentalism and nature writing. Nowhere is this more obvious than in the career of Ellen Swallow and her human ecology movement. Swallow was the first woman admitted to the Massachusetts Institute of Technology—in 1871, the year before *Zanita* was published. She became a professional chemist and went on to found the discipline of human ecology (or, as it is likely to be called today, home economics). A trained chemist deploying her expertise in the sphere "proper" to her, Swallow systematically analyzed the various components of the domestic environment and discovered the presence, even then, of harmful contaminants in water, air, and food. Seeking their sources outside the home and finding them in upstream water pollution, polluted wells, and industrial air pollution, she began to theorize the now-familiar ecological interactions linking home, community, and the surrounding "natural" environment. She analyzed these links in book after book, including *Air, Water and Food from a Sanitary Standpoint* (1904), *Sanitation in Daily Life* (1907), and *Euthenics: The Science of Controllable*

Environment (1910). Swallow envisioned the discipline of human ecology as the systematic study of these interactions for the improvement of the body, the home, and the local environment—domesticity expanded and refined into a bona fide science. But in a complex series of rhetorical and institutional battles—whose history has hardly begun to be written—the term *ecology* came to designate the outdoorsy and preponderantly male science we know by that name today, while human ecology evolved into home economics. Swallow's vision of a domestic environmentalism would lay dormant until the 1950s.[16]

A HOME IN THE WILDERNESS

We have, then, two marginalized domestic traditions, one literary and one environmental. *Zanita* can be situated in each. Following Kirkland, Yelverton brings the perspective of women's frontier experience to the form of the domestic novel; conversely, to the Cooper-style wilderness romance she brings the feminist perspective that Kirkland brought to the literature of the frontier. *Zanita* brings the home into the wilderness, but it also, as Zanita wreaks havoc in the Browns' residence in Oakland, brings the wilderness into the citified home. *Oikos* is counterpoised to *domus* in ways, as we shall see, that ultimately destabilize the underpinnings of each. The offspring of their union is not some happy accommodation of nature with society, but a truly destabilizing *wildness* that recalls the genuinely bewildering situation of a Mary Rowlandson—and for which the unruly female, Zanita, is the perfect emblem.

Zanita features an idealized, comfortably appointed late-Victorian household transplanted into the heart of a wild landscape—an image well calculated to resonate with readers brought up on authors such as Caroline Kirkland. Like Kirkland, Yelverton pointedly refuses to romanticize that home. In fact, when Sylvia is first guided to the Naunton homestead (by Kenmuir), she responds in hyperbolic clichés that parody and subvert the conventions of wilderness romance:

"And how did it get here?" I exclaimed, "that beautiful *bijou* cottage amid these fierce and ragged rocks? Was it borne through the air from Italy or Switzerland, on the wings of seraphs, like the Casa Santa de Loretto?"

"You've got to see my saw-mill, [responds Kenmuir,] and then you will know how it all came about."

"For goodness sake," quoth I, "don't destroy my poetic hallucination by suggestions of a saw-mill!" (14)

Yelverton deliberately demystifies the "settlement" of the wilderness by linking it visibly to the *commodification* of the wilderness—to the sawmill which, ironically, is run by the environmentalist Kenmuir.

Focusing as much on Yosemite's early society as on its scenery, *Zanita* features a running comparison of the homemaking and family life of the bourgeois Nauntons and Browns, the proletarian Radds, and an unregenerate neoprimitive Tory named Methley. As in Kirkland's writing, these comparisons provide a vehicle for exploring the difficulties frontier life poses for women. It is in particular the women—Placida Naunton and Nell Radd—who confront the frustrations of homemaking and child rearing in the wilderness. For them, Yosemite's mountain paradise affords no escape from the domestic round. While the men appear to flourish in their outdoor life, the women languish and suffer—and not always in silence.[17] Yelverton in fact depicts Nell as a boisterous shrew, a portrayal that perhaps speaks less to stereotypes of working-class boorishness than to the wilderness's fundamental antipathy to any more tender femininity. Nell at least *survives,* unlike her delicate counterpart Placida, who languishes in her wild surroundings until she simply fades away, dying slowly of a mysterious "consumption" (58). That she should thus vanish is not surprising. Her dainty, middle-class brand of femininity seems constructed entirely on her own negation—as absence and sacrifice, as her willingness to leave "all behind to come into this wilderness" with her husband, "when even her life was in danger from the Indians" (161). Her otherwise inexplicable death seems to express the essential hostility to "true" femininity of both the wilderness setting and the wilderness romance—of both the geographical place and the literary form. If the wilderness is where men can be real men, it is where the true woman cannot abide. Placida's eulogy is unwittingly and ironically symptomatic: "What a blank," intones the narrator, "she will leave behind her" (62).

Yelverton thus brings to environmental literature the same domestic and feminist perspectives that Kirkland brought to the frontier narrative and that Swallow would bring to ecology. In so doing, the novel blurs the boundaries that traditionally demarcate the natural and the cultural. Yosemite's outdoor, "natural" environment, to give one example, often seems to merge seamlessly into the novel's interior, domestic spaces. The narrator notes how skillfully Placida has integrated window views of the exterior landscape into her interior decorating; elsewhere the house is described as a landscape element that renders the valley scene more picturesque (14). In the same spirit, the Naunton family is *itself* picturesque, just another aspect of the delightful Yosemite scenery: "As I looked upon this artistic group," says the narrator, "I could not help believing that this family . . . was surely one of the natural features of the Valley" (19).

Zanita also departs from literary-environmental norms in its comparatively ungendered representation of the Yosemite landscape. Conspicuously absent is the familiar trope of the "virgin wilderness"; in its place is a rhetoric that, to the extent it is gendered at all, tends toward figures of domesticity. Rather than evoking the sense of a vast territory awaiting penetration and possession, the narrator tends to dwell on humanly scaled landscape features that invoke a sense of habitability; for example, a quiet outdoor niche whose "walls" are "elaborately tapestried" with moss, whose "ceiling" is decorated with lichens and whose "floor gleams in crystals and glittering spars" (52). This sort of description is typical of *Zanita* insofar as its domestic imagery seems geared toward the book's contemporary female readership without itself being as excessively gendered as, say, Cooper's landscapes.

In this consistent use of what might be called the trope of nature-as-domicile, *Zanita* may be compared with *A New Home*.[18] In contrast to Kirkland, however, Yelverton also turns the tables and brings the wilderness, in the person of her ungovernable protagonist, Zanita, into the urban home. This two-way traffic creates an opportunity for undermining some of the conservative tendencies of domestic frontier fiction—for instance, its reification of the middle-class family (portrayed as a "natural feature" in *Zanita*) and its easy faith in the "natural" progress of civilization. As we shall see, it suggests the possibility of a performative *wildness* that might counter the stabilizing force of Yosemite's *nature*.

CONTESTING INTERPRETATIONS

In *Zanita*, as in all literary environmentalism, the natural environment is itself a narrative. Peripheral to the novel's surface plot but central to my own reading is the picture Yelverton paints of the articulation and authorization of that narrative; that is, of early environmental interpretation in Yosemite. As in *The Last of the Mohicans*, there are passages in *Zanita* that rather explicitly thematize interpretation—mostly through the figure of Oswald Naunton, Yosemite hotelier and de facto leader of the local commercial guides. Oswald emerges as the valley's premier interpreter, holding forth in leisurely disquisitions that comically presage the later work of the National Park Service professional.

Early in the novel, for example, Sylvia, Kenmuir, and the Nauntons go out for a hike. The narrator describes the scene for her readers: "The Valley was some eight miles long, and about a mile and a half in width, inclosed by immense bulwarks of granite, always precipitous, and sometimes ascending vertically a mile in height." Thus far Sylvia hews closely enough to the facts, but soon she slips into a much more subjective depiction of Yosemite as a utopian counterpart of the fallen society "outside," a paradise from which "the rest of the great world was excluded" and within which "[n]o sound but nature's broke the stillness" (24).

Surely within such a natural sanctuary we might expect nature to speak to us directly. Surely amid such "stillness" we might expect to hear "no sound but nature's," to encounter the environment sans mediation. True to the interpretive genre, this pose suggests that through a transparent interpreter we will hear nature itself speaking—but what inevitably we find articulated within that silence are human voices and human concerns. Thus, when the hikers hear "the rap-a-tap-tap of the woodpecker" breaking the "stillness," the sound leads Sylvia to suggest that "one might fancy there were a number of carpenters at work" (24). This suggestion of laborers at work prompts Oswald to begin a lengthy declamation, a hyperbolic exercise in literary environmentalism. He begins in the stiff language of a Victorianized Natty Bumppo:

"There he goes," said my host [of the woodpecker]; "you can see him at work with his chisel beak and scarlet hammerhead. . . . [T]hese little birds have not only to provide their own winter food, but are fully conscious of the fact that the squirrels will rob them of the greater portion of their stores. And so it is in human nature . . . one half the world labors from dawn to dewy eve, and often by midnight oil, that the other half may prey upon them, and despoil them of the fruits of their labor. . . . Take the father of a family. For years he has passed six days of every seven sitting on that hard stool in that dismal counting-house, and has induced five or six young men, upon the alternative of keeping their spirit within their body, to do likewise; for the sole end and object that his lady wife and elegant daughters may sweep the street with their silks and velvets. . . . There is no difficulty in discerning that he is the woodpecker, and his lady wife and daughters are the squirrels."

Nor is there any difficulty in discerning the fact that Oswald's interpretation naturalizes a set of gender relations that might perturb a feminist like Sylvia. As if sensing this possibility, he immediately offers an alternative scenario that criticizes a less-than-admirable *masculinity*: "There is [also] 'the man of enterprise,' fashionably dressed, with the weightiest diamonds in his shirt-front; his buggy, or saddle-horse, awaiting his pleasure. He has started every sort of 'company' that a high-sounding name could be tacked to. He is a great talker, with an immense flow of language, and delights in the display of it. He has talked every one's money out of their pockets to supply his need. He never did one hour's labor, mentally or physically, but has lived all his life in affluence on his neighbors' acorns." When such "ravenous squirrels" as this caricatured entrepreneur "help themselves to . . . the hard-earned share of the laborer," it "falls pretty hard on the woodpeckers": "Look into that wretched garret, where dwells a mother, a son, and two daughters. The son . . . is loafing round the corner of the street, waiting for acorns to turn up without the seeking. The mother is trimming her pretty taper nails, and explaining to her daughters how she has always kept them unsplit, and of perfect filbert shape. The elder daughter is arranging dead men's beards into pads in her hair, to give her head the proportions of an idiot's. But the second daughter, who is the woodpecker of the family, is stitching away at the bodice of a dress. . . . Her nimble fingers, filbert nails all cut short, go as fast as the head of the little woodpecker boring his holes, to complete those seams, and bring home the acorns, upon which the rest of the family live idly" (25–26).

This sort of interpretation criticizes social relations even as it forecloses on any means of changing them. It presents its various subject positions as fully naturalized, as fixed within capitalist and familial orders that are as inevitable as the instinctive actions of woodpeckers and squirrels. Setting forth various notions of masculinity and femininity and positing them as fixed alternatives, it efficiently naturalizes class, gender, and race relations together: "[P]eople *never* change their natures," Oswald concludes, "anymore than the Ethiopian his skin" (26).

Clearly such interpretation owes less to Yosemite's natural environment than to the social conditions it supposedly transcends. It is also decisively shaped by Yosemite's *cultural* status as a public park—and by Oswald's particular financial concerns. The novel depicts him quite accurately as Yosemite's first homesteader, its first would-be property owner. His real-life counterpart, the British expatriate and former gold-seeker James Mason Hutchings, had settled there in 1863, just before the park's creation. Technically, Hutchings was a squatter; he knew full well that the valley had yet to be surveyed by the Land Office and was therefore not open for homesteading. (Clarence King's survey had simply delineated the park's boundary.) But he also knew that squatters could generally count on a liberal interpretation of the laws once their lands *were* surveyed, and he was banking on thus perfecting his title in the future (Runte 17–18). The Yosemite Park bill, however, threatened to derail Hutchings's plans because it allowed "authorized private individuals" the "privilege of building and operating tourist accommodations in the park," but only on the basis of ten-year leases. Hutchings was offered such a lease but refused it, insisting instead on what he believed were his property rights. The Yosemite Park Commission promptly declared him a trespasser and took him to court (Runte 23).

At stake for the Yosemite Commission, of course, was the new national park ideal as such, for Hutchings's success would clearly establish a dangerous precedent (Runte 24). While the commission took its case to court, Hutchings lobbied the California legislature, which sympathetically relayed his concerns to Congress (23). In Washington, a bill to perfect Hutchings's title quickly passed the House, which found persuasive his argument that the proposed leases would not suffice to motivate investors. Hard-working pioneers like Hutchings—rather like Oswald's industrious woodpeckers—"had built their cabins, planted their orchards and vineyards, and expended several thousand dollars in establishing for themselves a comfortable home," and California representative James A. Johnson argued that a government that would deny the disputed title "is not a Government of law, of justice, or of right between man and man; but is a plundering despotism, robbing its own citizens." Hutchings failed in the Senate, however, where it was predicted that privatization would ultimately allow Yosemite to "go into the hands of those who would levy tribute upon the travelling public, and make this beautiful valley odious for the extortions of its greedy and sordid possessors." "The irony," notes Yosemite historian Alfred Runte, "was that Congress, having disallowed private ownership in the park, nonetheless openly promoted private investment in its facilities. On the one hand, individual initiative was strictly curtailed; on the other, the Yosemite Park Act legally sanctioned and encouraged it." Thus from the very beginning the nation's "park experiment had been grounded in contradiction." [19] Hutch-ings himself had run into a similar contradiction—the conflict inherent in lit-erary environmentalism's alliance with capitalism. The preservation of land-scapes aims in part to preserve the grounds of interpretation, while the aim of interpretation is to preserve the grounds of capitalist patriarchy (and it is not hard to discern the tale of Hutchings's personal "dispossession" in his bitter and misogynist parable of the wronged woodpecker). What Hutchings discov-ered, to his dismay, is that in order to assure the continued functioning of the system as a whole it is sometimes necessary to sacrifice the commercial aspira-tions of the individual.

NATURAL REPUBLICANISM

If the novel figures Oswald Naunton as the valley's interpreter extraordinaire, it figures Zanita as the wild force that challenges and disrupts interpretation. In the scene just discussed, she quite literally interrupts her fa-ther's words by chasing a squirrel into the midst of his rapt audience. It falls to Sylvia to restore order and tactfully return the stage to Naunton. Taking advan-tage of the squirrel's presence to recall their earlier "moral squirrel conversa-tion," she asks Oswald if "squirrelism" is not in fact "practiced to a great extent amongst the Indian tribes in and about the Valley?" (In typical natural history fashion, Indians are deemed part of Yosemite's interpretable landscape.) "No," replies Oswald, "I cannot say it is to a greater extent than in civilized life" (29). What follows appears at first to be a series of liberal concessions on questions of race, class, and gender, with Oswald conceding, for example, "that the Indi-ans approach the nearest in their practice the pure idea of republicanism,— equality, fraternity, and indivisibility." Indian society, he claims approvingly, is not riven by class conflict, for the native peoples "live in tribes with *biens en com-mune*, and labor in common, too."

Oswald contrasts this state of affairs with that of civilized nations. After not-ing that poor women, like Indian women, are constrained to work just as hard as their menfolk, he concedes "that this difference increases as we emerge into the upper ranks of society; the wife of the citizen who has made wealth, and is able to hold on to it, lounges in her *causeuse*" while her less fortunate "fellow-citizen scours down her frescoed walls with chapped, bleeding hands, and aching bones" (30). Similarly, Oswald tells Sylvia, native society features an apparently admirable equality of the sexes. Not only are Indian women "quite as strong as the men,"

"they can walk as far, and ford rivers with the same ease. She, in truth, plays a more prominent part in life, and is more on an equality with her spouse than a white woman who is entirely dependent on her husband to lace her boots."

"That," I said, "is a very strong argument for woman's rights,—that in the primitive state a woman should be more equal than in the position in which civilization has placed her. Have they a vote, do you know?" I asked laughingly.

"I believe," he rejoined, "that some of the older and wiser squaws have 'a say' in the 'big talk.'" (31)

Oswald concludes with the observation that "the nineteenth century ought to blush to have to learn a woman's rightful sphere from a wild Indian" (31).

In a not-so-subtle contestation, Sylvia has maneuvered Oswald into naturalizing the sort of liberal feminism that was then, in the world outside the valley, coalescing around women's right to vote. But he does so in ways that can only strengthen a more generally conservative ideology of race and gender. His interpretation in fact participates directly in late nineteenth-century constructions of masculinity and whiteness, in which, as Gail Bederman has noted, "civilized" gender differences were held to be very pronounced, while "gender differences among savages seemed to be blurred." Darwinian science was held to justify "the belief that racial difference, civilization, and manliness all advanced together. Biologists believed that as human races slowly ascended the evolutionary ladder, men and women evolved increasingly differentiated lives and natures. The most advanced races were the ones who had achieved the most perfect manliness and womanliness" (27). "Savage women," therefore, were "aggressive"; they "carried heavy burdens, and did all sorts of 'masculine' hard labor" (25). And in *Zanita* we are thus not surprised to find Oswald noting that "two Indians I have in my employment perform any and every work indifferently, and seem to recognize no distinction between a man's and a woman's work" (31). Kenmuir, similarly, notes of the refined Egremont that "it is not likely he would allow [Zanita] to carry a burden like an Indian squaw" (174). In a scheme that so clearly maps race onto gender, the Indians' sexual equality is hardly an unqualified virtue: it functions as the mark of their savagery, just as

Egremont's chauvinism is not so much a fault as the mark of his racial and sexual superiority. The same might be said of the Ahwahneechees' economic egalitarianism, for in Oswald's interpretive scheme, a heightened appreciation of class difference is just as clearly a hallmark of civilization.

AN -OLOGY OF HER OWN

The interweaving of race, gender, class, and ownership so prominent in Oswald's interpretation is underwritten primarily by late nineteenth-century science. Science and interpretation work together to produce an environment that can discipline subjectivity, and Sylvia seems to understand the workings of such disciplinary power. Early in the novel, she complains that "[c]aprice had been *attributed to me* all my life through, as a schoolgirl, by my companions, and as a woman, by my husband; *until I had come to believe it formed a part of my character*" (3, my emphases). Significantly, *Zanita* is set in motion by just such a "capricious" act: Sylvia's decision to set off for Yosemite without her husband. She rather archly notes, however, that "it was not until my husband classified my action as a piece of caprice, that I came to regard it in that light" (3). The word *classified* is particularly salient, invoking as it does her husband's authority as a scientist in naturalizing her sense of a feminine self. She seems aware, nonetheless, that her "caprice" is really *not* natural but rather is repeatedly inculcated in a process of subjectification.

Sylvia's experiences with Zanita reinforce her sense that genders are constructed within disciplinary structures. At the Catholic school to which the girl is finally sent, the Ursuline mother superior stresses that a proper femininity is best inculcated in a conventual setting, where girls like Zanita find "difficulty in withstanding the order and resisting the moral discipline" (101). Surveillance reigns at the convent, where "a child's propensities are carefully observed, and every temptation spared her and avoided. The force of example is so strong, and the whole school in such perfect order, that a child must have an unwonted force of character to counterbalance it" (101–2). It is only in such an environment that Zanita appears at last to be *made* feminine.

From her husband, Sylvia learns a similar lesson about the "nature" of masculinity. John describes himself revealingly as "an unpoetical Professor of Geology" (131), identifying with a prosaic linearity of thought and highlighting an authority secured through his mastery of a scientific discipline. Because his science is crucial to his gender identity, he zealously marks it off as an exclusively masculine domain. In a typical aside, Sylvia complains that whenever *she* tries to cloak herself in the authorizing mantle of science, her husband "always work[s] out my nebulous theory by a little satire" (131). She seems perfectly aware that her husband identifies *as* scientist and *against* what he relentlessly characterizes as her pseudoscience.

If Sylvia longs for an "-ology" of her own, then, it is at least partly because she understands the workings of disciplinary power. She senses the possibilities of a science framed by her own perspective and capable of legitimating her own views, and her repeated claims to have found (or at least to have named) such a science are one of the running jokes of the novel. At one point she makes a halfhearted pitch for a science of names, or "*nomenclatology,*" as she chooses to call her "new science," insisting that "it has a right to an 'ology" (12)—that is, to be considered a bona fide discipline. Elsewhere she makes a similar case for "squirrelism" (29), phrenology (105), physiognomy (111), and what her husband mockingly terms "*Sylvia-Brownism,* or 'Landscape Religion'" (55). Occasionally, to be sure, she tries to use her husband's science toward her own ends,[20] but there are dangers in using the master's tools in this way; as we have seen, scientifically grounded constructions of femininity are too tightly bound up with linked formations of race and masculinity to be dismantled unilaterally. What Sylvia needs is not a *natural* science that objectifies both nature and women but a *human* science that could help her reframe gender on her own terms.

Where the aim of the Professor's science—and male science in general—would be to understand nature objectively, Sylvia's "-ologies" aim to understand people in their relations to each other—more particularly, men in their relations with women. Sylvia's hopes for phrenology are instructive: "I have often wished that phrenology could be reduced to a positive test, like astronomy or geometry; that we could put the human brain into a crucible, as we would a metal, and weigh the residuum of pure gold from the dross" (109). She laments that phrenology has not yet "reached the first practical principle of singling out a murderer from a martyr, a sinner from a saint" (110). Such a principle would be particularly useful to women, who routinely "trust [their] affections with those who trample them underfoot, and toss them adrift in scorn." "Why did not Providence," Sylvia wonders aloud, "shape a man's nose so that a woman could tell if he were true or false?" (110). As Yelverton must have discovered ruefully from her own disastrous marriage, women would benefit from the ability to read *men* as accurately as men claim to read *nature*. Not surprisingly, it is Egremont—Zanita's suitor and a perfect cipher of a man, in many ways a dead ringer for the youthful William Yelverton—who becomes the primary object of Sylvia's scientific desire.

Unfortunately, of course, however much Sylvia might wish to deconstruct hierarchies of gender and race, her commitment to science—even a science of her own making—assures that she will leave untouched the fundamental opposition by means of which all the other categories are founded: nature/culture. It will be left to Zanita to deconstruct that ur-binary, by means of an incipient ecofeminism that is potentially far more disruptive than Sylvia's liberal feminism.

ZANITA'S ECOFEMINISM

Zanita operates, as I have suggested, at the intersection of four late nineteenth-century discourses. It brings into conversation the language of early environmentalism, late nineteenth-century feminism, "savagery" and civilization, and the middle-class family. In each case, meaning is constructed upon the familiar binary opposition between nature and culture, the wild and the civilized. At the same time, however, the novel implicitly destabilizes that binary. The usual tension resides in the close and unavoidable linkage between the traditionally privileged term and its devalued counterpart—in the fact that the one is always necessary to define the other. Thus, to give just one example, Zanita characterizes the ability to appreciate *wild* scenery as a mark of the *civilized* individual.

A particularly acute tension haunts the "civilizing" of the "wild" child, Zanita, whose case reminds us vividly that the two terms of the nature/culture binary are not only hierarchized but also gendered. Culture, at the same time that it is privileged, is identified with the male, while the devaluing of nature is inseparable from its identification with the female. These patriarchal identifications have been so thoroughly naturalized within so many discourses (environmentalism not least among them) that it can take considerable effort to realize that they are, after all, only cultural constructs. Notably, as the ecofeminist Ynestra King has pointed out, it is precisely at the point where the woman-nature identification has been constructed as *most* natural—with the idea that mothering is "natural" to women—that the binary is *least* tenable. In fact, argues King, "the activities of women, believed to be more natural than those of men, are . . . absolutely social." Most crucially, she continues, "mothering is an absolutely social activity" because through it, "humanity emerges from nonhuman nature into society in the life of the species and the person. The process of nurturing an unsocialized, undifferentiated human infant into an adult person—the socialization of the organic—is the bridge between nature and culture" (116). Though Sylvia Brown, significantly, is a stepmother rather than a "natural" or "organic" mother, when she attempts to raise Zanita she clearly engages in this "socialization of the organic," in the bridging of the two terms of the nature/culture binary. In *Zanita*, child rearing thus becomes a particularly effective site—an unstable "border zone"—of both environmentalist and feminist contestation.

King argues that the denial and suppression of the cultural nature of mothering has been a self-serving patriarchal project; and not at all coincidentally, I believe, *Zanita's* plot foregrounds the working of this denial and suppression. For example, each time Sylvia attempts to reinscribe her "naturally" feminine activities—most conspicuously her mothering of Zanita—into the cultural and masculine discourse of science, she is ridiculed by her scientist husband. Thus when, in a typical scene, she makes a phrenological analysis of Egremont's character, the Professor responds sarcastically, asking if "there is no line or curve about him by which you could decipher the character of his grandmother? . . . Whether, for instance, she was fond of pickles?" (107). Significantly, Sylvia reminds us that this humiliating exchange took place while she "was working hard upon a manuscript of my husband's, preparing it for the press"— simultaneously emphasizing her exclusion from the discourse of science and her subordination in a hierarchy that privileges her husband's (cultural) work over her own (natural) work.

Sylvia repeatedly finds herself positioned at what King calls "the biological dividing line where the organic merges into the social" (116)—but, as in the example just cited, when she tries openly to cross that line she is rebuffed. She realizes, as King puts it, that "the basic prototype for the nature/culture dualism" is "the domination of men over women" (109); and it is around this basic ecofeminist tenet that *Zanita's* plot begins to revolve. In fact, the event that sets the novel in motion—Sylvia's spontaneous decision to experience the Yosemite wilderness—is described as a transition from feminine domesticity to masculine adventure prompted by a defiance of male authority: "Here was I," she says, "a lone woman having transgressed her husband's directions to await him in a civilized place, alone in the wildest part of the wild world" (13). To be "wild" is not merely to disregard the border between culture and nature but also to transgress the limits set for women by men.

Zanita's wildness is often characterized the same way. Early in the book, in fact, the Professor defines it precisely as her unwillingness to perform an appropriate gender. "Excuse me for doubting," he tells Sylvia, unconsciously revealing how gender is defined in terms of men's needs and expectations, "that, even under your most judicious treatment, she will ever make such a woman as a right-minded man would esteem and love" (74). Zanita is indeed an unapologetic tomboy who traffics freely across the gender line. Worse, she just as cavalierly ignores categories of race and species: she has a "Masonic understanding" with the black child Beppo (84); she socializes freely with Mu-Wah and the other local Ahwahneechees; she converses, or at least appears to converse, with animals. Later she carries on her transgressive intrigue with Egremont, and when questioned about the possibility of marrying him replies, "O no, Aunty! I could not be bothered!" (128)—casually dismissing not just the man but the entire institution of marriage and family. In *Zanita,* then, "wildness" serves not simply as a synonym for the term *nature* in the nature/culture system—nor to denote nature at its purest, as "wilderness"—but as a term that challenges the binary itself by rejecting its defining boundaries. To be wild is not at all to be natural but to reject the dualism within which nature is defined—and, as ecofeminism reminds us, within which it is simultaneously gendered and devalued.

Kenmuir's stance is instructive here. For all his radical environmentalism, he is no feminist. He shares the patriarchal expectations of the Professor, and he loves wild nature but not wild women, insisting only half playfully that he would as soon "be exposed to a female Puck, a Medusa, a banshee, an Ariel, a witch of Endor, all tied up in a bundle, as to be wedded to Zanita" (151). Elsewhere he is portrayed as having a genuine affection for her, but his language here—with its reference to witchcraft and monstrosity—suggests just how firmly he is attached to the dualistic order Zanita rejects. Kenmuir's environmentalism challenges the privileging of culture over nature but does not go so far as to challenge the gendering of nature as feminine, a gendering that is central to his own rhetoric. "O, no mother ever pressed her child in tenderer embrace" (6), he rhapsodizes at one point, or hurried "so gracefully, to bathe the upturned face of nature, and varnish with new brilliancy her enamelled breast" (8). This sort of figuration—which astutely mimics the highly gendered language of Kenmuir's model, John Muir—is characteristic of what I would call early deep ecology rhetoric. It challenges the separation of humanity from nonhuman nature but perpetuates the identification of nature with the feminine, typically blaming environmental destruction not on men but on the supposedly generic "man." One distinguishing feature of ecofeminist rhetoric, by contrast, is its awareness that under patriarchy nature and women are subordinated together. The rhetoric of Yelverton's novel is in this sense ecofeminist, its plot and language critiquing the woman-nature identification underpinning the early wilderness preservation movement.

ZANITA'S WILDNESS AND THE PERFORMATIVITY OF NATURE

The plot also suggests the performativity of both human gender relations and wild nature. Sylvia, searching for a respectable outlet for Zanita's habit of mimicry, proposes that the young woman study acting and learn "to personate Lady Macbeth, Ophelia, and Juliet" on the professional stage. This suggestion prompts the following exchange between Zanita and the love-struck Egremont:

"I would rather play Romeo. . . . I never could be so mawkish as Juliet and Ophelia."

"Do you think loving Romeo or Hamlet so absurd then?" said Egremont, making a desperate effort to look indifferent.

"No," replied the girl with perfect *sang-froid,*—considering that this was her *début* conversation on love with any young man,—"but the manner of it is ridiculous." (119)

Here Zanita does more than simply mock her suitor. She also calls attention to the performativity of the "natural" gender relations that, within the novel's imaginative framework, are so tightly intertwined with the relations between nature and culture. As Sylvia puts it in the chapter titled "The Episode of a Kiss," "the tenderest devotion and most sublime self-sacrifice is tendered with a kiss" shared by Placida and Oswald; she adds that such heterosexual performance marks "one of the grand dividing-lines between the animal and man" (54). In *Bodies that Matter,* Judith Butler makes much the same point when she says that "the matrix of gender relations is prior to the emergence of the 'human'" (7). Sylvia Brown, however, never seems quite sure that Zanita *is* human; perhaps more precisely, she sees Zanita as unraveling the matrix that makes both the natural and the human thinkable.

I argued at the end of my discussion of *The Last of the Mohicans* that Cooper's novel thematizes the performativity of "wilderness" as the "natural" body of the environment. Here I want to stress that such performativity is *citational.* That is, as Butler reminds us, "performativity must be understood not as a singular or deliberate 'act'" but "as the reiterative and citational practice by which discourse produces the effects that it names" (*Bodies* 2). The "binding power" of the performative speech of a judge, for example, is not "derived from the force of his will or from a prior authority"; rather "it is *through* the citation of the law that the figure of the judge's 'will' is produced." Similarly, the constitutive power of environmental interpretation is produced through the citation of some "law" of nature. And in either case that power is produced only within an "exclusionary matrix." It needs to produce some sort of out-group that by contrast can define the boundaries of the truly "human" in-group—but at the same time, the excluded category will always "haunt those boundaries as the persistent possibility of their disruption and rearticulation" (3, 8). The categorizations that both ground the subject and materialize the body depend upon "a repudiation whose consequences it cannot fully control" and are always potentially subject to a rearticulation by the resisting abject of "the very terms of symbolic legitimacy and intelligibility" (3).

In Yelverton's novel, it is Zanita who signifies this resisting abject, and what her performances disrupt is the interpretive articulation of the literary-environmental equation linking whiteness, masculinity, and possession. Her wildness is not itself constitutive (she is ever the abject, not the norm), but rather parodies the genuinely constitutive speech of the novel's authorized characters—Kenmuir, the Professor, and especially that environmental interpreter par excellence, Oswald Naunton. Like *The Last of the Mohicans*, Zanita thematizes the performativity of identities and the materialization of bodies; unlike Cooper, Yelverton also foregrounds the process of disruption. Zanita's stunts and antics repeatedly suggest "the *de*constituting possibility in the very process of repetition," the possibility of putting constitutive categories such as nature and culture into what Butler terms "a potentially productive crisis" (*Bodies* 10).

A practicing if unwitting ecofeminist, Zanita refuses both the nature/culture dualism and the woman-nature identification—and with them an array of other traditionally constitutive boundaries. Sylvia notes that Zanita "never had the smallest sense of propriety, or of the fitness of things" in general (158). The young woman rejects the trappings of femininity outright, being "self-reliant and self-sufficient" (76); she "never could be induced to take care of her costume; and of vanity, as far as *fixings* went, she had none" (77). Racial difference means nothing to her, and she likewise recognizes no division between the wild and the domestic, the natural and the human. When it appears that she has just killed the Browns' cat, she asks the maid if she won't "skin it, just like you do the rabbits" (88), refusing to acknowledge the patently constructed difference between rabbits, which may be slaughtered and eaten, and household pets, which may not. When we read that the "[l]ife of bird, beast, or man was alike indifferent to her" (89), or that she "would as soon have strangled her lover as her kitten" (128), the horror is not so much her cruelty as her refusal to make what strike us as "natural" distinctions.

Similarly, despite her affection for her Yosemite home, Zanita lacks any traditional concept of "nature" as the object of science or aesthetics. She "cares no more for scenery than science" (139) and "could perceive no beauty in earth, or sky, or rock, or river, nor yet in her own exquisite face" (89). Such indifference to beauty signals an aesthetics of performance rather than of representation. During her drawing lessons, we are told, "she usually caricatured" rather than faithfully copied her model (96), and this theatricality, in turn, lies at the center of her disruption of and resistance to citationality. As Butler puts it, "citation will emerge as *theatrical* to the extent that it *mimes and renders hyperbolic* the discursive convention that it also *reverses*" (*Bodies* 232), and Zanita's performances are consistently portrayed as hyperbolically disruptive. Thus her "power of mimicry" completely "demoralized and disorganized" the first school to which she was sent, until her "persistent insubordination" became "detrimental to the discipline" there (98).

Zanita's performances are equally disruptive of that other disciplinary apparatus, the church. Prior to services one morning in Oakland, she dresses herself up in a little boy's clothes, and dresses him in hers; their subsequent appearance completely scandalizes the assembled congregation (91). Asked to explain such conduct, she tells Sylvia disingenuously that "you said yourself that Tommy should have been a girl, and that it was a mistake that I was not a boy" (92). Here as elsewhere, she jolts comfortable essentialisms, reminding her mortified interlocutor of some unpleasant contradictions in her own gender ideology. When Zanita is summoned before the minister, she makes a similar shambles of his hollow morality. She is, in fact, a thoroughgoing deconstructionist with a keen eye for the *aporia*—with, as Sylvia puts it, "an absolute faculty for discovering a loop-hole through which she may create disorder" (105).

Among the many things that Zanita disrupts are the Professor's science and, most important for my purposes here, Oswald Naunton's interpretations. One of the striking things about her father's interpretive stories is just how stale and "sedimented" they seem. That is, just a few years after the park's formation, its interpretation is already predictable and formulaic, already a recognizable performance, already iterative and citational (and thereby *constitutive* of the identities that it not so subtly names). Significantly, whenever Oswald is interrupted and his interpretation is put into question, it is an upstart female who does so. First it was the comparatively docile Placida, who archly "broke in with the suggestion that if we were going to continue such disquisitions, we had better adjourn to a seat near the Yosemite Fall"—"'where the roar,' she added naively, 'would serve for applause at the end of Oswald's speech'" (26). "Naively" must here be read as "disingenuously," for both Placida and her companions know that the "roar" will also drown out her husband's wearisome pontifications.

Placida's intervention is perhaps just a bit of tact on the part of an alert hostess who senses that her guests have tired of a rambling host. Its aim, in any event, is simply to replace her husband's voice with that of an unmediated "nature" (the roar of the falls). Zanita's disruptions have much more symbolic heft. *Her* interruptions, mimic and hyperbolic and not the least bit tactful, call attention to the constructedness of "nature" itself—and to the mutability of the subjectivities it grounds. Thus when next she interrupts her father, she is figured as the very archetype of the transgressive female: "our Eden," complains Sylvia, "as of yore, was presently invaded by the unrestful spirit of Zanita" (29). Here the ungovernable child emblematizes not a readable and stabilizing nature but a much older sort of wildness—a mid-lapsarian *condition* in which, as Hélène Cixous puts it, "every structure is for a moment thrown off balance and an ephemeral wildness sweeps order away" (337). Such wildness clearly cannot be countenanced for long by a patriarchal literary environmentalism, and we are not surprised when Zanita is finally and violently dispatched by the novel's plot. Nor are we surprised that she winds up a beautiful corpse floating in Mirror Lake in the center of the valley (209)—objectified at last, a fully materialized component of the Yosemite scenery—or that by novel's end she has become just another story reiterated endlessly by the local guides.

Conclusion

Yosemite's Postnatural Landscape

Panoramas are not what they used to be.
—Wallace Stevens, "Botanist on Alp (No. 1)"

"We live," writes Bill McKibben, "in a postnatural world" (60). McKibben is right—although, as I argued earlier, his own account of that world seems not so much "post-al" as just another sacrifice of History at the altar of Nature. What might a *genuine* postnaturality look like? How might a post-natural environmental writing help rather than hinder us in revising the narratives we have come to call the environment? I have tried to show how early constructions of the environment enabled and naturalized a position from which to *mis*understand our relationships to the land and to each other, allowing literary environmentalism to serve not only a progressive ecological thinking but also a conservative social agenda. Must those constructions continue to serve that agenda? Or will they yet prove vulnerable to the sort of contestation figured by the bewildered captive, Mary Rowlandson; by Cooper's elusive Huron tribesman, Magua; and by Yelverton's "wild" child, Zanita? These final pages will examine the idea of postnaturality as it has been developed in Rebecca Solnit's *Savage Dreams*, a text that seems to me to demonstrate the considerable promise of a postnatural environmental writing.

Environmental Responsibility

Instead of depopulating her landscapes and naturalizing her environmental constructions, Rebecca Solnit engages the social dimensions of the environment forthrightly and responsibly. What might it mean to read and write the environment *responsibly*? To answer this question I must return briefly to the problem posed by Lafayette Bunnell's description of the "prospect" of Yosemite Valley. In his *Discovery of the Yosemite*, Bunnell aestheticizes the

Mariposa Battalion's genocidal activities, inviting his readers to understand the rightness of those actions through an appeal to the valley's natural beauty. "[R]efashioning the human subject from the inside," to recall Terry Eagleton's phrase, he interpellated contemporary readers in a way that prompted them to *feel* aesthetic beauty rather than *think about* political reality.

Such a situation is analogous to that analyzed by Myra Jehlen in a recent essay on the horrors depicted in Gustave Flaubert's *Salammbô*. "What," Jehlen asks, "would constitute a 'responsibility' of the reader of a text whose aesthetics seems to be grounded in such manifest evil?" Reading, she suggests, should "engage the imagination not only aesthetically but ethically as well" (10)—but what is the reader to do when the ethical and the aesthetic are opposed, or when the ethical seems at least to be thoroughly subordinated to the aesthetic? Bunnell is no Flaubert, and *The Discovery of the Yosemite* is no *Salammbô*, in terms of either literary sophistication or the extremity of the depicted atrocities. Nonetheless, it seems fair to characterize it, as Jehlen does *Salammbô*, as "a text that seems to have issued from a nightmare rather than a dream and seems to advance at each step in defiance of all duties save one," the "hardly moral" allegiance to beauty (10). More particularly, the extravagantly depicted violence of *Salammbô* produces something very like the effect Bunnell achieves in his depiction of genocide in Yosemite, "something that less repulsive accounts might not achieve, namely, a separation of exquisite form from hideous content and the subsequent triumph of form over content. The separation occurs when readers are repelled by the content and attracted by the form. . . . Flaubert has created a tension between the repellent unpleasantness of the scene described and the aesthetic attraction of the description as art [and] this tension works to enhance the aesthetic experience by making it stand apart, distinctively valuable and moreover ultimately redemptive of the repugnance engendered by the disgusting content" (11). In Bunnell's case, this "separation" is structured a bit differently; it is the scene we find attractive and the narration that is repugnant. Nonetheless, the abstraction of form from content produces the same tension Jehlen describes in the analysis quoted above.

I am not suggesting that "we"—readers hailed as Euro-Americans—are doomed to read *The Discovery of the Yosemite* with the same racist sensibilities that Bunnell's contemporaries presumably brought to the text. Clearly we are capable of maintaining a certain critical distance. But what of our reading of its intertext, the Yosemite landscape "itself," which Bunnell has also written for us, via precisely the same strategy of aesthetic abstraction? Can we completely divorce our appreciation of *this* text from the violence of its initial inscription? Little has happened in the intervening century to suggest that Euro-Americans have rejected the sense that Yosemite's beauty is "ultimately redemptive" of its repugnant history. (Certainly "we" have not during that time seriously entertained all the deserving proposals to return unlawfully seized native lands.) Our aesthetic responses, as Eagleton says, are not easily controverted. Jehlen puts it a bit differently: "When the beauty of the literary expression triumphs over the ugliness" it expresses, "it also triumphs over the reader's ethical impulse to condemn." Possibly the reader is even "brought to actually value" the ugliness, "since it permits such beautiful writing." Confronted with art that blossoms in the fertile soil of human suffering, the reader "abjures her or his moral responsibility in order to enjoy [the] dream" (11–12).

How, then, can the reader "be responsible toward" a text such as *Salammbô* or Yosemite Valley? Jehlen suggests that the contradictions enabling such aestheticism are "permanent" and "can only grow further apart"; she doubts whether we can do more than recognize the role of evil in much of our art. She considers this a "weak conclusion" (13), and indeed mere recognition may not seem like much. But when the problem is precisely the *repression* of discomfiting histories—as it is in traditional literary environmentalism—then recognition is surely part of the solution. If we think of Yosemite not as a fixed natural inscription but as continually reconstituted social text, then recognition may become *re*-cognition, a rethinking of the landscape's uses and meanings and a reentry into history. If that rethinking is performed in response to the region's history and politics—as opposed to some mythic essence of the landscape "itself"—it will constitute a *responsible* recognition. For a specific example, let us turn to *Savage Dreams*.

Landscapes in History

Rebecca Solnit does not use the term *postnatural*—the coinage appears to be McKibben's—but *Savage Dreams* nonetheless strikes me as genuinely postnatural environmental writing. It is not primarily concerned with changes in the biological configuration of life on the planet; it is not rooted in "ecology" or "nature." It is not about escaping to some mythic origin, but "about trying to come to terms with what it means to be living in the American West" of the here and now (xi). Where McKibben longs to forget human society, Solnit strives to recover a fuller political and historical consciousness, and her writing is explicitly concerned with "how what we believe blinds us to what is going on," in particular to "how the nuclear war that was supposed to be our future and the Indian wars of our past are being waged simultaneously" in the present (xi).

Savage Dreams categorically rejects the "problematic idea" of virgin wilderness (24). It does not cling to the idea of nature as eternal and separate; nor does it privilege particular landscapes on the basis of traditional aesthetic criteria. Rather it juxtaposes two landscapes that at first seem utterly unassimilable: the highly canonical (officially prized) Yosemite National Park in California, and the decidedly noncanonical (officially despised) Nevada Test Site northwest of Las Vegas. What relates the two is not nature but political struggle, the fact that both are flash points in the "hidden wars of the American West." Each is a fiercely contested site, and each has witnessed the unspeakable—genocide, on the one hand, and some nine hundred nuclear explosions, on the other. Each deepens the author's conviction that "political engagement [is] a normal and permanent state" (14).

For the writer of the postnatural environmental narrative, landscape must highlight rather than obscure the complexities of history and politics, and the Nevada Test Site does that well. It is a central target of the international anti-nuclear movement, useful for its ability to give concreteness to "[t]hat utter abstraction the Arms Race" (14). It is also part of a forty-three-thousand-square-mile tract that the Western Shoshone consider a part of their nation, land they have never ceded and are still actively trying to claim (30). The first half of *Savage Dreams* chronicles Solnit's participation in Native American land struggles and in the American Peace Test of the late 1980s and early 1990s. The narrative focuses not on the lyrical portrayal of landscape—there is some of that, but though beautifully wrought it is hardly central—but on Solnit's conversations with the various people contesting the landscape: her fellow nuclear protestors; government officials from the county, the military, the Bureau of Land Management, and the Department of Energy; and Western Shoshone tribespeople like the ranchers Mary and Carrie Dann.

The Danns' story is particularly instructive because of the way it complicates environmental politics, implicating traditional environmentalism in the larger structures of power that organize the West. The Danns have insisted upon grazing their cows on what they hold to be Shoshone land never ceded to the United States government. The resulting conflict between the two women and the Bureau of Land Management shows how environmental policies designed to protect the ecology of rangelands are inseparable from unresolved questions of sovereignty and the ongoing oppression of the Shoshone. Says Mary Dann of her first encounter with a BLM official: "[H]e was waiting for me in the house, and we talked, and he says, 'Do you know you're trespassing?' I told him I wasn't. I told him that the only time I'd consider myself trespassing is when I went over on the Paiute land. Then I would be trespassing, I says. I'm in our own territory, our own treaty. I told him about the treaty and showed him the map and he told me, 'Well that's a big territory.' And I told him, *Yes*" (159). It is not just the Danns and the BLM that are in conflict here, but also two histories. For the Danns, the environment figures as part of a tribal rather than a national history, a history in which the only genuine possibility of trespassing lay in the violation of preconquest agreements between her own people and the Paiutes. The tone is gentle, but challenging in its reminder that there is more than one story here to be told. One might at first find the phrase "I'm *in* our own *treaty*" a bit odd, conflating as it does the environment with the words by which that environment has historically been apportioned. But it makes perfect sense in literary-environmental terms, for a "treaty" is a discursive act that constitutes the sort of interwoven complex of land, people, and power that has been the subject of this book. Yoking history to landscape, Mary Dann sees land/history—"I told him about the *treaty* and showed him the *map*"—where the BLM official sees only land: "Well that's a big territory."

When the BLM threatens to confiscate the Danns' cows, the antinuclear protestors join forces with the two women. Since many of the protestors are themselves environmentalists with traditional views of ecological purity, including a distaste for cattle grazing on federal rangeland, the incident becomes a complex parable of environmental revisionism—one of many such instances of *Savage Dreams'* refusal to reduce the complexities of environmental politics to a simple image of a picture-postcard wilderness. Solnit's desert and mountain environments are free to exist and evolve within history, for the simple reason that they *are* history. As such they are not wholly available for the nature writer's mythic reinscription; they are places that have always been inhabited, places already invested with a multitude of stories. *Savage Dreams* is "responsible" precisely in its response to these stories: rejecting the traditional literary-environmental habits of repression and mystic appeal, Solnit insists that competing stories be recovered and told, that they be evaluated from an ethical rather than an aesthetic standpoint, and finally that their conflicting claims be negotiated.

In the second half of *Savage Dreams*, Solnit approaches Yosemite's mountain landscape with a political consciousness awakened in the politics of the Nevada desert. She finds Yosemite, too, a fiercely contested site, the center of struggles over that inseparable pair, land and the meaning of land. She acknowledges the work of traditional environmentalists trying to change the more destructive policies of the Park Service, but she complicates what is merely an *ecological* agenda by situating it within history. Citing the insights of such postmodern ecologists as Daniel Botkin, she points out that attempts to "restore" Yosemite to a "pre-contact" state are both incoherent and politically obnoxious: the valley as it was "discovered" by Savage and Bunnell was not a wilderness at all, but a garden that had been tended for centuries by native people. Efforts to "restore" Yosemite to a "wilderness" can thus be seen as continuous with earlier white attempts to naturalize the valley—attempts stretching back to the days of the Mariposa War.

Such a purely ecological approach to managing the park reinscribes an imperialist mythology under the guise of "protecting" the land. It also naturalizes a racist historiography predicated on the idea that Yosemite's Ahwahneechee Indians "became extinct" in the nineteenth century. Writing across this official grain, Solnit reveals that in fact, large numbers of native people have continued to live either in or immediately adjacent to the park, and that the federal government has seen fit to evict them on a recurring basis—not just in 1851 but also in 1906, 1929, and 1969. This is a decidedly different "prospect" from the traditional view still privileged by the National Park Service's own interpretations (288).

Such hegemonic interpretations can be challenged most effectively, of course, by the Ahwahneechee people themselves. Particularly instructive is a story related by Jay Johnson, a Park Service employee and an Ahwahneechee leader of the Mariposa Indian Council, which hopes "to get federal recognition for the 2,000 Southern Miwok still in the area" (290). In 1980, Johnson and four other Yosemite Indians visited the Smithsonian Institution, where they found an exhibit about their tribe (significantly enough, in the Museum of *Natural* History). Spying a display caption stating that the "Yosemites" had ceased to exist, Johnson tried to alert a Smithsonian employee to the error. The ensuing exchange speaks volumes about the social construction of the environment. As Solnit retells the story, Johnson informs a curator that the exhibit "is nice, but there's an error in the statement, and she says, 'Oh no, there can't be. Every little word goes through channels and committees and whatnot,' and I says, 'It's OK, but,' I says, 'It tells me that there are no more Yosemite Indians today.' She says, 'Well that's true, it's very sad but whatever's out there is true.' So I say, 'Well I hate to disturb you, but I'm a Yosemite Indian, and we're here on business for our tribe.' And she caught her breath and said, 'Ohhh, uh, let me call somebody,' and she called somebody who was in charge of exhibits, and I went and told her the same thing. If there's a statement saying that there are descendants of the Ahwahneechees living there today, all of us natives would be satisfied. But it hasn't been changed" (292–93). It should not be thought odd that Johnson, discursively effaced and literally dispossessed, would have been satisfied with such a seemingly minor concession as revising this caption—nor that the Smithsonian should be reluctant to revise it. Each side senses in this epistemological skirmish the relation between the interpretation *and* the ownership of the nation's most canonical landscape. An "extinct" tribe can make no claims, of either the historical or the legal sort.

By foregrounding the linkage between interpretation and ownership, *Savage Dreams* departs radically from what I referred to in chapter 1 as the "Great Books" tradition of literary environmentalism. In that tradition, the national parks function as an environmental canon, a collection of reverently preserved texts with seemingly transparent and unchallengeable meanings. Through the interlocking interpretive activities of institutions such as the National Park Service and the Smithsonian, those meanings are generated and disseminated as part of the larger formation of "cultural literacy," the highly selective complex of knowledge that, as E. D. Hirsch quite correctly claims, helped to "create" and serves still to "perpetuate" the nation (ix). But where the natural environment has functioned as a myth facilitating the landscape's appropriation and commodification, the postnatural environment may serve as a revisionist history, a new and more inclusive myth enabling the landscape's democratization and empowering traditionally subordinated classes of people. The environment in *Savage Dreams* is deployed in just these ways—not to perpetuate but to disrupt the prevailing fictions of nation, race, and gender, not least by restoring a voice to the abjected presences traditionally excised from them.

Such revision is a complicated and often messy process, and not necessarily conducive to the elegiac style of traditional nature writing. Solnit's landscape descriptions are often poetic, but she is wary of investing scenery with univocal, transcendent meanings or any sort of Edenic appeal. It is instructive to compare McKibben's traditional treatment of his Adirondack lake with Solnit's genuinely postnatural description of a swim in Lake Tenaya, in Yosemite National Park. In *The End of Nature*, McKibben writes that "[d]uring the week we swim across [the lake] and back, a trip of maybe forty minutes—plenty of time to forget everything but the feel of water around your body and the rippling, muscular joy of a hard kick and the pull of your arms" (49). This natural environment affords both a muscular performance of masculinity and a reassuring sense of withdrawal, away from history and society and into an insular, seemingly unified self. Solnit, by contrast, writes that she "finally got to Lake Tenaya, on a warm day in August. The water was marvelously clear. . . . Skeins of golden light slipped over the lake floor, and rounded boulders rose out of the water or hovered just below its surface. . . . It was an uncanny place. It was hard to trust that this cold, clear substance would bear me up if I immersed myself in it, or that I would emerge the same as I went in. In the gravelly shallows, eddies of fool's gold rose around me at every step, glittering in the bright light of the mountains. As the waves lapped at my feet, I tried to picture Tenaya and Bunnell standing there on a cold May morning 140 years before and wondered which shining rocks had moved the Ahwahneechee to name the lake Pyweack" (279). Where McKibben forgets history, Solnit vividly remembers it. And where McKibben might have discovered a longed-for solidity and assurance, Solnit offers a cautionary tale of instability and transformation. This is, first of all, a lake with not one but two names, bestowed upon it by two nations—a state of affairs that subtly calls into question the landscape's seemingly uncontested status as a "national" park. With its domestic imagery ("skeins") and its references to roundedness and immersion, this is also a decidedly feminine landscape, though certainly no longer the scene of the masculine subject's escape from a suffocating domestic order. Nor is it an attempt to imagine a stable, transcendent ground of identity and meaning; this is a landscape "hard to trust," sparkling with "fool's gold"—a perfect figure for the unreliability of the seemingly "natural" significations swirling around the subject. It is, finally, a *fluid* rather than a fixed scene, not a secure ground in which to affirm the identities more typically constituted through the environmental narrative. The narrator suspects that the lake will not "bear her up," and she fears unpredictable changes should she enter it. In its "bright light" and "marvelously clear" water we sense the power and the promise of a postnatural environment, one that will no longer reify subjects but transform them.

Notes

1. Whitman 401. This study owes much to Richard Slotkin, whose *The Fatal Environment: The Myth of the Frontier in the Age of Industrialization, 1800–1890* first prompted my thinking about the discursive functions of the term *environment*.

2. Analyzing a variety of contemporary ecological discourses in *The Chicago Gangster Theory of Life*, Ross has taken the lead in this country in exploring how environmentalism threatens a reactionary "revival of appeals to the authority of nature and biology." He notes the troubling historical flirtations of fascist groups with ecology and conservation (4) and suggests that "we may soon be engaged yet again in the struggle to prevent nature becoming the referee of our fate" (5). In *Earth Follies*, Seager cites specific examples of sexism and racism in the ecology establishment (176–85), in the animal rights movement (202–7), and in the theories of deep ecology (226–35).

3. I do not wish to oversimplify the positions in this debate. Not all contributors to *Reinventing Nature?* see contemporary theory as inimical to environmentalism, and in fact several of the collection's essays might have been equally at home in Cronon's *Uncommon Ground*. And despite their polemical tone, editors Lease and Soulé concede more ground to postmodern theory than is indicated by my brief caricature. Lease, for example, notes that environmentalists "sometimes fail to appreciate the degree to which their own concepts of nature are culturally determined" and stresses that "all the parties . . . have much to learn from each other and that cross-disciplinary contacts can promote . . . more effective conservation policies" (7).

In addition to the contributors to *Uncommon Ground* and *Reinventing Nature?*, a variety of other critics have weighed in on the growing debate about postmodernism and nature. For example, Lawrence Buell's *The Environmental Imagination* notes that "the theory that American idealization of nature and wilderness has acted as a kind of moral tonic or social conscience has come to seem increasingly suspect," to the point that the most recent criticism stresses "nature's function as an ideological theater for acting out desires that have very little to do with bonding to nature as such" (35). Unlike Cronon, Ross, and others, however, Buell "would question the increasing marginalization of the literal environment," arguing that "the conception of represented nature as an ideological screen becomes unfruitful if it is used to portray the green world as nothing more than projective fantasy or social allegory." I would suggest that the key phrase here is "nothing more than." To analyze ways in which nature has been *made to function* as "ideological screen" is not in itself to *reduce it to* such a screen—though perhaps some readers will think that I do just that in this book. Buell agrees that "American naturism" has an "imperial cast calling for continued scrutiny, but feels that such criticism generally has been too reductionist, making "insufficient allowance" for nature's "ideological multivalence" (36). The possibility of such "multivalence" is one of my own concerns in this study, though I conceive of it a bit differently, as the ongoing possibility of revising environmental narratives and reconstituting "environmentalized" subjects.

Several other critics whom I do not reference directly have nonetheless also helped to frame the fundamental questions now being explored by poststructuralist ecocritism such as my own. At the top of the list would certainly be Donna Haraway; it was *Primate Visions* that first led me to question my own assumptions about nature, wilderness, and gender. Patrick Murphy's *Literature, Nature, and Other: Ecofeminist Critiques* argues for the social and political value of bringing ecology into contemporary critiques of the discursive construction of the self. Only by doing so, he writes, can we hope to achieve "a gender heterarchical continuum in which difference exists without binary opposition and hierarchical valorization" (4). In "Body Politics in American Nature Writing: Who May Contest for What the Body of Nature Will Be?" Gretchen Legler applies Haraway's critique of nature as "source of insight and promise" specifically to nature writing, arguing persuasively that doing so can help us better understand the normative functions of a literature that generally "serves to strengthen boundaries between nature and culture, the self and the non-self" (72).

4. I realize that feminism and environmentalism are distinct movements, and in pursuing an analogy between the two I do not mean to erase important differences. Each movement has, however, had to respond recently to a similar critique of its grounding assumptions. (That environmentalism has responded so tardily suggests just how much less self-aware and self-critical it has been than feminism.) To further justify my citation here of Butler's arguments, I quote her own claim in *Bodies that Matter* that "the unanticipated appropriations of a given work in areas for which it was never consciously intended are some of the most fruitful" (19).

5. In the American West, displaced Native Americans were the primary victims of the creation of national parks; in the East the victims were as likely to be poor whites. See Bruce J. Weaver, "What to Do with the Mountain People?"

6. Wald 3, 299; Fliegelman 5. My thinking in this section draws broadly on the work of the so-called New Americanists, whose work is perhaps best exemplified in the book series of the same name now being published by Duke University Press.

7. Though created by federal legislation, Yosemite was in one sense not the first *national* park, because immediately after its creation the federal government ceded the site to the state of California for management. Yosemite would not be returned to federal jurisdiction until 1890, eighteen years after the creation of Yellowstone National Park, which had remained under federal control from the beginning (Nash 106). Several scholars, however, insist that Yosemite inaugurated the national park *idea;* see especially Huth 65–68.

8. "Literary environmentalism" as it is used in this book is a process of rendering natural landscape into disciplinary text that can help ground a stable American identity. In her excellent study *Writing Nature: Henry Thoreau's* Journal, Sharon Cameron demonstrates that while Thoreau viewed nature as a sort of language or syllabary for expressing human moods and thoughts, he nonetheless saw landscape as a *de*stablizing influence calling identity into question rather than stabilizing it. *Walden* seems often enough to write landscape as literary-environmental text, but even there, as Cameron points out (142), Thoreau tellingly admits that "Nature puts no question and answers none we mortals ask"—including, presumably, questions about identity. In the *Journal* Thoreau much more explicitly undermines the notion of nature as a stable ground of identity. Repeatedly, nature in the *Journal* "shies away from rigidification" and "has no fixed meanings" (61); Thoreau highlights the many times "the landscape resists the revelation it was about to confer" (113), and in the end he "relinquishes a belief in correlatives between nature and the mind not because he has no interest in them, but rather because . . . he finds them persistently unavailable" (162, n. 20).

In a similar vein, Scott Slovic notes perceptively that Thoreau "achieve[s] a sense of personal boundaries" not by discovering stable meanings in nature but rather by "becoming so alert to the idiosyncracies of his own emotional responses to nature" (28). Thoreau realizes that "the very significance of nature" is not transcendent but situational, "dependent upon the disclosure of the observer's relationship to the object observed" (29–30). Thus even though "Thoreau feels that he is working with a primal, potent form of language," that language is "not merely something to receive and interpret (as it was for the Puritans), but rather a medium for his own communication" (30).

In sum, both Cameron and Slovic reveal to us a Thoreau far more conscious than his contemporaries of what today might be called the problematics of nature and identity.

Chapter 1. **Canonizing Landscape**

1. Olmsted 21. I discuss Olmsted's views in greater detail in chapter 5.
2. Hirsch xiv. Hirsch's claim that the most crucial knowledge can be readily

identified and *defined* is itself problematic because the first of these terms implies a simple recognition of a fact and the second the *assignment* of a *meaning*. Hirsch's conflation of these terms indicates how the idea of cultural literacy naturalizes value judgments as simple "information." Interestingly enough, just as Olmsted invokes literacy in his theorizing of the environment, Hirsch argues for the importance of cultural literacy by citing its utility in comprehending environmentalist discourse (xiii).

3. This understanding of the links between literacy and the modern state is broadly informed by Raymond Williams's *Writing in Society;* Harvey J. Graff's *The Literacy Myth* and *The Legacies of Literacy;* Graff and Robert F. Arnove's *National Literacy Campaigns: Historical and Comparative Perspectives;* Elsa Auerbach's "Literacy and Ideology"; and Wlad Godzich's *The Culture of Literacy.*

4. With Congress at first reluctant to sponsor interpretive activities, the Park Service looked to outside funding to pay for them and created quasi-independent organizations to help coordinate them. In 1918 Charles D. Wolcott, secretary of the Smithsonian Institution, formed the National Parks Educational Committee, which with Mather's assistance created the nonprofit National Parks Association. Among the purposes of the association were "to interpret the natural sciences which are illustrated in the scenic features, flora and fauna of the national parks and monuments, and to circulate popular information concerning them in text and picture" (Mackintosh 6). To further such efforts, John D. Rockefeller helped fund the museum at Mesa Verde National Park in 1923; the Laura Spellman Rockefeller Memorial Fund and the Carnegie Corporation paid for interpretive facilities at Grand Canyon National Park, including a museum that opened in 1926; and the Loomis family, owners of the *Los Angeles Times,* funded a museum that opened in Lassen Volcanic National Park in 1929. The federal government did not fund a comparable facility until 1930 (Mackintosh 12).

5. Early on, interpreters were urged not to "rely upon a limited set of time-honored techniques without examining their current appropriateness" but instead to make use of "[c]urrent knowledge about human behavior in leisure settings" that will "suggest alternative interpretive strategies" (Field and Wagar 44).

6. Grant W. Sharpe notes that in addition to its overt political value in environmentalism, interpretation has an "often overlooked" "management aspect," affording a variety of concrete benefits ranging from "favorably promot[ing] the image of the agency which supplies it" (4) to providing "substantial assistance to law enforcement through educational persuasion" (18).

7. William C. Everhardt, as head of the National Park Service's Division of Interpretation and Visitor Services, advised his interpretive staff in 1965 not just to read Tilden's *Interpreting Our Heritage* but to reread it. "There isn't anything much better," he added in what was no doubt intended as less qualified praise (United States, *Inter-*

pretive Planning). Ten years later, Everhardt noted approvingly that "for nearly a generation the profession has been guided conceptually and philosophically by the teachings of Freeman Tilden, through his classic, *Interpreting Our Heritage"* (Sharpe xi).

8. For more information (and a sampling of opinions) on the renaming of the Little Bighorn National Monument, see "The Winners Get Their Due"; Karen Lynch's "Custer Loses Again"; Andrew Ward's "The Little Bighorn"; George Will's "Little Bighorn's Multiculturalism"; and James Kilpatrick's "Last Stand for Custer Battlefield?"

9. Unless otherwise indicated, information about Creationary Catastrophe Tours is taken from Cecil Allen Roy's Web site at http://www.tagnet.org/anotherview point/.

Chapter 2. **Ecocritical Theory**

1. Pack 58. The "Anecdote" may well be the most frequently analyzed of Stevens's poems, and the most persistent theme in its readings is that "a wild and disorderly landscape is transformed into order" by the "presence" of the jar. That order is not *natural,* however; it is wholly "a product of the human consciousness," and "acts in the imagination" rather than in the world (Baker 127). Order does not originate *in* nature, but is the effect of a "desire for wholeness" that "leads . . . toward surroundness" (Riddel 43). One critic writes that one of the poem's "critical points is that the jar, while it may reflect the hill on which it stands . . . is not nature" but a reflection, and "[o]nce nature is reflected, it is art—the domain of the imagination and not of the real world" (Perlis 47).

Yvor Winters disagrees with this prevailing view of the poem, finding it "a purely romantic performance," "an expression of the corrupting effect of the intellect upon natural beauty." "The jar is the product of the human mind," he stresses, "and it dominates the wilderness; but it does not give order to the wilderness—it is vulgar and sterile, and it transforms the wilderness into the semblance of a deserted picnic ground" (229).

2. Tu Wei-Ming 19. This passage's interdisciplinarity becomes more explicit when Tu Wei-Ming adds that "[f]ar-sighted ecologists, engineers, economists, and earth scientists, intent on developing a communal critical self-consciousness for 'saving spaceship earth,' have made an appeal to poets, priests, artists, and philosophers" (20). In a similar vein, another contributor to Tucker and Grim's *Worldviews and Ecology,* Thomas Berry, writes:

General ecological studies can be too abstract or too theoretical to constitute a recognized scientific discipline. Biological and geological studies can be too specialized. Environmental ethics is a much needed study, yet it cannot proceed in any effective manner without a larger understanding of the natural world. The . . . realm[s] of poetry and the natural history essay are important to establish the emotional-aesthetic feeling for the wonders of the natural world and to awaken the psychic energies needed. . . . But these humanistic insights are themselves mightily enhanced by a more thorough understanding of the identifying features and intimate modes of functioning of bioregions.

None of these studies can be done in isolation from the others. . . . The relationship of humans to the earth requires all these modes of inquiry, all these modes of expression. (236)

3. Foucault xv. Of course, some people have never found environmentalist discourse to make much sense. One thinks here of the irreducibility of the differences explored in John McPhee's *Encounters with the Archdruid,* in which, as the title suggests, one of the protagonists seems to find environmentalism utterly alien as a system of thought.

4. To demonstrate the extent to which my approach is indebted to Said, I quote the following from *Orientalism,* and invite the reader to substitute, more or less freely, "environment" for "Orient" and "literary environmentalism" for "Orientalism":

[I]t needs to be made clear about cultural discourse and exchange within a culture that what is commonly circulated by it is not "truth" but representations. . . . In any instance of at least written language, there is no such thing as a delivered presence, but a *re-presence,* or a representation. The value, efficacy, strength, apparent veracity of a statement about the Orient therefore relies very little, and cannot instrumentally depend, on the Orient as such. On the contrary, the written statement is a presence to the reader by virtue of its having excluded, displaced, made supererogatory any such "real thing" as "the Orient." Thus all of Orientalism stands forth and away from the Orient: that Orientalism makes sense at all depends more on the West than on the Orient, and this sense is directly indebted to various Western techniques of representation that make the Orient visible, clear, "there" in discourse about it. And these representations rely upon institutions, traditions, conventions, agreed-upon codes of understanding for their effects. (21–22)

5. Nash 5. There is the added problem that the very act of legally demarcating wilderness makes it less than truly "wild." As Stephen Greenblatt puts it in his treatment of Yosemite Valley in "Towards a Poetics of Culture," "[t]he wilderness is at once secured and obliterated by the official gestures that establish its boundaries" (9). Nonetheless there has been a *working* definition of wilderness in this country

ever since the Wilderness Act of 1964 fully codified the term. "A wilderness," according to the act, "in contrast with those areas where man and his works dominate the landscape, is hereby recognized as an area where the earth and its community of life are untrammeled by man, where man himself is a visitor who does not remain" (qtd. in Grumbine 377). Four elements of this formulation will prove important in this study. First, its stress on wilderness as uninhabited land, where "man" only "visits," effaces the history of early nonwhite presences on the land. Second, its universalization of "man" similarly obscures a set of nonmasculine presences on and interpretations of the land. Third, its binarism—the contrast it draws between the natural and the humanly altered landscape, and the sharp boundary that is thereby implied—helps reify the notion of a "natural" or "divine" inscription. Finally, the legislation's use of the classic form of the speech act—the way it declares that wilderness is "hereby recognized," that is, created through the perlocutionary force of its enunciation—links it to the imperialist performativity of the Spanish *Requerimiento* (discussed at length in chapter 4).

6. This study construes *ideology* in the Althusserian sense. James Kavanagh has summarized Althusser's view of ideology as follows: Ideology is a set of representations, "worked up in specific material practices," that helps to "form individuals into social subjects who 'freely' internalize an appropriate 'picture' of their social world." Ideology provides the subject "a fundamental framework of assumptions that defines the parameters of the real and the self," thereby making it possible for "men and women to 'see' their specific place in a historically peculiar social formation as inevitable, natural, a necessary function of the 'real' itself." My analysis of the ideology of literary environmentalism will thus concern itself "with the institutional and/or textual apparatuses that work on the reader's or spectator's imaginary conceptions of self and social order" as those apparatuses "interpellate" the reader into a given subjectivity (Kavanagh 310). For Althusser's conception of interpellation, see his "Ideology and Ideological State Apparatuses" (44–51).

Chapter 3. **Acts of Environment**

1. See Penelope 186–87. Instead of *incorporation* one might use other terms to denote the obverse of *penetration*, but, reflecting the asymmetry of a patriarchal lexicon, no such term is exactly complementary in the full range of its connotations. Marie Bonaparte uses the term *incorporating* in her own discussion of female sexual pleasure (*Female Sexuality* 105).

2. *Land* 4. Even at the most literal level, this desire to escape a burdensome history and society was conditioned by the capitalism one wished to escape, for the fantasies in question were circulated most widely by the colonial promoters themselves (9).

3. For details and a range of recent interpretations of the Pequot War, see Drinnon 35–57, Kibbey 92–94, and Nelson 12–16.

4. See M. Leach 1152, Legman 429–34, and Thompson 164, 213.

5. M. Leach 1152. Leach writes of this motif only as part of Native American folklore; Jay Mechling, in an analysis of contemporary alligator jokes, demonstrates that "the image of a toothed vagina" also circulates much more widely and is "still powerful in [Euro-]American male folk materials" (79).

6. For detailed accounts of King Philip's War, see Leach, *Flintlock and Tomahawk*, and Jennings, *The Invasion of America*.

7. For the Puritan, wilderness was not "natural" in the later, Enlightenment-conditioned sense of being "governed" solely by the "laws of nature"; it was thought of rather as ungoverned, chaotic. It is perhaps impossible for modern environmentalists to "believe" in wilderness in this earlier sense, any more than they can conceive of a place in the universe that is not subject to natural "laws." Even the chaotic is now considered to follow the predictable patternings described in modern chaos theory.

Chapter 4. **Performing Wilderness**

1. John F. Lynen writes, in economic terms that echo Audubon's own formulation, that Cooper's regret at the loss of wilderness was not mere "sentimental nostalgia," but arose "from the agonizing doubt whether civilization is worth the terrible price men pay for it" (174). Audubon, as late as 1835, could still question "[w]hether these changes are for the better or for the worse" (*Delineations* 5); Cooper by this time seemed far less ambivalent. In Roderick Nash's words, Cooper "held no brief for exploitation," and in Natty Bumppo he created a character who not only "honored the wilderness and used it respectfully" but also could serve as the author's mouthpiece in a repeated "condemnation of the exploiter" (76–77).

2. Philip Fisher notes that the "killing of a woman" in Cooper's novels is especially symbolic because "it wipes out the future" (56). In *The Last of the Mohicans,* the exemplary maiden and her partner, one of the Hurons' "bravest young men" (*Mohicans* 256), are the only Indian couple put forth by the novel, as are Alice and Duncan, as a procreative link to a racially unmixed future. Heyward is conveniently spared the burden of any responsibility for figuratively dooming an entire race by his failure to cure this woman: "A single look was sufficient to apprise the pretended leech, that the invalid was far beyond his powers of healing"; the "slight qualm of conscience which had been excited by the intended deception, was instantly appeased" (253).

3. Heyward's foil here is the aged Tamenund, regarded, like Washington, as the father "of a nation" (*Mohicans* 305). A figure "deeply venerated" and "well beloved,"

Tamenund has "the dignity of a monarch, and the air of a father" (294). The similarity of the two names is obvious enough, each with three syllables, each syllable of the one retaining a phonological correlate of the other: Wash/Tam, ing/en, ton/und. Predictably, the elderly chief's star is fading as that of the young white officer is rising.

4. My argument in this section draws upon Eric Cheyfitz's "Literally White, Figuratively Red," especially his comments on *The Last of the Mohicans'* figures of the book, writing, and orality (91–92 n. 17).

5. Barbara Mann, in fact, argues that Natty Bumppo "could only have been a mixed blood" (1), probably the son of a native woman and Major Effingham of *The Pioneers* (8).

6. According both Spaniard and native a precise place in a global teleology, the *Requerimiento* fixes identities for speaker and auditor, reaffirming the colonial in his familiar heritage and completely reconstructing the Indian into a "religious and legal fiction"—in Cheyfitz's words, a "pure figure" whose own specificities are "formally denied" (74). The document's narration of the deeds of the (church) fathers subsumes native histories into an all-encompassing patrilineage, claiming thereby a preexisting and eternal dominion over both native peoples and their lands. See also Stephen Greenblatt's discussion of the *Requerimiento* in *Marvelous Possessions* (97–98).

7. These differing stresses on ritual and iconoclasm have been seen as corresponding to contemporary Catholic and Protestant theological styles. See Kibbey 42–64.

8. *Mohicans* features two extended episodes that foreshadow Magua's demise, and in each the narrator is ambiguous as to the efficacy of the rifle and fails to "produce the body." During the battle at Glenn's Falls, a Huron sniper is wounded and dislodged from his perch in an oak tree. Heyward calls for a shot that would end the man's suffering, but Natty refuses to fire again, citing the need to preserve powder. Then, contravening his own advice, Natty makes as if to fire anyway. "Three several times the scout raised his piece in mercy, and as often prudence getting the better of his intention, it was again silently lowered. At length, one hand of the Huron lost its hold, and dropped exhausted to his side. A desperate and fruitless struggle to recover the branch succeeded, and then the savage was seen for a fleeting instant, grasping wildly at the empty air. The lightning is not quicker than was the flame from the rifle of Hawk-eye; the limbs of the victim trembled and contracted, the head fell to the bosom, and the body parted the foaming waters . . . and *every vestige of the unhappy Huron was lost forever*" (75, my emphasis). As will be true at the novel's climax, there is here no assurance that Natty's rifle "without question was the death" of this Huron.

9. This studied silence can be compared with the way, following an earlier battle scene, Natty goes around making sure his victims have in fact been dispatched,

making a "circuit of the dead, into whose senseless bosoms he thrust his long knife, with as much coolness, as if they had been so many brute carcasses." Natty has reason for this brutality. Just moments earlier, Magua had been engaged in a furious and seemingly fatal struggle with Chingachgook. Natty tried to pick off the Huron with Kill-deer, but—in yet another image of a category crisis, an extreme fluidity that occasions a figurative impotency—he found the two Indian bodies indistinguishable, too tightly intertwined to allow him sure aim. Chingachgook finally gets the upper hand and manages to stab his foe, apparently killing him. "Magua suddenly relinquished his grasp," we read, "and fell backward, without motion, and, seemingly, without life." Natty, "elevating the butt of the long and fatal rifle," then wishes to settle the matter with a blow to Magua's skull. However, "at the very moment when the dangerous weapon was in the act of descending, the subtle Huron rolled swiftly from beneath the danger, over the edge of the precipice, and falling on his feet, was seen leaping, with a single bound, into the center of a thicket of low bushes, which clung along its sides" (114). The precipice, the falling, the last-minute failure of the rifle—all these prefigure the circumstances of the novel's climax and warn us that rumors of Magua's death ought always to be considered premature.

10. My argument in this section elaborates on Cheyfitz's characterization of Natty Bumppo as a "consummate 'reader'" of nature (66).

11. The novel posits no successor to the skilled readers Natty, Chingachgook, and Uncas. The future belongs instead to Heyward, whose notions of language are quite different from Natty's. When, for example, Magua questions Heyward about the whereabouts of Uncas, whom Magua is hotly pursuing, Heyward's linguistic sophistication allows him to turn deferral into delay:

"Le Cerf Agile is not here?"

"I know not whom you call the 'nimble deer,'" said Duncan, gladly profiting by any excuse to create delay.

"Uncas," returned Magua, pronouncing the Delaware name with even greater difficulty than he spoke his English words. "'Bounding Elk' is what the white man says when he calls to the young Mohican."

"Here is some confusion of names between us, le Renard," said Duncan, hoping to provoke a discussion. "Daim is the French for deer, and cerf for stag; élan is the true term, when one would speak of an elk."

"Yes," muttered the Indian in his native tongue; "the pale faces are prattling women! they have two words for each thing, while a red skin will make the sound of his voice speak for him." Then changing his language, he continued, adhering to the imperfect nomenclature of his provincial instructors, "The deer is swift, but weak; the elk is swift, but strong; and the son of 'le serpent' is 'le cerf agile.' Has he leaped the river to the woods?"

"If you mean the younger Delaware, he too is gone down with the water."
(Cooper 91)

As Magua tries to pin it down, the signified repeatedly gets away from him. The signifier slides endlessly, and the exchange ends not with an absolute but with a conditional: "If you mean . . . " Heyward's strategy here exemplifies Cheyfitz's notion of colonial figuration as a way of "precisely not understanding the other" (74).

12. Samuels 89. My arguments concerning gender and performance in *The Last of the Mohicans* are indebted throughout to Samuels's insights in "Generation through Violence."

13. The co-performances at the beaver pond reaffirm John Lynen's contention that Cooper's wilderness landscapes, just like his plots and his characters, depend for any force they may have on our active cooperation as readers. The reifying traffic between "human values and natural forms" (187) is for Lynen rooted in our desire to make sense of the inconsistencies and gaps in the text. In Butler's terms, such "coherence is desired, wished for, idealized," and "this idealization is an effect of a corporeal signification" (*Gender* 136)—of a mask of fur, in this case, an outside that signifies but does not reliably correspond with an inside.

14. The overwhelming sense of a "natural" body is an effect, writes Butler, with "no ontological status apart from the various acts which constitute its reality" (*Gender* 136). And, as with cross-gender drag, the cross-species drag that so engages the reader of *The Last of the Mohicans* "implicitly reveals" a completely "imitative structure." In fact, "part of the pleasure, the giddiness of the performance is in the recognition of a radical contingency. . . . [This notion of] parody does not assume that there is an original which such parodic identities imitate. Indeed, the parody is of the very notion of an original, . . . a fantasy of a fantasy, the transfiguration of an Other who is always already a 'figure' in that double sense." The "original" is revealed as "an imitation without an origin," and what "postures as an imitation" is a "production," part of a "perpetual displacement" (138).

15. Butler 139. Certainly *The Last of the Mohicans* portrays its wild performances as culturally situated, directed toward specific interlocutors rather than any "universal." In order for Heyward to perform the Huron healer, for example, Chingachgook must reinscribe his civilized body as "savage," a process compared, appropriately enough, to *landscape* painting (228). "[T]he Sagamore can . . . make a natural fool of you," through a practice figured as fully artifactual, as an oxymoronic "making natural" that cannot be assimilated into any foundational notion of an unmade nature. Chingachgook, "long practised in all the subtle arts of his race," proceeds to draw upon Heyward "the fantastic shadow that the natives were accustomed to consider as the evidence of a friendly and jocular disposition," making sure that "[e]very line that could possibly be interpreted into a secret inclination for war, was carefully

avoided" (229). The Indian body that was earlier as transparent as its twin, the body of the wilderness, is now to be signified by an intentional alignment, not with any universal inscription, but with the customs and codes of a specific interpretive community.

Chapter 5. Four Views of Yosemite

1. For an accessible overview of the economics of nineteenth-century western land use, see Patricia Limerick's classic introduction to the "new western history," *The Legacy of Conquest.*

2. Muir 165. In a sense, the Yosemite region by the summer of 1869 *was* "full of humanity." Competition for Sierra pasturage had already become severe enough for Muir to complain of the fact that, "as several flocks had gone ahead of us, scarce a leaf, green or dry, was left; therefore the starving flock had to be hurried on" (7). Now and then his party encounters tourists (67), and Muir notes elsewhere of "several other camps and dogs not many miles" from his camp in the Tuolumne high country (161).

3. Muir is not the only nature writer to recast history as nature in this way. Gretchen Legler describes much the same phenomenon in noting how Henry David Thoreau treats the embodied Other in the landscape. Analyzing Thoreau's famous description of the shipwrecked bodies of the would-be Irish immigrants who had washed ashore on Cape Cod, she notes that "these raced and classed and sexed bodies are at the same time ironically 'naturalized' and removed from nature; they don't occupy the same privileged space in the landscape that Thoreau does because of his whiteness and maleness" (76).

4. For details on the Mariposa War, see Solnit 268–354, and Annie Mitchell's "Major James D. Savage and the Tulareños."

5. The accepted white historiography of Yosemite Valley implies that Indians ceased to live in Yosemite after the Mariposa War. Solnit points out, however, that a considerable number of native people continued to live either in or immediately adjacent to the valley, and that those people were evicted on a recurring basis—by military forces in 1851 and 1906, and by the National Park Service in 1929 and 1969 (288).

6. See Bunnell 297–99. Bunnell claims elsewhere that "Ten-ie-ya was the last chief of his people" (80), but in fact there remained several other leaders of the Yosemite tribe, and resistance continued after Tenaya's death (Solnit 281–82).

7. Rotundo, "Mount Auburn" 258; Sloane 45. In addition to these two sources, I have drawn in this section on Rotundo's "The Rural Cemetery Movement"; James J. Farrell's *Inventing the American Way of Death*; Stanley French's "The Cemetery as Cultural Institution"; Thomas Bender's "The 'Rural' Cemetery Movement"; and

David Schuyler's "The Evolution of the Anglo-American Rural Cemetery." Hans Huth has preceded me in discussing the movement's relation to environmentalism (60–62).

8. The American Association of Cemetery Superintendents, which preceded by twelve years the creation of the American Society of Landscape Architects, was in many ways the latter group's direct antecedent. In 1895, when the AACS changed the title of its official journal from *Modern Cemetery* to *Park and Cemetery*, the journal's editor noted that "the superintendents of our leading cemeteries" had long "recognized the fact that the requirements of the cemetery, apart from the burial of the dead, are very largely those of the park" (qtd. in J. Farrell 117).

9. Olmsted 13; see also Todd 145. Josiah Dwight Whitney, apparently fearing that the money requested by Olmsted for the new Yosemite park might be taken from funds earmarked for his own California Geological Survey, helped to suppress this report, which never reached the California legislature and remained lost until 1952 (Roper, "Yosemite" 13).

10. Wilkins, *Clarence King* 57; see also Roper, *FLO* 233–34.

11. As Patricia Limerick has pointed out, mining operations such as those at Mariposa provide a particularly clear window into this period of western history because they recapitulate the region's frenetic economic and social transformations in a sort of fast-forward review: "Mining placed settlements of white people where none had been before. It provoked major conflicts with Indians. It called territories and states into being and forced them to an early maturity. It drew merchandising and farming into its wake. As it changed from individual enterprise to a consolidated, industrialized business, mining threw the West into the forefront of industrialized life" (99–100).

12. In reality King was highly class conscious, a fact that manifests itself when he writes in modes other than that of the discovery narrative. Like Lafayette Bunnell, to give one example, King tries to dissociate himself from what he considers Yosemite's more vulgar visitors. In the following passage he has just passed near the famous Inspiration Point, which has provided generations of visitors their first view of the valley: "I always go by this famous point of view now, feeling somehow that I don't belong to that army of literary travellers who have here planted themselves and burst into rhetoric. Here all who make California books, down to the last and most sentimental specimen who so much as meditates a letter to his or her local paper, dismount and inflate" (127). On another occasion King wrote of the "vulgar gold-dirt" (154) of the mining districts in which he worked. This contempt for Mammon seems a hollow pose, considering how assiduously King strove for wealth later in his life. But at least in his belletristic writings he evidently felt compelled to mimic the sort of disinterested air that his wealthier friends could genuinely afford.

13. In this scene and elsewhere, the sexual undercurrent of King's adventures

with Cotter seems palpable. In addition to a genuine homosexual desire, it may mark a certain gendering of King's class anxieties, a conflation of the two men's socially proscribed class relationship with an equally "transgressive" gender relationship. But any attempt at a queer analysis of King would have to take into account his common-law marriage to a poor black woman, Ada Todd—a heterosexual but otherwise proscribed relationship crossing boundaries of both race and class. William Howarth terms this secret marriage "King's supreme fiction, the novel he never wrote" (King, *Mountaineering* xi), and contends that while "King detested this secrecy . . . he lacked the courage to defy prevailing social taboos. He also had a life-long preference for women of color, an appetite that conveniently preserved his own prestige and power" (xii). The marriage may thus have functioned more generally to compensate King for the feelings of social inadequacy he felt while circulating in the high society of Washington and Manhattan. Todd was more than twenty years younger than King (Wilkins, *Clarence King* 359)—which also would have bolstered King's sense of power and prestige. Wilkins notes that while King was attracted to women of color, whom he seems to have viewed as embodying "the archaic" he so much admired, "his role of voluptuary of the primitive and exotic . . . could swing to that of bitter misogynist" when it came to white women "of his own class" (*Clarence King* 359). For details, see King, *Mountaineering* xi–xii; and Wilkins, *Clarence King* 362–64, 408–11.

14. See Robertson 48–49, and Sanborn vii–xxii. Yelverton's husband left her shortly after their marriage and later, without benefit of a divorce or annulment, married another woman. William denied the legality of his first marriage, writes Sanborn, but nonetheless "asserted his right as Theresa's husband to keep her property and collect her income." One consequence of this was that Yelverton, in order to support herself, began to write professionally (xxi); in addition, her experiences contributed to the feminist undercurrent of works such as *Zanita*.

15. Kirkland and her husband settled in 1835 in what is now Livingston County, Michigan, approximately sixty miles northwest of Detroit. The couple moved back to New York City in 1843 after being swindled by the land agent hired to lay out their settlement. She later became editor of the *Union* magazine (Osborne 8).

16. The only book-length treatment of Swallow—Robert Clarke's *Ellen Swallow, the Woman Who Founded Ecology*—was written for a general readership during the ecology craze of the early 1970s and only hints at the institutional battles Swallow must have had to wage. For more information on Swallow, see G. Kass-Simon and Patricia Farnes, *Women of Science: Righting the Record* (150–57); Grace Farrell, "In Memory of Ellen H. Richards"; Alice G. Bryant, "Values for Which Mrs. Ellen H. Richards Stood"; Caroline L. Hunt, "Women of the Hour: Ellen Henrietta Richards"; and H. Patricia Hynes, "Catalysts of the American Environmental Movement" (37–39).

17. As Kirkland puts it, "women are the grumblers" on the wilderness frontier, "and they have some apology" (263). Nell Radd, who "has not the most placable of tempers in the world" (45), chafes volubly under the strain of trying to maintain a proper home in the wilderness. She gets little support from her romantic and nature-loving husband, who is too continuously enraptured to make much of a living. (He also has a drinking problem; he and Nell, in fact, recall Rip and Dame Van Winkle.) Nell grumbles incessantly, but when visitors call she nonetheless strives to set a nice table (47–48).

18. For example, Kirkland approvingly quotes Hazlitt's notion of nature as "a sort of universal home": "The heart reposes in greater security on the immensity of Nature's works, expatiates freely there, and finds elbow-room and breathing-space. We are always at home with Nature" (266). Elaborating on this conceit, Kirkland claims that, despite the rusticity of her and her husband's surroundings, "[w]e lacked not carpets, for there was the velvet sward, embroidered with blossoms. . . . nor canopy, for an emerald dome was over us, full of trembling light, and festooned and tasselled with the starry eglantine. . . . nor pillars, nor arches; for, oh! beloved forests of my country, where can your far-sounding aisles be matched for grandeur, your 'alleys green' for beauty?" (267–68).

19. Runte 24–27. Hutchings was not the only entrepreneur hoping to capitalize on his Yosemite claims; James C. Lamon had also built a cabin in the valley and appealed to both the state and federal legislatures to approve his claims. In doing so, notes Runte, both men strove to portray themselves "as struggling pioneers rather than frontier opportunists" (24).

20. At one point, for example, Sylvia deploys her husband's geological discourse to naturalize not her femininity but her feminism. "[T]here was a latent stratum of romance in my composition," she claims, that "would bubble up amid my daily cares and wrestle for a recognition, and enfranchisement of its own" (4). In a neat reversal, Sylvia "landscapes" her gender politics; having earlier posited her femininity as constructed—as hailed in the disciplinary environments of school and marriage—she here posits her feminist desire for "recognition" and "enfranchisement" as part of a "latent stratum," as undeniable as the geological realities of the valley landscape.

Works Cited

Adams, Ansel. "The Meaning of the National Parks." In *Ansel Adams: Our National Parks*, ed. Andrea G. Stillman and William A. Turnage, 15–18. Boston: Little, Brown, 1992.

Althusser, Louis. *Essays on Ideology*. London: Verso, 1984.

Another Viewpoint at Grand Canyon: Creationary Catastrophe Interpretive Tours. Electronic source: http://www.tagnet.org/anotherviewpoint/.

Audubon, John James. *Audubon and His Journals*. Vol. 1. Ed. Maria R. Audubon. New York: Dover, 1960.

———. *Delineations of American Scenery and Character*. Introduction by Francis Hobart Herrick. New York: Baker, 1926.

Auerbach, Elsa. "Literacy and Ideology." *Annual Review of Applied Linguistics* 12 (1992): 71–85.

Baker, Howard. "Wallace Stevens and Other Poets." *Southern Review* 1 (autumn 1935): 373–89. Reprinted in *Wallace Stevens: The Critical Heritage*, ed. Charles Doyle, 126–36. London: Routledge, 1985.

Bakhtin, Mikhail. *The Dialogic Imagination: Four Essays*. Austin: University of Texas Press, 1981.

Baym, Nina. "How Men and Women Wrote Indian Stories." In *New Essays on The Last of the Mohicans*, ed. H. Daniel Peck, 67–86. Cambridge: Cambridge University Press, 1992.

———. "Melodramas of Beset Manhood: How Theories of American Fiction Exclude Women Authors." *American Quarterly* 33 (summer 1981): 123–39.

Bederman, Gail. *Manliness and Civilization: A Cultural History of Gender and Race in the United States, 1880–1917*. Chicago: University of Chicago Press, 1996.

Bender, Thomas. "The 'Rural' Cemetery Movement: Urban Travail and the Appeal of Nature." *New England Quarterly* 47 (1974): 196–211.

Bennett, William J. *To Reclaim a Legacy: A Report on the Humanities in Higher Education*. Washington, D.C.: National Endowment for the Humanities, 1984.

Berlant, Lauren. *The Anatomy of National Fantasy: Hawthorne, Utopia, and Everyday Life*. Chicago: University of Chicago Press, 1991.

Bonaparte, Marie. *Female Sexuality.* London: Imago, 1953.

——. *The Life and Works of Edgar Allan Poe: A Psychological Interpretation.* Trans. John Rodker. Foreword by Sigmund Freud. London: Imago, 1949.

Bové, Paul A. "Discourse." In *Critical Terms for Literary Study,* 2d ed., ed. Frank Lentricchia and Thomas McLaughlin, 50–65. Chicago: University of Chicago Press, 1995.

Bradford, William. *Bradford's History of Plymouth Plantation 1606–1646.* Ed. William T. Davis. New York: Scribner, 1908.

Breitwieser, Mitchell Robert. *American Puritanism and the Defense of Mourning: Religion, Grief, and Ethnology in Mary White Rowlandson's Captivity Narrative.* Madison: University of Wisconsin Press, 1991.

Brower, David. "Hans Huth and His Story." *Sierra Club Bulletin* 33 (1948): 46.

Bryant, Alice G. "Values for Which Mrs. Ellen H. Richards Stood." *Medical and Professional Woman's Journal* 40 (August 1933): 214–18.

Buell, Lawrence. *The Environmental Imagination: Thoreau, Nature Writing, and the Formation of American Culture.* Cambridge: Harvard University Press, 1995.

Bumpus, Hermon Carey Jr. *Hermon Carey Bumpus, Yankee Naturalist.* Minneapolis: University of Minnesota Press, 1947.

Bunnell, Lafayette Houghton. *Discovery of the Yosemite and the Indian War of 1851 Which Led to that Event.* 1880. Reprint. Los Angeles: G. W. Gerlicher, 1911.

Butler, Judith. *Bodies that Matter: On the Discursive Limits of "Sex."* New York: Routledge, 1993.

——. *Gender Trouble: Feminism and the Subversion of Identity.* New York: Routledge, 1990.

Cadzow, Hunter. "New Historicism." In *The Johns Hopkins Guide to Literary Theory and Criticism,* ed. Michael Groden and Martin Kreiswirth, 534–40. Baltimore: Johns Hopkins University Press, 1994.

Cameron, Sharon. *Writing Nature: Henry Thoreau's* Journal. Chicago: University of Chicago Press, 1989.

Catlin, George. *Letters and Notes on the North American Indians.* Vol. 1. New York: Dover, 1973.

Cheney, Lynne V. *Humanities in America: A Report to the President, the Congress, and the American People.* Washington, D.C.: National Endowment for the Humanities, 1988.

Cheyfitz, Eric. "Literally White, Figuratively Red: The Frontier of Translation in *The Pioneers.*" In *James Fenimore Cooper: New Critical Essays,* ed. Robert Clark, 55–95. New York: Barnes and Noble, 1985.

Cixous, Hélène. "The Laugh of the Medusa." Trans. Keith Cohen and Paula Cohen. *Signs: Journal of Women in Culture and Society* 1 (summer 1976): 875–93.

Clarke, Robert. *Ellen Swallow, the Woman Who Founded Ecology.* Chicago: Follett, 1973.

Cleaveland, Nehemiah. *Green-wood Illustrated. In highly finished Line Engraving, from drawings taken on the spot. By James Smillie. With descriptive notices by Nehemiah Cleaveland.* New York: R. Martin, 1847.

Cooper, James Fenimore. *The Last of the Mohicans; a Narrative of 1757.* Ed. James A. Sappenfield and E. N. Feltskog. Introduction by James Franklin Beard. Albany: State University of New York Press, 1983.

Cronon, William, ed. *Uncommon Ground: Rethinking the Human Place in Nature.* New York: Norton, 1995.

Deposition in the case of Rubery vs. Grant and Simpson. *London Times,* 24 December 1874, 11.

Derrida, Jacques. *Of Grammatology.* Trans. Gayatri Spivak. Baltimore: Johns Hopkins University Press, 1974.

"Diamond Bubble and Its Bursting." *Nation,* 12 December 1872, 379–80.

Drinnon, Richard. *Facing West: The Metaphysics of Indian-Hating and Empire-Building.* New York: Meridian, 1980.

Duncan, James S., and Nancy G. Duncan. "Ideology and Bliss: Roland Barthes and the Secret Histories of Landscape." In *Writing Worlds: Discourse, Text, and Metaphor in the Representation of Landscape,* ed. Trevor J. Barnes and James S. Duncan, 18–37. London: Routledge, 1992.

Eagleton, Terry. *The Ideology of the Aesthetic.* Oxford: Basil Blackwell, 1990.

Farrell, Grace. "In Memory of Ellen H. Richards." *Journal of Home Economics* 21 (June 1929): 403–12.

Farrell, James. *Inventing the American Way of Death, 1830–1920.* Philadelphia: Temple University Press, 1980.

Field, Donald R., and J. Alan Wagar. "People and Interpretation." In *Interpreting the Environment,* ed. Grant W. Sharpe, 43–56. New York: Wiley, 1976.

Fisher, Philip. *Hard Facts: Setting and Form in the American Novel.* New York: Oxford University Press, 1985.

Fliegelman, Jay. *Prodigals and Pilgrims: The American Revolution against Patriarchal Authority, 1750–1800.* Cambridge: Cambridge University Press, 1982.

Fontana, Ernest L. "Cognition and Ordeal in Clarence King's *Mountaineering in the Sierra Nevada.*" *Explorations* 4 (July 1977): 25–30.

Foucault, Michel. *The Order of Things: An Archaeology of the Human Sciences.* New York: Pantheon, 1970.

French, Stanley. "The Cemetery as Cultural Institution: The Establishment of Mount Auburn and the 'Rural Cemetery' Movement." In *Death in America,* ed. David E. Stannard, 69–91. Philadelphia: University of Pennsylvania Press, 1975.

Fuller, Mary C. "Ralegh's Fugitive Gold: Reference and Deferral in *The Discoverie of Guiana*." *Representations* 22 (winter 1991): 42–64.

Garber, Marjorie. *Vested Interests: Cross-Dressing and Cultural Anxiety*. New York: Routledge, 1992.

Godzich, Wlad. *The Culture of Literacy*. Cambridge: Harvard University Press, 1994.

Graff, Harvey J. *The Legacies of Literacy: Continuities and Contradictions in Western Culture and Society*. Bloomington: Indiana University Press, 1986.

———. *The Literacy Myth: Literacy and Social Structure in the Nineteenth-Century City*. New York: Harcourt, 1979.

Graff, Harvey J., and Robert F. Arnove. *National Literacy Campaigns: Historical and Comparative Perspectives*. New York: Plenum, 1987.

"Grand Canyon Creationary Tours." Advertisement in *The Guide: Northern Arizona's Leading Tourist/Visitor Magazine* 7 (November 1998): 26.

Greenblatt, Stephen. *Marvelous Possessions: The Wonder of the New World*. Chicago: University of Chicago Press, 1991.

———. *Renaissance Self-Fashioning: From More to Shakespeare*. Chicago: University of Chicago Press, 1980.

———. "Towards a Poetics of Culture." In *The New Historicism*, ed. H. Aram Veeser, 1–14. New York: Routledge, 1989.

Grove-White, Robin. "Environmentalism: A New Moral Discourse for Technological Society?" In *Environmentalism: The View from Anthropology*, ed. Kay Milton, 18–30. London: Routledge, 1993.

Grumbine, Edward. "Wilderness, Wise Use, and Sustainable Development." In *Deep Ecology for the 21st Century: Readings on the Philosophy and Practice of the New Environmentalism*, ed. George Sessions, 376–96. Boston: Shambala, 1995.

Guillory, John. "Canon." In *Critical Terms for Literary Study*, 2d ed., ed. Frank Lentricchia and Thomas McLaughlin, 233–49. Chicago: University of Chicago Press, 1995.

Haraway, Donna. *Primate Visions: Gender, Race, and Nature in the World of Modern Science*. New York: Routledge, 1989.

Helps, Arthur. *The Spanish Conquest in America, and Its Relation to the History of Slavery and to the Government of Colonies*. Vol. 1. New York: Harper and Brothers, 1856.

Hirsch, E. D. Jr., Joseph E. Kett, and James Trefil. *The Dictionary of Cultural Literacy*. Boston: Houghton Mifflin, 1993.

Howe, Susan. *The Birth-Mark: Unsettling the Wilderness in American Literary History*. Hanover: University Press of New England, 1993.

Hunt, Caroline L. "Women of the Hour: Ellen H. Richards." *La Follette's Weekly Magazine*, 31 December 1910, 10–11.

Huth, Hans. "Yosemite: The Story of an Idea." *Sierra Club Bulletin* 33 (1948): 47–78.

Hynes, H. Patricia. "Catalysts of the American Environmental Movement." *Woman of Power* 9 (spring 1988): 37–41, 78–80.

Irigaray, Luce. *This Sex Which Is Not One*. Trans. Catherine Porter. Ithaca: Cornell University Press, 1985.

Jackson, Kenneth T., and Camilo José Vergara. *Silent Cities: The Evolution of the American Cemetery*. New York: Princeton Architectural Press, 1989.

Jehlen, Myra. "Flaubert's Nightmare." *Profession* 95: 10–13. New York: Modern Language Association, 1995.

Jennings, Francis. *The Invasion of America: Indians, Colonialism, and the Cant of Conquest*. Chapel Hill: University of North Carolina Press, 1975.

Johnson, Barbara. "Writing." In *Critical Terms for Literary Study*, 2d ed., ed. Frank Lentricchia and Thomas McLaughlin, 39–49. Chicago: University of Chicago Press, 1995.

Kalfus, Melvin. *Frederick Law Olmsted: The Passion of a Great Artist*. New York: New York University Press, 1990.

Kass-Simon, G., and Patricia Farnes. *Women of Science: Righting the Record*. Bloomington: Indiana University Press, 1990.

Kavanagh, James H. "Ideology." In *Critical Terms for Literary Study*, 2d ed., ed. Frank Lentricchia and Thomas McLaughlin, 306–20. Chicago: University of Chicago Press, 1995.

Keller, Evelyn Fox. *Reflections on Gender and Science*. New Haven: Yale University Press, 1985.

Kermode, Frank. "Institutional Control of Interpretation." *Salmagundi* 43 (1979): 72–86.

Kibbey, Anne. *The Interpretation of Material Shapes in Puritanism: A Study of Rhetoric, Prejudice, and Violence*. Cambridge: Cambridge University Press, 1986.

Kieran, John, ed. *Treasury of Great Nature Writing*. Garden City, N.Y.: Hanover House, 1957.

Kilpatrick, James. "Last Stand for Custer Battlefield?" *Baton Rouge Morning Advocate*, 22 July 1991, 6B.

King, Clarence. "Current Literature." *Overland Monthly* 5 (December 1870): 578–83.

———. *Mountaineering in the Sierra Nevada*. 1874. Reprint, with introduction by William Howarth. New York: Penguin, 1989.

King, Ynestra. "Healing the Wounds: Feminism, Ecology, and the Nature/Culture Dualism." In *Reweaving the World: The Emergence of Ecofeminism*, ed. Irene Diamond and Gloria Feman Orenstein, 106–21. San Francisco: Sierra Club, 1990.

Kirkland, Caroline. *A New Home—Who'll Follow? or, Glimpses of Western Life*. New York: C. S. Francis, 1840.

Kolodny, Annette. *The Land before Her: Fantasy and Experience of the American Frontiers, 1630–1860*. Chapel Hill: University of North Carolina Press, 1984.

——. *The Lay of the Land: Metaphor as Experience and History in American Life and Letters*. Chapel Hill: University of North Carolina Press, 1975.

Kroeber, Karl. *Ecological Literary Criticism: Romantic Imagining and the Biology of Mind*. New York: Columbia University Press, 1994.

de Lauretis, Teresa. *Technologies of Gender: Essays on Theory, Film, and Fiction*. Bloomington: Indiana University Press, 1987.

Leach, Douglas Edward. *Flintlock and Tomahawk: New England in King Philip's War*. New York: Macmillan, 1966.

Leach, Maria, ed. *Funk and Wagnalls Standard Dictionary of Folklore, Mythology and Legend*. New York: Funk and Wagnalls, 1972.

Legler, Gretchen. "Body Politics in American Nature Writing: Who May Contest for What the Body of Nature Will Be?" In *Writing the Environment: Ecocriticism and Literature*, ed. Richard Kerridge and Neil Sammels, 71–87. London: Zed, 1998.

Legman, G. *Rationale of the Dirty Joke: An Analysis of Sexual Humor*. New York: Breaking Point, 1975.

Leonard, Zenas. *Narrative of the Adventures of Zenas Leonard*. Clearfield, Penn.: D. W. Moore, 1839.

Limerick, Patricia Nelson. *The Legacy of Conquest: The Unbroken Past of the American West*. New York: Norton, 1987.

Lockhart, Gemma M. "Refighting the Battle of Little Bighorn." *USA Today*, 21 July 1992, 11A.

Lotman, Jurij. "The Origin of Plot in the Light of Typology." Trans. Julian Graffy. *Poetics Today* 1 (1979): 161–84.

Lynch, Karen. "Custer Loses Again." *Progressive* (September 1991): 11.

Lynen, John F. *The Design of the Present: Essays on Time and Form in American Literature*. New Haven: Yale University Press, 1969.

Mackintosh, Barry. *Interpretation in the National Park Service: A Historical Perspective*. Washington, D.C.: Government Printing Office, 1986.

Malotki, Ekkehart. "The Story of the 'Tsimonmamant' or Jimson Weed Girls: A Hopi Narrative Featuring the Motif of the Vagina Dentata." In *Smoothing the Ground: Essays on Native American Oral Literature*, ed. Brian Swann, 204–20. Berkeley: University of California Press, 1983.

Mann, Barbara. "Man with a Cross: Hawkeye Was a 'Half-Breed.'" *James Fenimore Cooper Miscellaneous Papers* 10 (August 1998): 1–8.

Mason, John. *A Brief History of the Pequot War*. Ann Arbor: University Microfilms, 1966.

McKibben, Bill. *The End of Nature*. New York: Random House, 1989.

McPhee, John. *Encounters with the Archdruid*. New York: Farrar, Strauss and Giroux, 1971.

Mechling, Jay. "The Alligator." In *American Wildlife in Symbol and Story*, ed. Angus K. Gillespie and Jay Mechling, 73–98. Knoxville: University of Tennessee Press, 1987.

Milton, Kay. Introduction to *Environmentalism: The View from Anthropology*, ed. Kay Milton, 1–17. London: Routledge, 1993.

Mitchell, Annie R. "Major James D. Savage and the Tulareños." *California Historical Society Quarterly* 28 (1949): 323–41.

Morgan, Keith N. "The Emergence of the American Landscape Professional: John Notman and the Design of Rural Cemeteries." *Journal of Garden History* 4 (1984): 269–89.

Muir, John. *My First Summer in the Sierra*. San Francisco: Sierra Club Books, 1988.

Murphy, Patrick. *Literature, Nature, and Other: Ecofeminist Critiques*. Albany: State University of New York Press, 1995.

Nash, Roderick. *Wilderness and the American Mind*. New Haven: Yale University Press, 1978.

Nelson, Dana D. *The Word in Black and White: Reading "Race" in American Literature, 1638–1867*. New York: Oxford University Press, 1993.

Nevius, Blake. *Cooper's Landscapes: An Essay on the Picturesque Vision*. Berkeley: University of California Press, 1976.

A New and Further Narrative of the State of New-England, being A Continued Account of the Bloudy Indian-War. London: Dorman Newman, 1676.

Olmsted, Frederick Law. "The Yosemite Valley and the Mariposa Big Tree Grove." *Landscape Architecture* 43 (October 1952): 13–25.

Osborne, William S. Introduction to *A New Home—Who'll Follow?* by Caroline Matilda Kirkland, 5–25. New Haven: College and University Press, 1965.

Pack, Robert. *Wallace Stevens: An Approach to His Poetry and Thought*. New Brunswick: Rutgers University Press, 1958.

Paine, Thomas. *The Works of Thomas Paine*. New York: W. H. Wise, 1934.

Pearce, Roy Harvey. *The Savages of America: A Study of the Indian and the Idea of Civilization*. Baltimore: Johns Hopkins University Press, 1965.

Pease, Donald. "National Identities, Postmodern Artifacts, and Postnational Narratives." In *National Identities and Post-Americanist Narratives*, ed. Donald Pease, 1–26. Durham: Duke University Press, 1994.

Penelope, Julia. *Speaking Freely: Unlearning the Lies of the Fathers' Tongues*. New York: Pergamon, 1993.

Perlis, Alan. *Wallace Stevens: A World of Transforming Shapes*. Lewisburg: Bucknell University Press, 1976.

Pratt, Mary Louise. "Scratches on the Face of the Country; or, What Mr. Barrow Saw in the Land of the Bushmen." *Critical Inquiry* 12 (autumn 1985): 119–43.

The Present State of New-England, With Respect to the Indian War . . . from the 20th of June, till the 10th of November, 1675. London: Dorman Newman, 1676.

Raymond, R. W. "Biographical Notice of Clarence King." *Transactions of the American Institute of Mining Engineers* 33 (1903): 619–50.

Reed, Ishmael. *Flight to Canada*. New York: Random House, 1976.

Rich, Adrienne. Introduction to *The Works of Anne Bradstreet*, ed. Jeannine Hensley. Cambridge: Harvard University Press, 1967.

Riddel, Joseph N. *The Clairvoyant Eye: The Poetry and Poetics of Wallace Stevens*. Baton Rouge: Louisiana State University Press, 1965.

Robertson, David. *West of Eden: A History of the Art and Literature of Yosemite*. Berkeley: Yosemite Natural History Association and Wilderness Press, 1984.

Roper, Laura Wood. *FLO: A Biography of Frederick Law Olmsted*. Baltimore: Johns Hopkins University Press, 1973.

———. "The Yosemite Valley and the Mariposa Big Trees: A Preliminary Report (1865) by Frederick Law Olmsted." *Landscape Architecture* 43 (October 1952): 12–13.

Rosenzweig, Roy, and Elizabeth Blackmar. *The Park and the People: A History of Central Park*. Ithaca: Cornell University Press, 1992.

Ross, Andrew. *The Chicago Gangster Theory of Life: Nature's Debt to Society*. New York: Verso, 1994.

———. "The Great White Dude." In *Constructing Masculinity*, ed. Maurice Berger, Brian Wallis, and Simon Watson, 167–75. New York: Routledge, 1995.

Rotundo, Barbara. "Mount Auburn: Fortunate Coincidences and an Ideal Solution." *Journal of Garden History* 4 (1984): 255–67.

———. "The Rural Cemetery Movement." *Essex Institute Historical Collections* 109 (1973): 231–40.

Rowlandson, Mary. *The Sovereignty & Goodness of God, Together, With the Faithfulness of His Promises Displayed; Being a Narrative Of the Captivity and Restauration of Mrs. Mary Rowlandson*. Cambridge: Samuel Green, 1682. Reprinted in *So Dreadfull a Judgement: Puritan Responses to King Philip's War, 1676–1677*, ed. Richard Slotkin and James K. Folsom, 301–69. Middletown, Conn.: Wesleyan University Press, 1978.

Roy, Cecil Allen. *Another Viewpoint at Grand Canyon, Creationary Catastrophe Interpretive Tours*. Electronic source: http://www.tagnet.org/anotherviewpoint/.

Runte, Alfred. *Yosemite: The Embattled Wilderness*. Lincoln: University of Nebraska Press, 1990.

Said, Edward. *Orientalism*. New York: Pantheon, 1978.

Samuels, Shirley. "Generation through Violence: Cooper and the Making of Americans." In *New Essays on* The Last of the Mohicans, ed. H. Daniel Peck, 87–114. Cambridge: Cambridge University Press, 1992.

Sanborn, Margaret. Introduction to *Zanita: A Tale of the Yo-semite*, by Theresa Yelverton, vii–xxxvi. Berkeley: Ten Speed Press, 1991.

Saussure, Ferdinand de. *Course in General Linguistics*. Trans. Wade Baskin. New York: Philosophical Library, 1959.

Schuyler, David. "The Evolution of the Anglo-American Rural Cemetery: Landscape Architecture as Social and Cultural History." *Journal of Garden History* 4 (1984): 291–304.

Seager, Joni. *Earth Follies: Coming to Feminist Terms with the Global Environmental Crisis*. New York: Routledge, 1993.

Sharpe, Grant W., ed. *Interpreting the Environment*. New York: Wiley, 1976.

Shepard, Paul. *Man in the Landscape: A Historic View of the Esthetics of Nature*. College Station: Texas A & M University Press, 1991.

Shklovsky, Viktor. "Art as Technique." In *Contemporary Literary Criticism*, ed. Robert Con Davis and Ronald Schleifer, 55–66. New York: Longman, 1989.

Sloane, David Charles. *The Last Great Necessity: Cemeteries in American History*. Baltimore: Johns Hopkins University Press, 1991.

Slotkin, Richard. *The Fatal Environment: The Myth of the Frontier in the Age of Industrialization, 1800–1890*. New York: Atheneum, 1985.

Slovic, Scott. *Seeking Awareness in American Nature Writing: Henry Thoreau, Annie Dillard, Edward Abbey, Wendell Berry, Barry Lopez*. Salt Lake City: University of Utah Press, 1992.

Snyder, Gary. *The Practice of the Wild: Essays by Gary Snyder*. San Francisco: North Point Press, 1990.

Solnit, Rebecca. *Savage Dreams: A Journey into the Hidden Wars of the American West*. San Francisco: Sierra Club, 1994.

Soulé, Michael E., and Gary Lease, eds. *Reinventing Nature? Responses to Postmodern Deconstruction*. Washington, D.C.: Island Press, 1995.

St. Armand, Barton Levi. "The Book of Nature and American Nature Writing: Codex, Index, Contexts, Prospects." *ISLE: Interdisciplinary Studies in Literature and Environment* 4 (spring 1997): 29–42.

Stevens, Wallace. *Harmonium*. New York: Knopf, 1953.

Struckman, Robert. "Looking at Little Bighorn: Indian Tour Guides Lend New Perspective." *Denver Post*, 4 July 1998, 24A.

Sundquist, Eric, ed. *American Realism: New Essays*. Baltimore: Johns Hopkins University Press, 1982.

Thomashow, Mitchell. *Ecological Identity: Becoming a Reflective Environmentalist*. Cambridge: MIT Press, 1995.

Thompson, Stith. *Motif-Index of Folk-Literature*. Bloomington: Indiana University Press, 1956.

Tilden, Freeman. *Interpreting Our Heritage: Principles and Practices for Visitor Services in Parks, Museums, and Historic Places*. Chapel Hill: University of North Carolina Press, 1957.

Todd, John Emerson. *Frederick Law Olmsted*. Boston: Twayne, 1982.

Tompkins, Jane. *Sensational Designs: The Cultural Work of American Fiction, 1790–1860*. New York: Oxford University Press, 1985.

Tu Wei-Ming. "Beyond the Enlightenment Mentality." In *Worldviews and Ecology*, ed. Mary Evelyn Tucker and John A. Grim, 19–29. Lewisburg: Bucknell University Press, 1993.

Tucker, Mary Evelyn, and John A. Grim, eds. *Worldviews and Ecology*. Lewisburg: Bucknell University Press, 1993.

Underhill, John. *Newes from America; or, A New and Experimentall Discoverie of New England*. London: Peter Cole, 1638.

United States. National Park Service. *Interpretive Planning Handbook: A Preliminary Draft (Advance Copy for Current Development Program)*. Washington, D.C.: Government Printing Office, 1965.

———. *A Personal Training Program for Interpreters*. Washington, D.C.: Government Printing Office, 1976.

Veeser, H. Aram, ed. *The New Historicism*. New York: Routledge, 1989.

Wald, Priscilla. *Constituting Americans: Cultural Anxiety and Narrative Form*. Durham: Duke University Press, 1995.

Walter, Cornelia W. *Mount Auburn Illustrated. In highly finished Line Engraving, from drawings taken on the spot, by James Smillie. With descriptive notices by Cornelia W. Walter*. New York: R. Martin, 1851.

Ward, Andrew. "The Little Bighorn." *American Heritage* 43 (1992): 76–87.

Warren, Robert Penn. *Audubon: A Vision*. New York: Random House, 1969.

Weaver, Bruce J. "'What to Do with the Mountain People?': The Darker Side of the Successful Campaign to Establish the Great Smoky Mountains National Park." In *The Symbolic Earth: Discourse and Our Creation of the Environment*, ed. James G. Cantrill and Christine L. Oravec, 151–75. Lexington: University Press of Kentucky, 1996.

Weaver, Howard E. "Origins of Interpretation." In *Interpreting the Environment*, ed. Grant W. Sharpe, 23–42. New York: Wiley, 1976.

Westbrook, Max. "Myth, Reality, and the American Frontier." In *Under the Sun: Myth and Realism in Western Literature*, ed. Barbara Howard Meldrum, 11–19. Troy, N.Y.: Whitston, 1985.

Whitman, Walt. *Leaves of Grass: Inclusive Edition*. New York: Doubleday, 1948.

Wilkins, Thurman. *Clarence King: A Biography*. Albuquerque: University of New Mexico Press, 1988.

———, ed. Introduction to *Mountaineering in the Sierra Nevada*, by Clarence King. Philadelphia: Lippincott, 1963.

Will, George. "Little Bighorn's Multiculturalism." *Baton Rouge Morning Advocate*, 18 July 1991, 6B.

Williams, Raymond. *Writing in Society.* London: Verso, 1983.

"The Winners Get Their Due." *Time,* 9 December 1991, 33.

Winnicott, D. W. *Playing and Reality.* New York: Basic Books, 1971.

Winters, Yvor. *The Anatomy of Nonsense.* Norfolk, Conn.: New Directions, 1943. Reprinted in *Wallace Stevens: The Critical Heritage,* ed. Charles Doyle, 224–52. London: Routledge, 1985.

Wirth, Conrad L. "Securing Protection and Conservation Objectives through Interpretation." Memorandum of 23 April 1953. Reprinted in *Interpretation in the National Park Service: A Historical Perspective,* by Barry Mackintosh, 105–11. Washington, D.C.: Government Printing Office, 1986.

Worster, Donald. *Nature's Economy: A History of Ecological Ideas.* New York: Cambridge University Press, 1994.

Yelverton, Theresa. *Zanita: A Tale of the Yo-Semite.* Introduction by Margaret Sanborn. Berkeley: Ten Speed Press, 1991.

"Zanita: A Tale of the Yo-Semite." *Nation* (July–December 1872): 326–27.

"Zanita: A Tale of the Yosemite." *New York Times,* 8 November 1872, 3.

Index